# To Live Like a Moor

THE MIDDLE AGES SERIES

Ruth Mazo Karras, Series Editor
Edward Peters, Founding Editor

A complete list of books in the series
is available from the publisher.

# To Live Like a Moor

Christian Perceptions of Muslim Identity
in Medieval and Early Modern Spain

## Olivia Remie Constable

Edited by Robin Vose

Foreword by David Nirenberg

**PENN**

UNIVERSITY OF PENNSYLVANIA PRESS

PHILADELPHIA

Published by
University of Pennsylvania Press
Philadelphia, Pennsylvania 19104-4112
www.upenn.edu/pennpress

Printed in the United States of America on acid-free paper
1 3 5 7 9 10 8 6 4 2

Library of Congress Cataloging-in-Publication Data

Names: Constable, Olivia Remie, author. | Vose, Robin J. E.,
    editor. | Nirenberg, David, 1964- writer of foreword.
Title: To live like a Moor: Christian perceptions of Muslim
    identity in medieval and early modern Spain / Olivia
    Remie Constable; edited by Robin Vose; foreword by
    David Nirenberg.
Other titles: Middle Ages series.
Description: Philadelphia: University of Pennsylvania Press,
    [2018] | Series: The Middle Ages series | Includes
    bibliographical references and index.
Identifiers: LCCN 2017026803 | ISBN 9780812249484
    (hardcover: alk. paper)
Subjects: LCSH: Muslims—Spain—History. | Muslims—
    Spain—Public opinion—History. | Christians—Spain—
    Attitudes xHistory. | Muslims—Spain—Social life and
    customs—History. | Muslims—Spain—Ethnic identity—
    History. | Christianity and other religions—Spain—
    Islam—History. | Islam—Relations—Spain—
    Chrisitanity—History.
Classification: LCC DP103 .C68 2018 | DDC 946/.02—dc23
LC record available at https://lccn.loc.gov/2017026803

# CONTENTS

Foreword, David Nirenberg     vii

Editor's Preface     xiii

Chapter 1. Being Muslim in Christian Spain     1

Chapter 2. Clothing and Appearance     15

Chapter 3. Bathing and Hygiene     63

Chapter 4. Food and Foodways     104

Editor's Afterword     140

Notes     145

Bibliography     193

Index     219

Editor's Acknowledgments     225

DAVID NIRENBERG

In 1492 Fernando and Isabel accepted the surrender of the city-kingdom of Granada, the last redoubt of Muslim political power on the Iberian Peninsula, granting in return to the conquered the right to continue practicing their religion. In 1501 officials of the same monarchs broke that promise and offered the region's Muslims a "choice" between conversion to Christianity or expulsion from their homes and lands in the Peninsula. Tens of thousands chose conversion, giving birth to what would become a new religious category in Spain, that of the Moriscos, as the converts and their descendants came to be known.

The creation of this new category (made much larger over time by the eventual forced conversion of Muslims living in Valencia, Aragon, and other regions of the Peninsula) raised any number of new questions. Among these were questions of what it meant to be Muslim, what it meant to be Christian, and what aspects of a person's behavior or belief needed to change in order to make the transition from the one to the other. Today we often speak of "religious identity" as if the phrase—with its etymological implication of the subject's religious "oneness," "unity," or "sameness"—were unproblematic. But what these mass conversions of Muslims to Christianity catalyzed was a debate about precisely what such spiritual "oneness" required of the individual. This basic question, already posed sharply a century earlier but in a different flavor with the forced conversion of the Peninsula's Jews to Christianity, was the bellows that raised the issue of Christian perceptions of Muslim identity to a red-hot heat.

Addressing the converts at around the time of their baptism, Hernando de Talavera, Granada's first archbishop, took a position on this question: "So that no one might think that you still adhere to the sect of Muhammad in your heart, it is necessary that you conform in all things to the good and honest ways of good and honest Christian men and women, including their manner of dressing, wearing shoes, doing their hair, eating at tables, and cooking their food."[1] Note how the model of religious subjectivity implicit here approaches a totalizing "identity." In order for the interior spiritual state (the heart) of converts to be legible as Christian to someone else, their exterior, so to speak, had to "conform in all things" to the exterior of known, nonconverted Christians ("old," "clean" Christians, in the vocabulary of Talavera's contemporaries).

The book before you is, among other things, an exploration of the consequences that flowed from the emergence and imposition of this model of religious subjectivity. It focuses on many of the same registers of culture as in Hernando de Talavera's exhortation: dress, food, manners, and other aspects of behavior whose relationship to faith was neither simple nor obvious to contemporaries (or to us). Through this exploration it shows us what Christians (and to a lesser degree, Muslims) perceived as "Islamic," and how that perception changed as a consequence of these mass conversions. All kinds of cultural practices become meaningful. Baths, for example, emerge as signifiers of Islam, napkins and tablecloths become banners of Christianity. Couscous can condemn a descendant of converts who eats it as "Muslim" before the Inquisition but be included in a royal chef's cookbook as an exotic delicacy. Painstakingly piecing together these fragments of culture, Olivia Remie Constable reveals to us how a society built and rebuilt its images of Islam, and with what consequences, for Muslims and for Christians both.

In this task she was inspired by a remarkable predecessor, himself a member of the very first generation of Moriscos: Francisco Núñez Muley, born into an elite Muslim family in Granada shortly before the city's surrender to the Catholic Monarchs in 1492. Many years later, in 1567, the now venerable Morisco took up his pen to protest prohibitions recently promulgated by royal officials on certain activities by Moriscos—frequenting baths, speaking Arabic or possessing Arabic books, using their old family names, singing their traditional songs, or wearing their traditional dress. According to the officials, these activities were Islamic or Islamizing. They threatened or belied the Moriscos' Christian faith and therefore had to be abandoned by them, whether of their own volition or by force. In page after page of his memorandum, Núñez Muley argued that these aspects of Morisco culture were local customs, not carriers or determinants of what we today would call religious identity. Ancient communities of Christians in the Holy Land, he pointed out, spoke Arabic and dressed in local garb but were no less Christian for that. Foods and foodways were not matters of faith but of habit and taste; baths were a question of hygiene, not of Islam, for Moriscos who labored in fields and mines.

Núñez Muley's passionate and precocious critique of these totalizing Christian models of Muslim "identity" appeals to the present antiessentialist generation of historians, who have learned to think of culture as construction, but it went unheeded in its own day. The prohibitions on dress, food, language, and so on were imposed on the Moriscos, with tragic results: violence, rebellion, massacre, and eventually expulsion. This book is a history of those cultural practices, a history that Núñez Muley did not—could not—write. Would the outcome have been different if Christian authorities had been able to read Remie Constable's history rather than Núñez Muley's polemic? The question may seem perverse, but I ask it to make a point: *To Live Like a Moor* is a book that teaches us about a history with enormous consequences for Muslims and Christians alike. How we learn to think about that history today may not change the fate of the Moriscos, as Núñez Muley tried to do, but it may very well help us change our own "fate," as we think about similar questions about religion, Islam, and Christianity in our day.

*To Live Like a Moor* is the last book we can hope for from Remie Constable's pen. Indeed she was not able to complete the manuscript before her untimely (she was fifty-three) death in 2014. She bequeathed the task of preparation for publication to her student Robin Vose, to whom we as readers owe an enormous debt. (Professor Vose describes the precise contours of his editing in the following preface.) It seems fitting here, in the first pages of her final work, to dwell for a moment on its elder siblings, for her career was fruitful and extremely distinguished, although too brief.

The honor of primogeniture belongs to her Princeton doctoral dissertation, published as *Trade and Traders in Muslim Spain: The Commercial Realignment of the Iberian Peninsula, 900–1500* (Cambridge, 1994). The title alone makes clear the subject and vast scope of that book, although no title could reveal the riches it contained. For already in this first book Professor Constable displayed the characteristic virtues that mark all her subsequent work: a special focus on the material conditions of life, a willingness to embrace time spans of a length that make most historians blanch, and a technical ability to work with a vast array of sources, from Arabic chronicles to the ledgers of Genoese merchants, from pilgrimage narratives to ships' manifests.

*Trade and Traders* was a book very much alert to the lessons of the founding giants—Fernand Braudel, Charles Verlinden, Roberto S. Lopez, and Shelomo

Dov Goitein—who taught the historical profession about the enduring importance of the movement of commerce as a mode of what we might call cultural
production and intercultural exchange. It was equally influenced by the next
generation in this field, some of them Constable's teachers at Princeton,
such as Abraham Udovitch and Mark Cohen. But unlike the work of these
great predecessors, it was marked by equally deep commitments to the western
European and the Islamic medieval traditions, and to sources both Latin and
Arabic. In this sense the book marked the emergence of a new generation of
historians of the Mediterranean, one eager to explore the interaction between
Christendom and Islamdom along as many axes as possible.

Remie Constable was not only a founder of this generation, she was also
particularly gifted at discovering new axes for it to explore. I think it is on
page 43 of *Trade and Traders* that readers first encounter what seems merely a
detail of some of the treaties negotiated between the Almohads and the Genoese: these often included provisions regarding the establishment of *funduqs*
(translated here as "hostelries") for Genoese merchants in Almohad lands. It
is difficult to imagine trade agreements today spending much time on hotels
for business travelers, but by page 119 we learn that one anonymous author
reported as many as sixteen hundred such establishments in early thirteenth-
century Islamic Córdoba, while others reported roughly one thousand in Almería: places "where merchants, travelers, single men, foreigners, and others
may stay."

I am not sure if Professor Constable already knew as she wrote those pages
that in these *funduqs* she had found the foundations for her next book, *Housing the Stranger in the Mediterranean World: Lodging, Trade, and Travel in Late
Antiquity and the Middle Ages* (Cambridge, 2003). Again her penchant for titles both clear and illuminating makes evident the vast scope of the book,
which used the long history of "hotels"—from the ancient Greek *pandocheia*
so scathingly criticized by Plato in his *Laws*, to the *funduqs* of classical
Islam and their final transformation into *fondacos* at the hands of European
commercial powers like the Catalans and the Venetians—to explore a long
and shifting history of exchange and interaction between communities of
disparate faiths.

Like *Trade and Traders*, the book was a major contribution to the long
tradition of scholarship on commercial institutions from which she in some
sense descended. But it is also a monument of scholarship in the tradition of
another of her teachers, John Boswell, who captured her attention (as he did
that of so many others, including me) during her undergraduate years at Yale.

Much as Boswell had done in works like *The Kindness of Strangers* (1988), on the abandonment of children in western Europe, but on an even wider canvas that included the Islamic as well as the Christian world, Constable proceeded to create a pointillist portrait of a vast but hitherto overlooked cultural formation out of an accumulation of tiny shards of detail expertly recovered from a seemingly endless library of heterogeneous sources. Is it fanciful to detect a hint of homage in the echo between titles?

If for the sake of brevity I mention only her monumental monographs, it is not for lack of contributions in other genres. Remie was also mistress of the short form, and published pieces—such as her article on the medieval slave trade as an aspect of Muslim-Christian relations, or her essay on chess and courtly culture—chiseled and compressed on fundamental topics that others might have stretched into a book. She also translated her pedagogical gifts into print, editing a collection of documents for the classroom that has become the broad gate through which a generation of students enters into the rich "multicultural" history of medieval Iberia.[2]

The present book, unlike Professor Constable's previous works, is not primarily about commercial institutions or relations. Its arch extends over fewer centuries, and its emphasis is more melancholic: more a history of how exchange was impeded than how it was facilitated. But like all of her engagements with the past, this one is focused on the ever-shifting cultural formations that mediated interactions between Muslims and Christians (and Jews as well, though these were less often the focus of her attention) in the medieval Mediterranean and especially Spain. It is easy enough to see how it grew out of her previous engagements. *Trade and Traders* already pivoted around the great shift that occurred in the relative fortunes of Iberian Islam and Christianity, and *Housing the Stranger* contained revealing pages about how that same shift transformed the meaning and function of the *funduq* of Valencia.

But it is also easy enough to see how these differences illustrate yet another of Professor Constable's great virtues as a historian: because she was always on the qui vive for new approaches and interests emerging in the profession, her work could put the medieval material she mined so well to the service of historians discovering those emerging topics even before they knew they wanted it. To pick but one example, whatever period they work in, the many historians who are becoming interested in the cultural work done by material culture—dress, food, housewares and furnishing, the things and objects we bear about our lives as we construct them—will find much inspiration in these pages. So too will those whose attention is increasingly tuned to questions of Islamic "diasporas" in Christian Europe, both past and present. There is a great deal to learn from this book, which cannot help but remind readers who knew its author in life (and I suspect also the many more readers who did not) what a sharp loss we have all suffered with the too early silencing of such a generous, learned, distinctive, and humane historical voice.

"Perceptions" of Islam, and their development over time, form the topic of this book. But where others have explored such perceptions above all as they were expressed in a select corpus of contemporary theological, legal, or literary texts, Olivia Remie Constable's approach here was rather that of a wide-ranging social historian.[1] The author's ability to glean evidence from a dizzying array of archival documents, manuscript and printed volumes, architectural remains, and material objects permitted her to weave together precisely the sort of nuanced and colorful tapestry that best represents the complexities of lived—as opposed to idealized—experience. "A long process of hunting and gathering," she once called her method; or "trying to piece together a jigsaw puzzle of unknown design, in which many of the pieces are missing and some of the available pieces are borrowed from other apparently similar puzzles."[2] From legal and economic documents to chronicles (both royal and more localized) and cookbooks, religious treatises, travelers' accounts, poetry, artistic representations—Olivia Remie Constable was able to draw on all these and more to work out a more comprehensive and nuanced sense of just how medieval and early modern Iberian Christians' perceptions of their Muslim neighbors actually manifested and changed over the course of more than five centuries.

The tensions evident between any one source's depiction and the composite images resulting from a more expansive and inclusive approach are reflected in Constable's conscious decision to frame her analysis (at least initially) around the testimony of a single Morisco elder: Francisco Núñez Muley. Taking her lead from his passionate denunciation of the Christian regime's criminalization of heretofore licit practices widespread among the formerly Muslim population of Granada, she identified three major categories of behavior that were deemed to be unacceptable markers of "Islamic" identity by the middle of the sixteenth century: the adoption of certain types of clothing and appearance, certain approaches to bathing and hygiene, and use of traditional Arabic forms of communication (including naming and musical performance as well as speech and text). Yet a fourth category, left unmentioned by Núñez Muley in this text, also emerges in many other sources as an equally important area of dispute and a marker of difference: certain types of food preparation and consumption. This latter category had to be given due consideration, even if it did not always strike one relatively acculturated and privileged male witness as being worthy of comment, if a full picture of past experience was to be effectively rendered.

Constable's great original insight and research contribution with this book was to document how day-to-day cultural habits—especially habits that were *bodily* in nature, and in particular those that could be specifically linked to *female* bodies—became a primary focal point of anti-Muslim sentiment from the later Middle Ages to the beginning of the early modern period. Quite apart from their concerns over Islamic theological beliefs, Spanish Christians became increasingly antipathetic to the ways in which Spanish Muslims (and many of their converted Morisco descendants) dressed, bathed, spoke, and ate. These seemingly innocuous daily practices served as lightning rods for struggles over distinctiveness, assimilation, and the limits of toleration in the Iberian Peninsula. It was both by listening closely to what Francisco Núñez Muley had to say and by going beyond his singular perspective to see how other aspects of the same problem actually emerged over a long period of time that Remie Constable was able to bring together and make coherent such a vast mass of otherwise discordant information on such a very important topic. The result is a careful presentation of how and (where possible) why attitudes fitfully evolved to arrive at the tragic experiences of Núñez Muley's generation and the subsequent final expulsion of their children and grandchildren from Iberian soil.

*   *   *

The decision to seek publication of a work that, while near completion in many ways, remained unfinished at the time of its author's illness and death, was not taken lightly. There was, in particular, a problem with one of the four analytic sections originally intended for study. Constable had completed much of her research on the topic of language, naming practices, and songs, however the draft chapter laying out this information existed only in an incomplete outline. After much discussion, first with Remie herself and later with several of her closest confidants, it was reluctantly decided that only the three most complete of the four sections, those on dress, bathing, and food, should be submitted for publication as a coherent piece of scholarship that could stand proudly on its own merits. This meant leaving out a key planned chapter on evolving Spanish Christian perceptions of the Arabic language, and related linguistic and musical performances, as markers of religious identity. The importance of these topics to the original project remains evident in Professor Constable's introductory chapter, and there seemed no reason to hide it or to gloss over the resulting gap.

The virtue of this approach has been to retain, as much as possible, Remie Constable's own voice. The editor's role has been deliberately minimal. For the most part, it was limited to careful checking and rechecking of references, polishing and standardization of format, and completion of occasional unfinished thoughts (usually following meticulously recorded prompts from the author's own notes). Brief conclusions were imposed on each chapter for the sake of closure—Constable had deliberately left them open-ended because she was always adding more data, and consequently adjusting her ideas, to the very end. The only substantial research contribution by the editor appears in subsections relating to the use of henna (in Chapter 2), the impact of syphilis on questions of bathing hygiene (in Chapter 3), and the use of implements such as forks (in Chapter 4); further bibliographical information on modern debates over Islamic veiling was also added to Chapter 1. All these additions were scripted by Olivia Remie Constable's notes, with generous hints and clues to be followed, but any errors or distortions inadvertently introduced therein should not be held to her account.

## CHAPTER I

# Being Muslim in Christian Spain

In 1567, seventy-five years after the Christian conquest of Granada, an elderly gentleman in that city sent a memorandum to the city's chief administrator defending a set of customs—visiting bathhouses, wearing local dress, using old family names, possessing Arabic books, and singing traditional songs—that had recently been prohibited by Christian authorities. The gentleman, Francisco Núñez Muley, had been born into an elite Muslim family in Granada, probably around 1490, shortly before the city's surrender to the Catholic Monarchs, Fernando and Isabel, in 1492. He had converted to Christianity as a young man, and by 1502 he was employed in the household of the archbishop of Granada. By the time he was writing his memorandum, he must have been nearly eighty, with a lifetime of experience of what it meant for Muslims, and converted Muslims ("New Christians," or *moriscos*), to live under Christian rule in sixteenth-century Spain.

The subject of Núñez Muley's memorandum, which contemplates the meaning of traditions of bathing, dressing, naming, language, and music, closely parallels the subject of this book.[1] To what degree were such practices entwined with religious belief, local culture, or political allegiance, and how did perceptions of their meaning change over time during the period from the twelfth to the sixteenth century in Spain? The condemnation of cultural practices in 1567 and Núñez Muley's vigorous arguments for their continuation draw attention to the permeable, narrow, and shifting line between what was perceived as being Muslim or Christian in late medieval and early modern Spain. Then as now, there were many beliefs and practices that were seen as defining characteristics of one religion or the other, especially articles of doctrine and ways of life that were explicitly set forth in holy texts and books of religious law and tradition. But every religion also has other customs and

habits, whether local or widespread, that have come to be associated, sometimes very strongly, with that faith tradition, even though they may have little
basis among official aspects of belief. Foodways provide a good example of
this duality. On the one hand, there are strict and widely recognized religious
dietary laws set out for Jews and Muslims regarding kosher and halal butchering practices and the avoidance of pork products. On the other hand, there
are many regional food traditions that can also be associated with Jews and
Muslims, without being universal, exclusive, or religiously required. Enjoying
kebabs, falafel, or hummus might fall into this category today; in late medieval
Spain, this was true of eating eggplants and couscous.

The same is true for traditions of cleanness and purity, where there is a
difference between the religious requirements of ritual washing before prayer
and the customary and pleasurable cleansing of one's body in the warm water
and steam of a bathhouse. Yet both practices are related in their valuation of
hygiene, and they are closely culturally linked to each other.

Many of the practices that Núñez Muley was called upon to defend fell
into this often indefinable and sometimes controversial borderland between
religious requirement and customary tradition. Christians in sixteenth-century
Spain could catalog a broad set of activities, described as "customs," "superstitions," "ceremonies," and "rites" (*costumbres, supersticiones, ceremonias, ritos*),
that they saw as characteristic of Muslim life, which included and yet went well
beyond canonical Islamic requirements. For example, the 1554 Synod of Guadix included a list of *supersticiones y ritos* practiced by New Christians. All
were condemned, both those that were overtly Islamic rituals (such as fasting
during Ramadan) and others (such as painting the hands with henna) that
were categorized as merely superstitious but not heretical.[2]

In preparing the 1567 edict in Granada, Old Christians argued that
converted Muslims must abandon all elements of their former life, not only
official beliefs but also long-term habits. The chronicler Luis del Mármol
Carvajal, a Christian contemporary of Francisco Núñez Muley in Granada,
explained their reasoning in that "because the Moriscos have been baptized
and are called Christians, and they have had to both be *and appear to be*
Christians, they have left behind the clothing, language, and customs that
they once used as Moors."[3]

Similar reasoning and language would continue through the Morisco
expulsions in the early seventeenth century. Francisco Bermúdez de Pedraza
later recalled how Morisco customs (*costumbres de los moriscos*) had to be re-
formed, since the local people "appeared to be Christians but were actually

Moors" (eran Cristianos aparentes y moros verdaderos), holding to "the rites and ceremonies of their sect" (los ritos y ceremonias de su seta) including food-ways, prayers, and music (*zambras*).[4]

The 1567 ban on what Old Christians perceived as Islamic customs—especially the prohibition on dress, veils, and shoes—caused consternation within the New Christian community and Núñez Muley was commissioned to draft a rebuttal. Strikingly, his defense rested on economic and cultural arguments, not religious associations. Not only would it be a hardship for New Christian women to have to buy entirely new wardrobes, but he emphasized that these clothing practices were merely elements of local culture and style; they were not based on faith traditions. "Their style of dress, clothing, and footwear," he states, "cannot be said to be that of Muslims, nor is it that of Muslims. It can more rightly be said to be clothing that corresponds to a particular kingdom and province." (El ábito y traxe y calçado no se puede dezir de moros, ni que es de moros. Puédese de dizir ques traxe del Reyno y provinçia.)[5]

All regions have their own particular styles, Núñez Muley argued, and thus Granadan dress was distinct from the fashions elsewhere in Castile, just as clothing in Morocco was different from styles in Turkey. Yet at the same time, dress was not linked to religion, since Christians in Jerusalem dressed just like their Muslim neighbors. Likewise, the practice of female veiling was shared by both Old and New Christians in Granada, where many women from Old Christian families routinely veiled their faces if they wished to walk in the street unrecognized.[6]

Christianity, he insisted, "is not found in the clothing or footwear that is now in style, and the same is true of Islam," so that "from all that I have just pointed out, your Most Reverend Lordship will certainly be convinced, as it is true, that the natives' style of clothing and footwear has nothing at all to do with either support for or opposition to Islam."[7]

Núñez Muley was in a very tricky position, and his line of argument was necessarily somewhat disingenuous. Whether or not they were strictly "religious," many of the practices that he defended were indeed holdovers from the previous century, when Granada was a Muslim city and its citizens were Muslims. The Naṣrid kingdom of Granada had survived for two and a half centuries (from 1232 until 1492) as the final outpost of Muslim-controlled territory in the Iberian Peninsula until its last Muslim ruler surrendered to Fernando and Isabel. But by the time Núñez Muley was drafting his memorandum, Granada had been officially Christian for three-quarters of a century, and its inhabitants were all baptized Christians, whether from Old

Christian families (*cristianos viejos*) or relatively recent converts (*cristianos nuevos*). At least two generations had passed since the early sixteenth-century edicts requiring conversion or expulsion, so only the very oldest among New Christian citizens, like Núñez Muley himself, had actually been born Muslim. Nevertheless, New Christians in Granada still thought of themselves as "natives" of the city (*naturales*, in Núñez Muley's words), as opposed to the Old Christian incomers, and they preserved many of their distinctive local customs, including traditions of bathing, fashion, music, names, and language. But, as Núñez Muley's argument makes clear, there was nothing to be gained for the Morisco community by linking these practices to Islam, since everybody was now technically Christian. Indeed, in an age in which the Spanish Inquisition was a present and fearful fact of life, it was highly desirable to discourage any linkage with Islam.

Yet despite Núñez Muley's protestations in his memorandum, it is reasonable to assume that many New Christians did, in fact, associate these practices with their Muslim heritage and that Old Christians were not incorrect in believing that certain ways of life distinguished the two Christian populations from each other. It is likewise reasonable to posit that neither group, Old or New, was a solid or undifferentiated bloc. Many Moriscos (the ones sometimes called crypto-Muslims in modern scholarship) actively resisted acculturation and conversion, and they preserved traditional ways precisely because they knew them to be Islamic, while other more assimilated New Christians may have held to their customs more from habit and tradition. Even members of the most highly assimilated group, including Francisco Núñez Muley (who himself knew little or no Arabic, and who has sometimes been described as a collaborator because he served under the postconquest administration),[8] still clearly felt that these older traditions and practices were an important part of Granadan life.

Within Old Christian society there must also have been a spectrum of opinion about the practices in question, with some people shunning anything that might be perceived to bear a taint of Islam, while others willingly dressed in local clothing styles, ate regional foods, visited bathhouses, and listened to popular music. Even Christian clerics differed in their approaches to these traditions. Shortly after the 1492 conquest, we are told that the first archbishop of Granada, Hernando de Talavera, incorporated local music (*zambras*) into Corpus Christi processions and tried to win over Muslim converts by preaching the Gospel and inviting them to dinner so as to inculcate table manners and other Christian customs (*costumbres cristianas*) by example.[9] Meanwhile, his more conservative colleague Cardinal Francisco Jiménez de Cisneros ordered the burning of Arabic books and successfully pursued the forced conversion of the Muslim population of Granada.

Debates, disputes, disagreements, and indecision about the best strategies for Christian-Muslim relations were nothing new, although there were changes over time and differences according to region. By the early 1500s, Christians and Muslims had lived in the Iberian Peninsula for eight hundred years, through periods of warfare and relative peace, sometimes separate and sometimes side by side. For much of this period, they had maintained separate polities under Christian or Muslim rulers, although Christians and Jews also lived in Muslim territories while Muslims and Jews lived in the Christian kingdoms. But mere adherence to a religion does not imply unity, and there were regional political, cultural, and linguistic differences that were unaligned with religion, leading to warfare between Christian states, or between Muslim states, as well as between Christians and Muslims. In the eleventh century, for example, the northern Christian states (Castile, León, Galicia, Catalonia, and others) were often as hostile toward each other as they were to Muslim states, while Muslim rulers of the disparate Taifa kingdoms fought against each other as much as against their Christian neighbors. In the later Middle Ages, consolidation of territories clarified the Christian-Muslim frontier conflict, but did not resolve inter-Christian disputes.[10] By the later thirteenth century, three major political entities emerged: the Naṣrid kingdom of Granada, the Crown of Castile (consolidating the older regions of León, Castile, Asturias, Galicia, Murcia, and Andalusia), and the Crown of Aragon (encompassing Aragon, Catalonia, Valencia, the Balearics, and other Mediterranean colonies), alongside the separate and smaller Christian kingdoms of Portugal and Navarre (the latter of which would become part of the Crown of Aragon in 1512). In 1492, Fernando and Isabel added Granada to the regions held within the Crown of Castile, putting the entire Iberian Peninsula in Christian hands for the first time since the Islamic conquests of 711.

The period of Fernando and Isabel, who were granted the joint title "los Reyes Católicos" (the Catholic Monarchs) by Pope Alexander VI in 1496, has been celebrated as the culmination of a long process of Spanish unification, but in reality unity remained elusive and differences did not disappear under their rule. The Crowns of Castile and Aragon would not be politically unified into the nation-state of "Spain" until 1516, with the death of Fernando and the accession of Carlos I (Emperor Charles V), the grandson of Fernando and Isabel. Even this merger did not quell unrest, and there were

Morisco uprisings in Granada, Valencia, and Aragon throughout the century, creating a feeling of disunity and insecurity. Many Christians feared that the Moriscos could become a fifth column, and that they might receive outside aid from Muslim rulers in North Africa or from the powerful Ottoman sultan.

In many respects, the conquest of Granada paved the way for religious unification of the Peninsula, with the expulsion of the Jews in 1492 and increasing pressure on Muslim communities to convert, but Christianization would also prove to be a long struggle. The surrender treaty negotiated with Granada in late 1491 had promised that Muslims could continue to live in Granada, to practice Islam, and to maintain their traditional ways of life. But this policy changed within a decade of the conquest, as hard-liners such as Cardinal Cisneros successfully argued for new requirements of conversion or expulsion. In 1501, in the wake of a local uprising in 1499–1500, Cisneros oversaw an edict ordering the conversion of all Muslims in Granada, followed a year later, in 1502, by an extension of the policy to Muslims throughout Castile.

These proclamations caused many Muslims to leave Spain, but large numbers remained, submitted to baptism, and became New Christians, or Moriscos. These two synonymous terms are controversial, in large part because many of the converts were, in almost all respects, still essentially Muslim. They practiced their faith either covertly (adhering to the Islamic doctrine of *taqiyya*, or permissible dissimulation) or relatively openly, especially in regions like Valencia where mosques still existed even after further conversion edicts were passed in the 1520s. Scholars like L. P. Harvey have therefore argued that this group, sometimes called crypto-Muslims, should simply be called Muslims.[11]

But people like Francisco Núñez Muley do not fit comfortably within this rubric, since all evidence points to the fact that he considered himself to be a true Christian, albeit a New Christian. He uses the term *cristianos nuevos* to designate his compatriots, describing them as "the said natives of this kingdom [who have] converted to our holy Catholic faith" (los dichos naturales deste Reyno se convirtieron a nuestra santa fe católica).[12] The persuasive force of his memorandum itself rests to some extent on an assertion of the New Christians' loyalty and Christian faithfulness, as well as his own insistence that "my intention [in writing] . . . is to serve the Lord our God, the Holy Catholic Church, and His Majesty."[13]

In contrast, Núñez Muley describes Muslims as Moors (*moros*) and Islam as the sect of the Moors (*la seta de los moros*). This vocabulary is obviously designed to reinforce his argument that certain customs were regional rather than religious, but these terms must reflect contemporary usage to some degree. Meanwhile, most Old Christians used the word *moro* for any person who was religiously, culturally, politically, linguistically, or ethnically linked with Islam in Spain or North Africa, usually Muslims but often including converts.

The term *moro*, like *morisco*, frequently had a derogatory flavor. *Morisco* was also a contemporary usage, but its meaning is confused by having two separate senses. It could either (as a noun or adjective from about 1500 onward) refer to a New Christian, or (as an adjective, and an older usage) pertain to anything to do with *los moros*. Thus, for example, a piece of clothing described as a *capa morisca* could either be a cloak in the style worn or made by New Christians or, more generally, any cloak in a Moorish style. This double meaning can sometimes be confusing, but it does not detract from the legitimacy or utility of the term when used, as by Luis del Mármol Carvajal, in the sense of "the Moriscos who have been baptized and are called Christians" (los moriscos tenian baptismo y nombre de cristianos) even though they may not act or dress like Old Christians.[14]

Cardinal Cisneros and his contemporaries were well aware of the obstacles to conversion and assimilation if New Christians in Castile preserved their older customs and habits, and he moved, unsuccessfully, to ban them in 1516. A second ban on Muslim clothing, language, and customs in Granada, imposed in 1526, was postponed for forty years after local Moriscos petitioned Charles V and paid over eighty thousand ducats to the crown.[15]

During the early 1520s, Muslims in Valencia and Aragon also faced forced baptism and suppression of their customs and usages.[16] And opposition to any practices perceived as Islamic, including traditional Morisco modes of dress and appearance, bathing, foodways, names, and the use of Arabic, continued to appear throughout the sixteenth century, both in royal documents and inquisitorial records. Then in January 1567, precisely timed to coincide with the seventy-fifth anniversary of Granada's surrender, the Audiencia of Granada issued its proclamation banning Morisco dress, language, names, bathhouses, and other traditional customs. The original text of this edict does not survive, but evidently it revived many of the bans originally promulgated by Charles V in 1526.[17]

Reactions to the 1567 decree included not only Francisco Núñez Muley's carefully argued memorandum but also the launching of a major rebellion among Moriscos in the Alpujarras in 1568. Neither effort achieved its desired effect. There is no evidence that Christian authorities paid any serious attention to Núñez Muley's appeal, and the Alpujarras revolt was put down after two years, followed by the deportation and relocation of many Granadan Moriscos to other areas of Castile in 1570. Meanwhile, uprisings in Aragon and Valencia led to forced disarmament of Moriscos in these regions and an intensification of efforts to enforce Christianity and suppress Islamic practices. Whether these goals were even achievable became an increasingly hot topic for debate among Christian administrators and clerics, with the majority eventually deciding that it would never be possible to assimilate the Old and New Christian populations. Between 1609 and 1614, during the reign of Felipe III, the entire Morisco population was expelled from Spanish territories.

The Morisco period in Spain lasted for roughly a century, from the conversions of the early sixteenth century until the expulsions of the early seventeenth. It was only the final chapter in the story of Muslim life under Christian rule in the Iberian Peninsula, yet this Morisco chapter was dramatically different from what had gone before. Until about 1500, and even after the conquest of Granada, Muslims had been able to live openly as Muslims (*mudéjares*) in the Crowns of Castile and Aragon, although it was often a struggle to maintain the requirements and customs of their Islamic identity. The difficult question of how to continue to live a fully Muslim life under Christian rule became a pressing issue in Iberia from the conquest of Toledo in 1085 by Alfonso VI of Castile, through the watershed victories of Fernando III of Castile and Jaume I of Aragon in the first half of the thirteenth century that consolidated most of the Iberian Peninsula in Christian hands, to the conquest of Granada by Fernando and Isabel in 1492.

From the late eleventh century to the late fifteenth century, it was generally assumed that subject Muslim populations living within the Crowns of Castile and Aragon would continue to be just that: Muslim. They could continue to practice their faith traditions and to live their daily lives much as they always had, even though now under Christian lordship. Latin and Romance documents often mentioned that certain things could continue as they had in the time of the Moors (*en tiempo de moros*), although life would never really be the same. Christian rulers normally allowed at least some mosques to remain in operation; Muslim communities could live according to their own religious law and custom (*sharīʿah* and *sunnah* in Arabic, *xara* and *çuna* in later medieval Romance texts); the call to prayer continued; halal butchers were permitted; Muslim schools, cemeteries, bathhouses, and pious endowments stayed in operation; Muslims could go on pilgrimage, they could observe Ramadan, they could circumcise their children, and they could continue to use Arabic and call themselves by traditional Islamic names.

But was this really enough to live a fully Muslim life? In fact, many Mudejars found their lives increasingly restricted and impoverished, their religious practices curtailed, their communities segregated, and they were largely cut off from the larger Islamic world. Within the Muslim community outside of the Iberian Peninsula, especially in North Africa, many Islamic jurists argued that despite Christian promises of continuity for the *shari'ah* and *sunnah*, it was not actually possible to live as a true Muslim under Christian rule. They urged that all Muslims should leave Christian lands, and many Mudejars complied, emigrating to Naṣrid Granada, North Africa, or the eastern Islamic world.[18]

Many other Mudejars chose to remain in Spain, whether by preference, economic necessity, family commitments, or for other reasons. Continued Muslim life in Spain is recorded in a small number of texts produced by their own community and a much larger body of Christian sources, mainly legal and economic materials, relating to Mudejar affairs and legislation. The realities of Mudejar existence did not remain unchanged in the four centuries between 1085 and 1492, and there were significant regional variations between the large Mudejar populations in Valencia and Aragon, and somewhat smaller ones in Castile and Andalusia. Although these men and women continued to live as Muslims, it is clear that their access to religious and cultural traditions became more restricted over time as Christians around them became gradually less tolerant of public and private practices that they associated with Islam. This shifting context and changing attitudes about certain aspects of Muslim life will be discussed in more detail throughout this volume.

The eve of the sixteenth century ushered in fundamental changes for Muslim life in Spain. After the conquest of Granada, the long-standing though contested toleration of Muslim customs and religious practice under Christian rule quickly shifted into a zealous Christian conversation about how to eradicate these pernicious symbols of Islamic identity. By 1500, most Christian authorities in Spain had come to the conclusion that it was impossible to be Christian and yet still live one's daily life in a fashion that many people perceived as Muslim (*vivir como moro*). This was true not only in Granada, where Núñez Muley composed his memorandum in response to the 1567 restrictions, but also in Valencia and other regions of the Peninsula where there were New Christian populations. Among Old Christians, urban administrators, bishops and local clergy, inquisitors, kings, and queens were all openly concerned about backsliding among converts; secret Muslim rituals practiced at home behind closed doors, in bathhouses, and elsewhere; furtive teaching of Arabic and Islamic texts to children; continued adherence to Muslim dietary laws and fasts; attendance at traditional festivals, weddings, and musical events; clandestine funerary practices and circumcisions, as well as many other aspects of earlier Islamic life, especially concerning clothing and appearance. These worries about residual Islam were quite aside from concurrent and significant concerns about improper or insufficient Morisco knowledge of Christian prayers, rituals, practices, and doctrine. And these anxieties were reflected in repeated statutes prohibiting perceived Islamic practices, reiterated throughout the sixteenth century.

Although at first glance such early modern legislation seems a dramatic break from the medieval past, in fact, this new push to eliminate Muslim "rites and customs" was merely the mirror image—reversed yet fundamentally the same—of earlier laws concerning Muslim life and practice. Before 1500, Christian legislation had been largely intended to maintain clear barriers between Muslims and Christians, with laws explicitly designed to assist segregation and to prevent assimilation, intermarriage, social and sexual mixing, or any confusion of religious identity. For example, medieval sumptuary laws in Spain, at least since the rulings of the Fourth Lateran Council in 1215, had functioned to preserve easily recognizable visual markers of identity in line with differences of religion: Jews must wear a star on their clothing or a particular style of hat or cap; Muslims should wear distinctive types of dress, cut their hair in a certain way, or wear a crescent moon symbol on their clothes. After 1500, and following the wave of forced conversions, the same basic impulses dictated that all baptized Christians should look, dress, pray, eat, and otherwise conduct themselves in the same way. In Granada, according to the edicts of 1567 "with respect to clothing, it was ordered that they [the Moriscos] not make any new dresses, veiled gowns, hose, or any other sort of dress such as those that they wore during the Muslim period; and that all the clothing that they cut and made in the future be like that worn by Christians."[19] If there was no longer any difference of religion, nor should there be any distinctions in dress or daily life.

Because of this, in the sixteenth century, a whole group of practices that had once been open, acceptable, and even required aspects of Muslim culture, even under Christian rule, now became newly dangerous signals of imperfect Christian belief and probable markers of crypto-Islam. Inquisition records and episcopal correspondence from the early sixteenth century onward are filled with accusations not only of the inadequate Christianization of Moriscos (such as not knowing prayers, working on Sundays, failing to attend mass and confession, or avoiding baptizing their children) but also of outright Islamic practices (including prayer, circumcision, fasting, abstaining from pork and alcohol, reading the Qur'ān in Arabic, and ritual washing), together with a whole host of other more customary and cultural activities (things like visiting bathhouses, dressing in traditional clothing, veiling of women, eating couscous, dancing and singing *zambras*, staying up all night at parties [*laylas*], using henna to tint one's hands and feet, sitting on the floor to eat, or wearing sandals and jewelry decorated with amulets and folk patterns). This new inquisitorial and administrative attention to Morisco *ritos*, *costumbres*, and *supersticiones* provides the context for Francisco Núñez Muley's decision to argue his defense on the basis of culture and local tradition, while suppressing any associations with Islam.

Lines differentiating religion and custom are still often unclear today, but apparent parallels between past and present can be misleading. Regulations on female veiling provide a case in point. In the contemporary Islamic world, there is ongoing debate about the interpretation of passages in the Qur'ān (such as *sūrah* 24, *āyah* 31) and *'aḥādīth* in regard to veiling, and the degree to which women should be covered when they go out in public. Muslims likewise differ over whether the wearing of a veil is a religious requirement for all women or a personal choice to be made by individual women.[20] The origins of the tradition are also a matter for dispute among scholars, whether female veiling was an innovation of the early Muslim community or a practice adopted from Christian fashions common in late antique Syria and Egypt.[21]

Ironically, in the modern Muslim world, laws requiring the veil may lead some women to wear it as a legal necessity or a habit rather than as a dictate of personal faith, whereas women elsewhere who veil by choice usually do so with an explicitly religious rationale. Meanwhile, in western Europe, there has been much recent condemnation of the wearing of the veil (whether in the form of a *hijab*, *niqab*, burka, or other regional style) on the grounds that veiling is inconsistent with prevailing local expectations and law. In April 2011, veils that hide the face were banned in France, on the basis that they oppress women, they are a violation of individual liberties, and they present a conspicuous religious symbol at odds with French expectations of a secular society. Face veils were also banned in Belgium a few months later, and other European countries are discussing the issue. All of these measures have met with resistance and lawsuits from Muslims living in Europe.[22] Controversy over Muslim women's clothing has also been at the center of debates in North

America, especially in Quebec where efforts to ban veils and other religious symbols culminated in the 2013 promotion of a "Charte de la laïcité."[23]

A facile comparison between restrictions imposed in twenty-first-century Paris or Montreal and sixteenth-century Granada might seem to suggest intriguing similarities, but ultimately, this comparative exercise is elusive. The contexts of these legislative acts are profoundly different, as are the beliefs about humanity and society on which they are based. Contemporary Western arguments about the veil are overtly grounded in assumptions about equality, openness, and security within a modern secular society, even while anti-Islamic and anti-immigrant sentiments may lurk just below the surface of this discourse. In contrast, legislators in sixteenth-century Granada made no bones about their anti-Islamic and pro-Castilian Christian opinions. Most early modern Christians saw Muslims and Islam in Spain as a recently defeated enemy and a righteously obliterated religion, while many suspected that crypto-Muslims were still dangerous as a potential military and religious fifth column. Christian administrators and inquisitors cherished a mutual goal of creating, by force when necessary, a single unified Catholic Spain. To achieve this goal, in the wake of mass conversions, many saw it as equally necessary to stamp out all earlier habits and customs possibly associated with Islamic life. The reactions to these acts of restrictive legislation, modern and early modern, are likewise fundamentally different. Modern Muslims have responded with appeals to their rights to freedom of religious practice and expression. Francisco Núñez Muley, in contrast, knew that there was no freedom of religion, and in consequence he argued that these practices were not an expression of religious belief.

The details of Francisco Núñez Muley's defense of Granadan cultural practices in terms of styles of dress, haircuts, use of henna, and visits to bathhouses, will be discussed in the individual chapters of this book devoted to these topics, along with one other distinctive aspect of Muslim custom and practice (mentioned only very briefly in his memorandum): the continuity of Andalusi foodstuffs, foodways, and table manners. Núñez Muley's arguments reflected their particular late sixteenth-century Granadan context, but the customs and practices that he defended had a much longer history. In the chapters that follow, I will examine the legislation, perceptions, and debates about Muslim appearance (Chapter 2), bathing (Chapter 3), and foodways (Chapter 4) in Christian Spanish kingdoms from the late eleventh century until the late sixteenth century.

Over this five-hundred-year period, there were remarkable changes in Christian attitudes about the continuation of Muslim rites and practices under Christian rule, from a relatively easy acceptance in the twelfth and thirteenth centuries, to increasing hostility during the fourteenth and fifteenth centuries, to eradication in the sixteenth century. This was true both for outright aspects of Islamic law and faith, which were always completely separate from Christian norms, and the more ambiguous aspects of daily life, such as foodstuffs and popular music, that could fairly easily assimilate across the borders of faith. Thus, ordinary habits that had been widely shared by Christians, Muslims, and Jews in Iberia during much of the medieval period, such as regular visits to community bathhouses, became tainted as filthy, disreputable, and un-Christian by the late medieval and early modern period. This book will trace these changes and consider their causes, looking not at the overtly religious aspects of Islamic practice (which are easy to explain) but at the more equivocal but deeply ingrained habits of daily life, which, though widely recognized as Muslim, could also be argued as being merely regional and customary.

In the final clauses of his memorandum, almost as an afterthought after the signature, Francisco Núñez Muley posits two counterfactual situations in order to drive home his point. First, Núñez Muley asks what would happen if

there should be established a decree requiring all Christians to dress like Moriscos and wear their footwear; to cease celebrating weddings in the Castilian way and instead begin celebrating them as Moriscos do; to have no other music but the Morisco *zambra* and the instruments that accompany it; to bathe in the Morisco baths and to hire only Morisco bath-workers and no others; to speak no Castilian whatsoever but only Arabic; to cease using any Castilian names or surnames; to keep the doors to their homes open at all times. Furthermore, this decree would prohibit women from leaving their faces uncovered in public and require them to cover them as Morisco women do, and it would prohibit Christians from possessing any contracts, registers, or land titles in Castilian—all of these would have to be written in Arabic.[24]

Second, he follows on this long hypothetical suggestion by asking, what if instead of requiring Castilian Christians to speak Arabic, they were required to speak and write in the Genoese dialect of Italian, would they comply? No, he answers. Even though Genoese is not that different a language from Castilian (certainly "much closer to Castilian than Arabic is"), and both the Castilians and the Genoese are Christian, "they would not comply, but rather they would die and suffer under burdens and punishments."[25]

These two hypothetical scenarios are revealing in the degree to which they seek to turn the issue at hand from a question of religious identity (Christian vs. Muslim) to one of linguistic and regional identity (first Granada and Arabic vs. Castile and Castilian, then Castilian vs. Genoese). By extension, the Moriscos were also willing to die and suffer to preserve their regional identity, language, and customs, even while being Christians. Like Francisco Núñez Muley's memorandum, this is also a book about identity and the structures that support our understandings of identity, but unlike his work, it includes religion as one among many factors creating identity in medieval and early modern Spain.

CHAPTER 2

# Clothing and Appearance

Do clothes make the man—or the woman? Should it be possible to know a person's identity or religion simply from his or her appearance, and can certain clothes, hairstyles, and other aspects of visual identity be mandated by custom and law? Throughout the medieval period, the desirable answer was generally "yes." Different groups of people should look different, with different vestimentary traditions, whether through self- or communal regulation (according to their own laws, habits, and personal desires) or mandated by external legislation. Prescriptive legal sources, both religious and secular, from medieval Islamic, Jewish, and Christian spheres, all indicate medieval sentiments in favor of the immediate visual identification of religious, social, and economic distinctions through regulations on dress, hairstyles, veils, belts, shoes, beards, jewelry, and other aspects of personal and collective appearance. One of the most famous iterations of these opinions, codified at the Fourth Lateran Council in 1215 and requiring distinctive "signs" for Muslims and Jews, did not stand alone in the legal tradition.

Meanwhile, the lawyers, clerics, and administrators who upheld sumptuary laws were themselves far from alone in supporting the importance of differential visual identity in medieval and early modern Spain. Artists (and, by extension, their audiences) in Christian and Muslim regions were likewise familiar with the conventions for representing Christian and Muslim appearance, whether in luxury manuscripts produced at the court of Alfonso X of Castile, or in frescoes of courtly scenes adorning the ceilings of the Alhambra Palace in Granada. While it may be argued that neither law nor art necessarily reflected actual lived experience in medieval and early modern Spain, nevertheless, both genres expressed clear and well-understood expectations that Muslims, Christians, and Jews should be visually distinguishable from each other.

And just as different groups should look different, so too members of the same community should appear as such. Thirteenth-century Castilian law had dictated not only that Muslims should dress differently from Christians but also that newly converted Christians ("christianos novos") must no longer dress as Moors ("nin vistan commo los moros").[1] Three centuries later, on the eve of mass conversions in the early sixteenth century, the first archbishop of Granada, Hernando de Talavera, likewise advised that New Christians should conform outwardly to Christian ways of life, and lest they be suspected of harboring Muslim belief in their hearts, they should appear as good and honest Christians in their dress, shoes, and hairstyles.[2] Sixteenth-century opinion in this matter was founded on medieval precedents, with one adviser to the emperor Charles V in 1526 recommending that Morisco dress be prohibited because "people and things identify themselves by the signs that they carry, and thus they are judged to be those whose signs they bear."[3] It follows, therefore, that the 1567 law in Granada requiring that the Moriscos "may not wear Moorish clothing" (no traygan vestido de moros), but they must "conform with Old Christians in their dress" (conformen en los trajes con los cristianos viejos) was directly related to a much older discourse about legislating the visual distinction of identity.[4] Pedro de Deza, the president of the Granadan Royal Audiencia who was in charge of implementing the 1567 ordinances, thus argued that the retention of Moorish styles (ropas a la morisca) "was dishonest, and it did not look right that Christian women should go around dressed like moras."[5]

When Francisco Núñez Muley was called upon to defend the rights of New Christians to wear traditional styles, he was forced to find a new focus for this familiar line of argument, by reorienting the discussion from religious to regional distinctiveness. In trying to disassociate the long-held presumption that people of different religions were, and should be, visually distinct because of religion, he argued that "the style of dress, clothing and footwear of the natives cannot be said to be that of Muslims, nor is it that of Muslims. It can more rightly be said to be clothing that corresponds to a particular kingdom and province . . . it follows from what I have just said that Christianity is not found in the clothing or footwear that is now in style, and the same is true of Islam."[6] These arguments ran counter to centuries of legislation and assumptions linking belief and appearance. And yet Núñez Muley's arguments also had good grounding since there were many different regional styles of dress in early modern Spain. Styles in Granada were different from those worn by New Christians elsewhere, stemming from the fact that this region had been very recently conquered, while Mudejars in Valencia, Aragon, and northern Castile had been living under Christian rule for centuries. Evidence from these regions indicates that Muslims had long dressed in styles that were often similar to those of their Old Christian neighbors—even while religious and secular legislation required differential appearance. By the sixteenth century, many New Christians in northern and eastern Iberia had more or less given up Morisco styles (*el traje a los moriscos*).[7]

Some identity requirements were purely external and easily changed, such as styles of clothing; others were also temporary, but somewhat more long term, such as particular styles for hair and beards; still others were permanently inscribed on the body, as with circumcision in particular.[8] Inherent differences in appearance, such as skin color, might also be seen as important visual markers, but these could not be legislated or altered. Meanwhile, certain invisible elements that were believed to create identity—such as the importance given to purity of blood (*pureza de sangre*) in early modern Spain—were a different matter again.[9] The case of Granada was thus particular, and this region would become the focal point for early modern attention to Morisco dress. But it was not entirely unique, and it is important both to consider the particularities of Granadan experience on their own terms and to situate them in a wider context.

\* \* \*

The more changeable aspects of visual identity could be easily shared, and there is a common and understandable tendency for people living in the same place at the same time to dress in similar fashions. Much of medieval sumptuary legislation therefore addressed the problems entailed by the social and economic muddling of visual identity. As has frequently been pointed out, repeated laws requiring differential styles of clothing may suggest that, in fact, people routinely ignored these rules. We know, for example, that many Christians in late medieval Spain liked to wear elements of what was commonly identified as "Moorish" dress, despite strictures against such things, while Mudejars did not always wear the particular clothing and hairstyles that were dictated by Christian authorities to signal their Muslim identity. Sharing was less likely in the case of permanent bodily signs, which could not be assumed without inflicting pain, and which would have remained the same even when identity changed. In 1526, when Moriscos in Granada were first required to abandon "Moorish" forms of dress, many adult male converts would still have been circumcised. But, needless to say, this inscribed sign of residual Islamic identity would rarely have been visible in the public sphere (except perhaps in a bathhouse). Old Christian authorities could not demand its removal, although they certainly tried to ensure that Morisco boys did not undergo the procedure.

Many rulings regarding communal visual identity were directed internally, issued by political and religious authorities toward members of their own communities to create solidarity and conformity, whether these were requirements for circumcision or sumptuary laws dictating clothing and hairstyles. Other laws were imposed by a ruling community that wielded power over a subject community (whether or not these subjects were actually a numerical minority). Both sorts of rules had very ancient roots, and many elements of legal thought that became common in the medieval Mediterranean world can be found in Roman law and other earlier traditions.

As regards Christian-Muslim relations, legislation on the proper dress and deportment of Christians and Jews living under Muslim rule (*dhimmīs*) can be traced back to the first century of Islam, in the so-called Pact of 'Umar (Shurūṭ 'Umar).[10] This famous document is thought to have been promulgated by either the caliph 'Umar I (d. 644) or 'Umar II (d. 720), and it would be widely disseminated throughout the later medieval Islamic world, including al-Andalus, as a long-term template for Muslim-*dhimmī* relations. The categories for distinction were clearly, and strictly, envisioned along religious lines. Along with other provisions relating to behavior and daily life, Christians and Jews were not allowed to wear Muslim clothing, shoes, turbans, or hairstyles; instead, they were required to dress with a distinctive type of belt and to clip their hair in a particular way.[11] Although there is plenty of evidence to suggest that these rules were not always strictly or universally enforced, and that many *dhimmīs* actually dressed and looked much like their Muslim neighbors, the legal initiatives of the Pact of 'Umar survived over many centuries.[12]

The most influential medieval Latin Christian statement on visual distinction was promulgated by Pope Innocent III at the Fourth Lateran Council in 1215. Toward the end of the records of the council, in canon 68, the pope noted that in some Christian regions "a difference of dress distinguishes Jews or Saracens from Christians, but in certain others such confusion has developed that they are indistinguishable." He therefore decreed that all Muslims and Jews "of either sex in every Christian province and at all times shall be distinguished from other people by the character of their dress in public." He went on to explain that not only should non-Christians avoid rich and elegant clothing, or anything that might appear to set them above Christians, but that wearing distinctive clothing would avoid the possibility of any confusion of religious identity during daily interaction or—more critically—any confusion that might lead to forbidden sexual contact. Because of similarity of dress, Innocent warned, "it sometimes happens that by mistake Christians unite with Jewish or Saracen women, and Jews or Saracens with Christians."[13] His words reflected significant anxieties about confusion of appearance, mistaken identity, and the possibility of sexual mixing that had become common in western European thought by the later twelfth century in the wake of warfare, trade, and increasing encounters between Christians and Muslims.[14]

These rulings initiated a flurry of subsequent sumptuary legislation throughout Latin Europe, dictating the signs that Jews and Muslims should wear in order to be visually distinguished from Christians. The long-term ramifications for Mudejar dress and appearance in Christian Spain will be discussed in more detail below. But what is clear is that the dictates of Lateran IV confirmed and institutionalized, for the rest of the medieval period, widespread acceptance of the idea that Christians and non-Christians should look different.

## Clothing After Conquest

In 1499, seven years after their conquest of Granada, when King Fernando and Queen Isabel returned to visit that city, they were greeted by the "admirable" scene of a great crowd of people that included (according to their chronicler, Alonso de Santa Cruz) thirty-thousand Muslim women (*moras*) wearing traditional white veils (*almalafas*).[15] It must have been a stunning sight and distinctly different, visually, from the kind of crowd that might have greeted their entrance into Burgos, Barcelona, Madrid, or other towns where the Muslim population was very low. The original capitulations of Granada, drawn up late in 1491, had allowed the Muslim inhabitants of the conquered city to remain Muslim and to preserve their distinctive religious and customary ways of life, including clothing, foodways, language, and bathing. This and the other late fifteenth-century treaties that the Catholic Kings negotiated with cities throughout the former Nasrid kingdom had all assumed, initially, that the newly subject inhabitants would remain Muslim and assume a status very like that of Mudejars living under Christian rule elsewhere in the realms of

Castile and Aragon. So there was little surprising or problematic in the fact that the crowds in Granada who gathered to greet the monarchs in 1499 were dressed in the traditional fashions closely associated with their Islamic faith.

But problems and unpleasant surprises were about to appear, and the process of forced conversion of Muslims in Granada and other parts of the Crown of Castile, undertaken in 1500–1502, would profoundly change long-standing assumptions about visual distinction and identity. After conversion, New Christians were encouraged to abandon the earlier ways that had marked them as Muslim and to look, dress, speak, and act like Old Christians. Hernando de Talavera, appointed as the first archbishop of newly Christian Granada in 1493, was especially attentive to the nuances of dress and deportment, having already written a sumptuary treatise for Christians in 1477, which he revised and published in 1496 after moving to Granada.[16] Talavera sought to "domesticate" his converted flock (*para domesticarles*) and to teach them Christian ways.[17] Among these, "he made sure that they dressed in Castilian styles [*que se vistiessen a lo Castellano*], and he gave cloaks, shoes, and hats to poor men, and shawls and skirts [*mantos y sayas*] to their wives."[18] Talavera was much more sympathetic to the local population than was his colleague Francisco Jiménez de Cisneros, who would become infamous for his hard-line attitude toward enforcing conversion and the abandonment of Muslim ways.[19]

Early capitulation treaties, in which Muslim communities in the region of Granada agreed to convert to Christianity, made practical provision for the difficult shift from Muslim to Christian ways of life, including clauses relating to butchers, bathhouses, language, and clothing. Similar documents drawn up with converted communities in Baza, Huéscar, and Vélez Rubio in 1500 and 1501 all promised that New Christians "would not be pressured to buy and wear new clothes until those that they and their wives currently owned had worn out.[20] We also find negotiations for a delay nearly three decades later, when Muslims in Valencia (in 1525) and elsewhere in the Crown of Aragon (in 1526) likewise faced forced baptism. New converts in Valencia pleaded to retain their styles of clothing "which are so different from the clothing of Christians, especially as regards female clothing. Because the change of dress and the loss of these articles of clothing would be a great hardship, and no provision had been made to cover the loss, they requested a grace period of forty years before being forced to abandon their clothing." In reply (in a treaty ratified in 1526 but published in 1528), the king and the Inquisition granted them "a period of ten years in which to use and wear the clothes that they currently had, after which they would have to switch to Christian styles."[21]

The grant of ten years may have been based on earlier experiences in Castile, where there seems to have been a decade of uncertainty about the point at which Morisco clothing could be considered to be "worn out" and whether items could be mended and refashioned to prolong their useful life. An ordinance issued by Queen Juana in 1511, addressed to all New Christians in the kingdom of Granada ("men and women, old and young"), ordered not only that they must give up wearing Moorish-style clothing ("ropa de vestir a la manera de los moros") and dress like Old Christians, but also that "no tailor, for any reason or in any way, shall cut or make any clothing for the newly converted to wear except in the style of Old Christian dress."[22] However, a loophole was immediately found in this ruling, so in 1513 Juana issued another decree noting that for the past two years, Old Christian and Mudejar tailors had claimed that the 1511 law did not apply to them; from here onward, she "ordered that another decree be made that Old Christian and Mudejar tailors not be allowed to make Moorish-style clothing [ropas moriscas]."[23] Juana then went on, in this decree and in another document issued on the same day (July 29, 1513), to prohibit both New Christian and Old Christian women from wearing almalafas or any other form of veil that covered their faces.[24] This would be the first in a long series of edicts against the almalafa and female veiling, which will be discussed in more detail in a separate section below.

The first comprehensive set of postconquest ordinances and restrictions relating to New Christian life was issued in Granada by Charles V in December 1526, and the Inquisition was charged with enforcement of this legislation. Although the original edict's extant text included no clauses relating to general Morisco clothing, other aspects of their visual identity—female face veiling and the almalafa, painting hands and feet with henna, and wearing ornaments in the shape of a hand inscribed with Arabic letters—were specifically addressed and prohibited.[25] Nevertheless, a later account of this edict in Prudencio de Sandoval's Historia de la vida y hechos del emperador Carlos V (published in 1604) did give equal weight to clothing, recalling the requirement that "they were to put aside and leave off wearing the marlotas [loose open garments with sleeves] that they were accustomed to wear in place of skirts [sayas], and the linen almalafas that they wore in place of

shawls [*mantos*], and all Moriscas and Moriscos were to dress themselves as
Christians . . . and no tailor should dare to fashion clothes, or jeweler to create ornaments, in a Moorish style."[26] The ordinances of 1526 were in any
case sufficiently broad-ranging to create a shock wave through the New
Christian community in Granada, and a petition was made to the emperor for
a grace period to lessen the impact of his decree (not unlike the contemporary
plea from New Christians in Valencia). Their appeal met with success, and
the edict was put on hold for forty years—in return for a hefty payment to the
crown from the New Christian community in Granada.[27]

The struggle over clothing was an uphill battle for both sides in the middle
of the sixteenth century. Many New Christians steadfastly retained their traditional styles of dress; royal legislation was not necessarily effective, fines and
penalties could be ignored, and the Inquisition had promised not to intervene
during the grace period negotiated in 1526. Clothing, also, was easily changed,
and people who dutifully dressed in Christian fashions for public activities might switch back into their more comfortable and familiar older-style
clothing when they returned home. Royal letters sent to the archbishop
and Audiencia of Granada in 1530 lamented the backsliding of New Christian women, who had resumed dressing in Moorish clothing ("se han vuelto
a poner el [hábito] morisco") and in so doing "had forgotten Christian doctrine
and committed many sins and offenses."[28] Later in the same year Charles's
empress, Isabella of Portugal, wrote directly to the New Christian community in Granada urging that they give up their past beliefs and errors in their
ways of life, especially "the clothing and styles that you wore in the time
when you were not Christians." The letter even took on something of a personal tone, underlining Isabella's concern over the issue: "we charge and en-
treat you to abandon these garments, and from now on to clothe and to dress
yourselves and your children in clothing and styles after the manner that Old
Christians wear in this kingdom, because as well as being something very
important for the salvation and improvement of your souls, this will also give
me much pleasure."[29]

Perhaps some New Christians heeded her request, but a quarter century
later, in 1554, the canons of the Synod of Guadix repeated similar accusations
that some Moriscos were switching back and forth between the two different
styles of clothing as evidence of their bad faith. By the middle of the sixteenth
century, concerns about faith and identity had taken on new importance in
light of the Reformation. Martín Pérez de Ayala, bishop of Guadix and con-

vener of the synod in 1554, was also a participant at the Council of Trent and well aware of such problems. The Guadix synod gave specific instructions about clothing reforms and six months to put them into effect, after which "nobody should dare to wear Morisco clothing or styles, and they should especially abandon veils [*savanas* or *sábanas*], *marlotas*, and head coverings [*atavio de las cabeças*], and they must put on shawls, skirts, and head coverings [*mantos y sayas y tocas*] in the Christian style."[30]

These rulings set the scene for the crackdown in 1567, when even more comprehensive restrictions on Morisco life were imposed in Granada. First, the legislation addressed those who made clothes. Henceforth, "no one among the newly converted in the said kingdom or among their descendants would be able to make or cut new *almalafas* or *marlotas* or any other types of shoes or clothes that were used or worn in the time of the Moors. And any new clothes that are made must conform to the styles that are worn by Old Christians, namely *mantos* and *sayas*." The edict went on to lay out penalties, in prison terms and monetary fines, for first, second, and third offenses. Next, it addressed those who wore *almalafas* and *marlotas*, and permitted (once again) a grace period that allowed one year of further wear for fancy silk garments and two years for ordinary unornamented clothing. After that, nobody could wear such clothes, and they would be liable for the same penalties as those imposed on tailors. Finally, even while women continued to wear their *almalafas* during the grace period, they must be sure that their faces remained uncovered.[31]

This, then, was the situation that Francisco Núñez Muley was called on to address in his memorandum to the Audiencia in Granada, and which led him to try to disentangle the bond between religion and clothing styles. Ultimately, this was a lost cause, but the strategies of his argument illuminate various sides of the debate over Morisco clothing: religious, cultural, moral, economic, and visual. Núñez Muley began by reviewing the history of restrictions on clothing, going back to Queen Juana's attempts to prevent tailors from making clothes in traditional styles and other early sixteenth-century decrees "prohibiting the wearing, weaving, and elaboration of Morisco clothing."[32] These rulings were never implemented, he says, not because of Morisco intransigence, but because Old Christian leaders of the city were either unaware of the new laws, or were opposed to them, or restrictions were suspended in return for payment. At the same time, from an economic perspective, people recognized that "overwhelming harm would be done to the natives by taking away their traditional style of dress, and great injury would also be done to those merchants who have invested their wealth in purchasing cloth for such clothing."[33] Pressing this fiscal argument, Núñez Muley estimated that 150,000 people would be required to purchase new clothes, of whom only a small fraction (he claims four or five thousand) would have the money to do so. Another option might be to cut up Morisco clothes and sew them together again as Christian-type garments, but the differences in the two styles made this impracticable. In the end, he concluded, lots of perfectly good clothes would have to be thrown away, and this (to make one last compelling point) would "greatly diminish royal rents as well as all things related to the taxes paid to the Royal Crown."[34]

The primary issue that Núñez Muley had to contend with was the long-held correlation between clothing styles and religious faith. As he argued, "the prelates contend that the preservation of the traditional style of dress and footwear of the natives of this kingdom is tantamount to a continuation of the ceremonies and customs of the Muslims. I can only say, My Lord, that in my modest judgment (which has nonetheless helped me to reach old age) these reports are wholly without merit."[35] This launches him into his argument (quoted at the start of this chapter) that traditional clothing styles were in fact merely an expression of regional identity, not religious affiliation. In support of this, he points out that clothing styles vary between different regions of Castile and in other Christian kingdoms and provinces, just as styles differ between Granada, Morocco, and Turkey, even though all inhabitants of the latter two lands are Muslim, so "it follows that one cannot establish or state that the clothing of the new converts is that of Muslims." Furthermore, Christians from Jerusalem have been seen "wearing clothing and head coverings similar to what is worn in the Maghreb and resembling in no way what is worn in Castile—and yet they are Christians."[36]

Finally, regarding style, he observes that fashions change over time and thus modern Morisco everyday clothes were much closer to Castilian styles (being shorter, lighter, and cheaper) than they had been at the start of the century. This is in contrast to costly festive garments, only brought out for weddings and celebrations, which—he admits—tend to be carefully preserved and passed down from generation to generation.[37] New Christian men had quickly adopted new styles and now "wear wholly Castilian clothing. If the natives' hearts were truly obstinate, then they would no doubt think that changing their style of dress would compromise their religion . . . and yet the men do not dress now as they used to." According to Núñez Muley, this shift was a relatively easy process since male clothes and shoes wear out quickly and need to be regularly replaced in any case, and "seeing that the Castilian style of dress is better and more suited to men . . . they began to wear Castilian clothing as they do today by their own free will and without any complaint whatsoever. This has been the custom here for over forty years," despite which New Christians have not yet received any relief from the special taxes and re-strictions that still set them apart from Old Christians.[38] Women's fashions were a different matter, and traditional styles persisted into the later sixteenth century, especially wearing the distinctive and enveloping *almalafa*, and Núñez Muley spoke forcefully about the benefits of modesty and protection, afforded to both Old and New Christian women, provided by covering their heads and faces.[39]

Underlying all of Núñez Muley's arguments were the assumptions that local styles differed and fashions changed over time. He does not question the fact that clothing types common in Granada were unlike the fashions of Cas-tile, and that these distinctions played a strong role in visual identity—whether this identity was interpreted as religious or regional. He also makes strong claims about personal choice and free will, suggesting that people wear certain clothes because they are comfortable, fashionable, or affordable, not merely because church or state sumptuary laws require adherence. As in the rest of his memorandum, Núñez Muley makes the case for the weight of tra-dition, local ("native") identity, and the practical aspects of daily life over those of religious belief in influencing the clothing choices of New Christians. Núñez Muley's argument was that people in different regions will naturally look different, regardless of religion, while people sharing regional identity will gradually come to share vestimentary traditions over time (whether Christians in Jerusalem wearing local styles, or New and Old Christian women in Granada veiling their faces). Thus, the difficulty in Granada was merely that coalescence of dress had not yet happened, because habit and economic dis-incentive had so far led many New Christians—especially women—to pre-serve their long-held regional fashions.

Núñez Muley's memorandum had no apparent effect in mitigating con-temporary edicts against wearing *almalafas, marlotas,* and other elements of Morisco dress. But it did not fall on entirely deaf ears, since Luis del Mármol Carvajal mentioned Núñez Muley's appeal in his history of the Morisco re-bellion in 1568.[40] Diego Hurtado de Mendoza went further, in his more sym-pathetic history of the same wars, by elaborating Núñez Muley's arguments about regionalism in the voice of a fictional Morisco "of very great natural

authority and ripe and mature counsel," who pointed out that "they order us
to leave off our Moorish clothes and dress in the Castillian manner. Even
amongst the Christians, the Germans dress in one manner, the French in another, the Greeks in another, the friars in quite a distinct manner and the
Christian boys dress quite differently from the Christian men. Amongst the
Christians, each nation, each profession, each group and rank and station of
mankind has a distinct way of dressing, and they are all Christians, and we
are Moors and so we dress in the Moorish fashion: it is as if they wish us outwardly to conform even when we are not conforming in our hearts."[41] One
might think that this argument would have had a certain logical traction,
because it was objectively true and would appeal to the professed rationalism
of contemporary thought. Nevertheless, it failed to change assumptions, based
on customs and legislation that had been firmly in place for many centuries,
that Christians and Muslims did in fact dress differently because of their different religious traditions.

*   *   *

The pull of distinctive clothing presented a real problem in an age when
religious and secular authorities wished to establish conformity in both external appearance and internal belief. This was very different from the medieval concerns, expressed in the Fourth Lateran Council, which had worried
about an inevitable pull toward the assimilation of visual identity. Visual
confusion of identity was a bad thing in 1215, when the overall desire was
to preserve difference where difference existed. Crusaders needed to know
that they were fighting the right enemies; tax collectors needed to be able to
identify non-Christian subjects; preachers should be able to target their
audience; jurists knew that different codes of law applied to different
groups; and above all people must avoid jumping into bed with somebody of
a different faith.

Overall, religious difference was a persistent fact of medieval Iberian life.
Despite a strong rhetorical and polemical impulse urging the conversion of
Muslims, there were no actual widespread, concerted, or successful efforts in this
direction before the sixteenth century.[42] Instead, while rulers such as Alfonso VI
and Alfonso X of Castile and Jaume I of Aragon may have wished—on some
level—to rule over entirely Christian kingdoms, they were also well aware
not only of the practical obstacles to mass conversions but also of the economic and structural advantages to maintaining their subject non-Christian

populations. Thus, Mudejars should look different from Christians, as a reflection of their Muslim identity; just as later Moriscos, being New Christians, must look the same as their Old Christian coreligionists.

## Visual Identity in Medieval Spain

The effort to preserve difference, as opposed to mandating assimilation, resulted in medieval attitudes toward vestimentary legislation that were profoundly different from those of the sixteenth century (even while both traditions arose from the same basic premises about visual identity). In the wake of the Lateran IV rulings in 1215, Christian legislators all over Europe established dress codes and signs by which Jews and Muslims could be easily identified.[43] Jews were the exclusive focus for such laws in most regions of western Europe, where there were no Muslim communities. Both subject religious communities were present in Spain, but even here vestimentary rules were not always equally applied to the two groups. Legislation relating to Jews in Castile and Aragon tended to focus on special signs (often stars) to be worn on clothing, particular colors (frequently yellow), and peculiar hats, but laws for Muslims more often required distinctive styles of clothing or hair. Only occasionally, as in a law of 1408 from Castile that ordered Muslims to wear badges in the shape of crescent moons, were Mudejar rules directly parallel to those of their Jewish contemporaries.[44] Sometimes, Muslims were not even cited in Iberian laws relating to visual distinction. This was the case in the *Siete Partidas*, a comprehensive law code commissioned by Alfonso X in the later thirteenth century, which mandated that "Jews shall bear certain marks in order that they may be known" (los judíos deuen andar sennalados por que sean connoscidos) without mentioning any similar law for Muslims.[45]

The reasons for this disparity in the thirteenth century are unclear. One might posit that by the time of the Lateran rulings, Jews in Spain already had a long history of life and assimilation under Christian rule, whereas Muslim subjects were still a relatively recent phenomenon, dating only from the last decades of the eleventh century. Muslim communities in Castile and Aragon also often maintained ties with family, business associates, and coreligionists in Andalusi regions still under Muslim control and in North Africa, and these connections may have fostered ongoing differences in dress and appearance. Mudejars, on the whole, were less acculturated with their Christian neighbors and less urbanized than were their Jewish counterparts, and this may have

lessened Christian worries about confusion of identity. However, this situation appears to have changed over time, as one might expect, as generations
of Muslims continued to live under Christian rule in Castile and Aragon and
began to adapt their external appearance to their local context. So it is noteworthy that only in the later thirteenth century, two hundred years after the
conquest of Toledo and many decades after the Fourth Lateran Council, did
Iberian Christian legislation begin to focus serious attention on Mudejar dress
and hairstyles. Before that, all evidence indicates that Muslims in Christian
Spain generally dressed according to their own vestimentary systems and that
they maintained a distinctive visual identity by their own choice.

There are three main sources for evidence telling us about visual distinctions in clothing and personal appearance in medieval Spain: sumptuary legislation, descriptions of dress in chronicles and literature, and depictions in
art and sculpture. There are also other items of textual evidence, including
wills, sale documents, and personal inventories that document clothing but
usually say less about identity. Material evidence also survives, in the form of
medieval articles of clothing and Andalusi textiles preserved in Christian
tombs and treasuries. Virtually all of the textual sources on clothing and appearance date from the thirteenth century and after. Although one might
think that twelfth-century *fueros* (as one example) would be a rich source for
details of legislation about differential Muslim and Christian dress, they are
not. This silence may further suggest that the visual distinction between
Muslims and Christians was not perceived as a legal problem in Christian Spain
before the later thirteenth century.

Almost all such evidence relating to differences of Christian and Muslim
appearance in later medieval Christian regions is mediated through Christian
perceptions and is found in sources produced by Christian authors and artists. The exception, textiles woven and embroidered in Andalusi ateliers, nonetheless reflects Christian appreciation and use of these materials. Although
we have some visual and textual data on clothing and appearance from al-
Andalus and Naṣrid Granada, for example, in legal texts (*ḥisba* treatises and
*fatwa* collections) or images (illustrations in the tale of Bayāḍ and Riyāḍ [see
Figure 1], or paintings of Muslim and Christian warriors on ceilings in the
Alhambra), these sources are very limited in number as compared to their
Christian-context counterparts.

Notably, however, there are a few Andalusi sources that discussed clothing and religious identity before the development of Christian concerns in the
thirteenth century. Arabic legal writings about *dhimmī* clothing were gener-

Figure 1. *Ḥadīth Bayāḍ wa Riyāḍ* (ca. 1240). Vatican Arabo 368, fol. 22r. Andalusi depiction of contemporary Muslim garb, showing men's and women's head coverings. © 2017 Biblioteca Apostolica Vaticana

ally based on the aforementioned Pact of 'Umar, a text that was familiar to Andalusi jurists and others. The early twelfth-century Sevillian market inspector Ibn 'Abdūn reiterated the regulation that Christians and Jews should dress differently from Muslims, but he also remarked that one ought not to sell used clothes that had belonged to a Christian or Jew without clearly informing the buyer about their origins.[46] Apparently the appearance of the clothing was not sufficient in itself. In Córdoba, another early twelfth-century jurist, Ibn Rushd (d. 1126; the grandfather of Averroës), answered a query about whether it was necessary to wash clothes that had belonged to a Christian before wearing them for Muslim prayer. His answer turned on the issue of whether or not the Muslim wearer knew that the clothes had previously been worn by a Christian.[47] Both of these cases suggest that in al-Andalus, at least, there were often no obvious differences in styles of clothing worn by Muslims and their local Christian (*dhimmī*) neighbors.

The first Iberian statute to reflect the rulings of Lateran IV appeared in the canons of the Council of Tarragona in 1239, with a brief statement that "Jews and Saracens must distinguish themselves from Christians in matters of dress," and that interfaith wet-nursing and cohabitation were prohibited.[48] This idea was considerably elaborated in later secular legislation sponsored by Alfonso X of Castile at the Cortes of Seville in 1252, which ordered that "wherever there are Moors who live in towns that are also inhabited by Christians, they must be sure that their hair is clipped all around their heads, and parted in the middle without any longer pieces [*sin tapet*]. They should wear beards, as is mandated by their law, and they may not wear any items made of *çendal*, nor any white, green, bright red, or dark red fabrics, nor white or gold shoes."[49] The Cortes of Valladolid, in 1258, for their part issued a long list of sumptuary legislation that was almost entirely aimed at Christians, with only one brief entry on Muslim clothing and another on Jewish garb. As in Seville, Muslims who lived in towns with Christian neighbors must trim and part their hair in a certain way (this time *sin copete*), wear long beards according to Muslim tradition, and avoid wearing *çendal*, white or tinted cloth (except as had already been specified for Jews), and white or gold shoes.[50] Ten years later, almost identical rules about male clothing, hair, and beards were issued by the Cortes of Jerez in 1268, but an additional clause was added noting that Muslim women (*moras*) were to dress in the same fashions and colors that had been prescribed for Jewish women (*judías*). Non-Christian women were allowed to wear colored or white clothing, with otter-fur trim, but not scarlet or orange, or ermine-trimmed items and other expensive adornments, golden shoes, or sleeves made of gold and silk.[51]

These detailed regulations on clothing (as opposed to those for hair and beards) all emphasize color, fabric, and ornamentation rather than what we would think of as "style"—in other words, unlike sixteenth-century legislation, particular types of garment (such as the *almalafa* or *marlota*) were not singled out for prohibition. All of these colored, expensive, and gilded items were reserved for the Christian nobility and royalty, and thus these clothing rules were probably less aimed at restricting Muslim dress than at enforcing hierarchy and protecting noble entitlements.[52] Ordinary Christians were also prohibited from wearing richly adorned and expensive clothing.[53] Nevertheless, in all three of these pieces of Castilian legislation, the clause limiting its application to "those Moors who live in towns that are populated by Christians" suggests that another intended aim was to prevent any possible confusion (in line with Innocent III's stated goals), not merely to penalize or humiliate non-Christians.

Medieval sumptuary laws always reserved elaborate and expensive dress for members of society's elite, and cost was almost certainly more important than perceived religious origin. Indeed, exotic or foreign fabrics gained value through their rarity. We know from textiles and clothing preserved in tombs at the convent of Santa María Real de Las Huelgas, in Burgos, that the Castilian royal family owned and appreciated Andalusi luxury fabrics.[54] Here again, the richness and exclusivity of the materials was presumably what made these items suitable and indeed desirable for royal attire and burial, rendering any actuality of "Muslim" origins irrelevant.

At the same time, there clearly were differences in style and types of clothing worn by Muslims and Christians in thirteenth-century Castile, and these would generally have provided immediate visual identification without the need for legislation. This is suggested in ordinances from Seville in the early 1270s specifying that new converts to Christianity (*los christianos novos*) must no longer dress as Muslims.[55] Presumably Old Christians were not supposed to dress in Muslim styles either. Visual differences between Muslims and Christians, both men and women, are explicitly depicted in thirteenth-century Castilian art, most notably the *Cantigas de Santa María* and the *Libro de ajedrez*, both manuscripts closely associated with the court of Alfonso X (see Figures 2 and 3).[56] Details of hair, beards, skin color, robes, turbans, veiled faces, bare feet, and hands painted with henna (sometimes holding books with Arabic writing) all drew attention to real distinctions that may have been even more prominent in the Christian imagination and artistic presentation than in everyday life.[57]

Much medieval Christian legislation merely stated that Muslims and Christians should dress differently, but there were a number of more precise statements about how this difference should be expressed. As already noted, thirteenth-century Castilian laws tended to emphasize social hierarchy, expressed in terms of particular types and colors of clothing and fabrics, distinctive hairstyles, and the wearing of beards by Muslim men. Unlike Jews, Muslims in this place and period were not required to wear special signs or symbols on their clothing. Neither, at this point, did Castilian legislation mention particular garments that might be traditionally associated with Muslims. Thus, while legislation for Muslims was undoubtedly restrictive, it is not clear that it was more restrictive than sumptuary legislation for many Christians. Nor

Figure 2. *Libro de ajedrez* (ca. 1283). Escorial Codex T.I.6, fol. 18r. Castilian depiction of Muslim women; note use of henna on fingers. © Patrimonio Nacional

Figure 3. *Libro de ajedrez* (ca. 1283). Escorial Codex T.I.6, fol. 17v. Castilian depiction of Muslim men; several of the figures seem to have henna-dyed beards. © Patrimonio Nacional

is there any indication that Muslims were not able to wear garments (except for luxury items) other than those that they would normally have worn, so long as they were not distinctively Christian.

Hair was a different matter. On the one hand, the distinctive haircut described as being "cut short all around the head" (what Elena Lourie has described as "a special pudding-basin haircut") was surely a humiliating requirement and not something that could be easily changed or hidden.[58] On the other hand, Muslims may already have often worn their hair differently than did Christians, and possibly preferred to have it cut by members of their own community. Jaume I's grant of immunity from royal taxes and seigneurial dominion to a Muslim barber from Vall de Gallinera in 1259 (in return for an annual fee paid to the crown) suggests that this man traveled widely, pursuing his craft in the Muslim communities of Valencia and beyond, and he may have cut hair in certain distinctive styles.[59] In the first half of the fourteenth century, Muslim men in the Crown of Aragon were forbidden to wear their hair in a style called the *garceta*, in which the hair was allowed to grow in locks on either side of the face, in front of the ears and falling to about halfway down the ears, then cut back behind to reveal the ears.[60] The *garceta* (which may have been similar to the *copete* and *tapet* mentioned in Castilian documents) was favored by Christian men in the thirteenth century, and the style appears in contemporary images.[61] But fashions change, as do laws, so that by the middle of the fourteenth century many Muslim men would suddenly be required to adopt the *garceta* (instead of avoiding it) as a sign of their non-Christian status. Nothing was ever said about hairstyles for Muslim women.

Beards presented a different issue, though again exclusively a matter of male appearance, and they appeared much less frequently in Christian legislation than did hair. This makes it especially noteworthy that early Castilian legislation required Muslim men to wear long beards, with the recognition—quite correctly—that this was part of Muslim tradition, which from the beginning had been intended to distinguish Muslims from non-Muslims. Islamic *'aḥādīth* reported the Prophet Muhammad's injunction that Muslim men should allow their beards to grow, while keeping their mustaches trimmed, because this was "the opposite of what the pagans [or polytheists, *al-mushrikūn*] do."[62] Beards did often signal difference; they continued to be commonly worn by Muslim men in thirteenth-century Spain, presumably by choice as much as requirement, while their Christian contemporaries were often—but not universally—clean shaven. Thirteenth-century images normally showed young Christian men without beards, although older men might have them (and one of the most famous beards in medieval literature was, of course, sported by the great Castilian hero Rodrigo Diaz de Bivar, El Cid).[63]

Despite the early expression of Lateran IV rulings at the 1239 church council in Tarragona, secular legislation from the Crown of Aragon did not regulate Muslim appearance until the final quarter of the thirteenth century.[64] In the late 1270s, the *Costums de Tortosa* echoed Castilian rulings—though with the notable variation of singling out particular articles of Muslim clothing. Mudejar men were to have their hair cut short all around the head and allow their beards to grow long and, unless they were working, should wear long loose tunics with sleeves (*aljubas* or *al-jubbas*) and other loose sleeved garments (*almeixias* or *almejías*). Muslim women were to dress as did their Jewish counterparts, in something called an *aldifara*.[65] Nothing was said about color, fabric, or ornament.

Mention of the *garceta* first appeared in the final decade of the thirteenth century, in Catalonia in 1293, when King Jaume II of Aragon wrote to the bailiff of Lérida with instructions that Muslims could wear their hair long (in contrast to the "pudding bowl" cut), but without the *garceta* (*sin garceta*), so long as they looked different from Christians. Apparently the local bishop had recently complained that there was not sufficient visual distinction between the two communities.[66] This 1293 ruling may not have been very effective, since less than a decade later (in 1300 or 1301) the king not only had to reemphasize differential Muslim hairstyles in Lérida (this time requiring that hair be cut short all around the head), but he also had to remind Christians in the city that they should not wear Muslim dress.[67] Nevertheless, it would be the first of a deluge of legislation regulating Muslim hair that would continue throughout the fourteenth century in the Crown of Aragon. This preoccupation with hair, and especially with the *garceta*, was very prominent in fourteenth-century legislation from the regions of Aragon, Catalonia, and Valencia, even while there was very little attention given to Muslim hair in contemporary Castilian law.

Legislation on Muslim hairstyles must have existed in Valencia before 1301, when a Catalan Muslim from L'Espluga de Francoli was arrested and enslaved on a visit to Valencia because he was not wearing the correct haircut (and could not pay the fine). His seigneurial lords, the Templars of Barberá, complained to the king and obtained his release.[68] This case was probably related to Jaume's other rulings about Muslim hairstyles in Catalonia and Aragon, made in that same year. At the Cortes of Zaragoza (also in 1301), he required that all Muslim men in Aragon, Ribagorza, and La Litera must wear their hair cut short around the head, and without the *garceta*.[69] A year later, he wrote to the bailiff of Albalate de Cinca (near Huesca), reiterating these requirements, and in 1306 in Calatayud, he ordered that the bailiff general of Aragon ensure that all Muslims cut their hair differently from Christians, in accord with the recent rulings of the Cortes of Zaragoza.[70] This latter ordinance was now to include those Muslims living near the border with Castile, whom the king had earlier released from this requirement during a period of warfare between the two Christian kings.

While Jaume's attention to this matter suggests a desire to coordinate legislation relating to Muslim hairstyles throughout the Crown of Aragon, it also indicates a tendency toward regional differences in appearance both within his own territories and across the border with Castile. These may have been slight but sufficiently recognizable for a Muslim to be identifiable when he traveled from one place to another. Regional difference could also provide a rationale for exemptions, especially for those who had money and influence. In 1345, Pere IV granted permission to Yahya de Bellvís (a member of a wealthy Muslim family in Aragon and Valencia) to wear his hair in the style customary in Castile, and thus be exempt from Aragonese laws regarding Muslim hairstyles, because he lived in Medinaceli and traveled throughout Castile.[71] A decade later, in 1355, another member of the Bellvís family pleaded exemption from Valencian laws regarding hairstyle on the grounds that his branch of the family was from Aragon.[72]

This latter plea was probably in response to a sudden change in Valencia law, imposed under Pere IV in September of 1347, that now required Muslims to wear the *garceta*—a reversal of the earlier prohibition.[73] This about-face immediately spurred a flurry of court cases and appeals involving Mudejars, their lords, urban administrators, and royal officials, as Muslim men were apprehended in Valencia for not wearing the *garceta*. In October, for example, the king heard the case of a Muslim from Alfama who was apprehended in Murviedro for not wearing the *garceta*; Ramoneta, the seigneurial lord of Alfama, had interceded on his behalf, pleading that he had been excused from wearing the *garceta* because of a wound (presumably to his head). Such cases would persist over the next two decades in Valencia, and it is clear that many Muslims (or their patrons) simply paid for an exemption.[74] Eventually, in 1373, the king became tired of all of this legal fuss. Claiming that ambiguous appearance was still causing too many problems, he revoked all of the earlier privileges and exemptions given to individual Muslims and Muslim communities regarding dress and hair. Muslims in Valencia were to wear "a certain haircut" (certa scisione crinium), presumably the *garceta*, and they must dress as Muslims; that is, in the *aljuba*, not in Christian clothes.[75] Nevertheless, some differential treatment apparently continued. In 1389 Prince Martí (later Martí I) wrote to the governor of the kingdom of Valencia to reprove him for too rigorously punishing Muslims in the Serra d'Eslida for not wearing the *garceta*, while other (more wealthy) Muslims in the region were not so heavily penalized for this infraction.[76]

This ongoing legal wrangling in Valencia testifies to confusion, inconsistency, and resistance, especially because (as was clear from the Bellvís appeal in 1355) laws in Aragon had in fact continued to insist that Muslims must not wear the *garceta* (a fact reiterated in Zaragoza in 1360)—long after the reversal of this policy in Valencia.[77] Perhaps in an effort to resolve these differences, Pere IV eventually changed the law in Aragon also, now requiring the *garceta* for all Aragonese Muslims in November 1386, just two months before his death.[78] Not surprisingly, his successor, Joan I, faced an onslaught of complaint and opposition to this change immediately upon his ascent to the throne, especially after he reaffirmed laws imposing distinctive styles of hair and dress. There were Mudejar revolts in Zaragoza and Huesca in 1387, with protesters claiming that these laws were not the custom in Aragon and that they were only being imposed in order to generate income (presumably for the benefit of those selling exemptions and imposing fines).[79] In Huesca, at least, the new king quickly backed down, ordering in September 1387 that officials in the city should stop requiring that local Muslims cut their hair short all around the head (*sarcenati*) or that they wear any other distinctive signs. He explained his decision based on the argument (undoubtedly presented to him by the Mudejar population) that this policy was not only unusual in Huesca but also that it would lead to the depopulation of the city's *aljama*.[80] Three months later, Joan followed up on this order and wrote to the bishop of Huesca to remind him that he could not require local Muslims to cut their hair or wear the *clenxia* (a style similar to the *garceta*).[81]

During the first half of the fourteenth century, legislation in Castile—as in Valencia and Aragon—tended to require yet another particular style of Muslim haircut (usually described as with a single part, cut short all around the head, and without the *copete*), along with rather vague statements that Mudejars must also wear some kind of distinctive sign (in line with the rulings of Lateran IV).[82] The Castilian sumptuary ordinances that had been so prominent in the thirteenth century, however, were not restated until the reign of Pedro I (1350–69), when attention refocused away from hair back to clothing, textiles, and ornamentation. In 1351, at the Cortes of Valladolid, Pedro ruled that too many Jews and Muslims were dressing in high-quality imported woolen cloth, half-length cloaks, and adornments ("panos de viado e a meytad e con adobos") making them indistinguishable from Christians. Henceforth, Castilian Muslims over the age of thirteen were not allowed to wear those types of clothes, nor any garments ornamented with gold or silver.[83] After his succession to the throne, Enrique II restated these policies at the Cortes of Toro, in 1371, though with somewhat less precision: Muslims were not allowed to wear luxury textiles, and they must display unspecified signs to distinguish them from Christians. There was no mention of hair.[84]

Elsewhere in the Peninsula, there was also a shift away from policies regarding hair to those concentrating on clothing in the final decades of the fourteenth century. Although laws in the Crown of Aragon continued to mention the *garceta*, they also began to introduce other distinctive signals of Muslim identity—perhaps because the regulation of hair had proved too difficult on its own. In 1373, Pere IV had required that Muslims in Valencia wear *aljubas*, harking back to laws requiring this garment from a century earlier in the *Costums de Tortosa*. Another ordinance from the same year also required that Valencian Muslim men wear the *aljuba* and cover their heads with a blue cloth ("tovallola blava en lo cap"), while—in an unusual additional clause—Muslim women should veil their faces.[85] At about the same time, Muslims in Portugal complained to King Pedro I (1357–67) about laws requiring them to wear the *aljuba* and *burnūs* (*albornoz*) because the sleeves of these garments got in their way when they were working.[86] In 1384, Pere IV restated that clothing, vestments, and hair were all important in the demarcation of Muslim appearance.[87]

Unlike their coreligionists elsewhere, Muslims in Catalonia experienced almost no regulation of their hair or clothing for most of the fourteenth century, although in theory the regulations established in 1301 were still in effect. This changed in 1388, about a year after Joan I came to the throne, when he ordered that all Muslims who lived and worked in Lérida must wear the clothing and hairstyles established by the Constitutions of Catalonia, with the intention of differentiating them from Christians. It appears that the king was responding to the fact that local Mudejars had not been sufficiently distinguishing themselves from their Christian neighbors.[88] Two years later, in March 1390, the king went much further at the Cortes of Monzón, issuing a new law that all Muslims in Catalonia over the age of ten must wear a yellow band of cloth on their right sleeve (or a red band if the garment that they were wearing happened to be yellow). These rules were repeated in Tortosa the following November.[89] The new regulation was innovative and yet in line with the general move back toward the legislation of visual distinction through signs and clothing, rather than hair, which characterizes the end of the fourteenth century.

Needless to say, Catalan Muslims complained vociferously about this new law, and the king agreed to suspend it pending further investigation in January 1391.[90] Six months later, however, he issued a new decree, this time in Zaragoza, requiring that Muslims in Aragon must wear the *garceta* along with red or yellow armbands. This caused such an uproar among Aragonese Mudejars that an ambassador from Granada even arrived to intervene on their behalf.[91] Although Joan acknowledged the ambassador's intercession and promised not to impose the law, other documents indicate that he reiterated these statutes from Monzón and Zaragoza several times over the next few years, though possibly they were not always enforced.[92] Differential imposition is certainly suggested in an exemption issued in 1396, in which the king allowed Aragonese Muslims to take off the yellow band when they were traveling in Catalonia.[93] It also seems likely that the yellow band was not commonly enforced in Catalonia given the irritation expressed by Catalan Muslims after the death of Joan in May 1396, when the queen regent María de Luna, wife of his successor Martí I, briefly reimposed the "good customs" established at Monzón. As soon as Martí arrived from Sicily to assume the throne, the *aljamas* of Catalonia appealed this legislation and received freedom from wearing the yellow band in 1397.[94] Shortly thereafter, in 1401, Martí ordered Muslims in Aragon to wear distinctive signs, but there was no further mention of the despised colored armbands.[95]

Ever since the edicts of the Fourth Lateran Council, it had been common for Jews in Spain (as elsewhere in Europe) to be required to wear specific insignia on their clothing, often yellow stars or circles. However, there were no parallel laws establishing distinctive vestimentary symbols for Iberian Muslims until nearly two centuries later, with the colored armbands required in the Crown of Aragon. Before this, edicts that Muslims wear "distinctive signs" had been vague, and more explicit legislation focused on particular styles of clothing and hair that were supposed to be different from Christian fashions. Initially, at least, Muslims were forbidden from wearing certain styles (such as the *garceta* or gold ornamentation on their clothing) rather than required to add specific markers of their identity, perhaps because it was assumed that they were already sufficiently visually distinct from their Christian neighbors.

This assumption seems to have changed in the course of the fourteenth century, as indicated by new legislative initiatives mandating that Muslims wear the *garceta* and colored armbands.

Even more explicit markers would be instituted in Castile in the early fifteenth century, with a new series of vestimentary laws issued by Queen Catalina in 1408, in her role as regent for her young son, the future Juan II. This legislation was aimed at "all of the Moors in my kingdoms and seigneurial lands, and those that are studying in them, and traveling through them," and it ordered that "men must wear over their clothes a cowl [*capuz*] made of yellow cloth, and a symbol cut of cloth in the shape of a crescent moon, in cornflower blue [*color torquesado*], of this size [here there is a picture of a moon provided], that is to be worn openly below the right shoulder in such a manner as to be fully showing. And women must all wear the same [blue moon] symbol . . . large enough so that it is obvious, worn openly on all their clothes below the right shoulder, in such a manner as to be fully showing." The ordinances went on to list certain types of clothing and shoes that Muslims were not allowed to wear, much along the lines of earlier Castilian sumptuary regulations.[96] This law requiring yellow cowls and blue lunettes would be reaffirmed by Juan II in 1437 and repeated in later Castilian legislation into the reign of Fernando and Isabel.[97]

As well as mandating these distinctive symbols, Queen Catalina would also go on to establish the most rigorous and detailed prescriptions for Muslim clothing that had yet been set down in law anywhere in the Peninsula. Her legislation enacted in Valladolid in January 1412 contained three paragraphs devoted to the textiles, styles of clothing, and length of garments that Muslims and Jews should or should not wear. Another paragraph was devoted to hair and beards, both of which should henceforth be worn long and uncut "as had been the custom long ago."[98] These rulings were in line with an increasing emphasis on rules about clothing in the fifteenth century, and they also mark a shift in that they cover both Muslims and Jews under the same ordinance. The appearance of both groups was restricted in similar ways, to distinguish them from Christians, while the yellow stars and blue moons were established to differentiate them from each other. Later legislation from the reigns of Juan II, Enrique IV, and Fernando and Isabel would likewise group Muslims and Jews together, ordering them to wear public signals on their clothing, to dress differently from Christians, and to avoid luxury textiles and clothing adorned with pearls, silver, or gold.[99]

This repeated legislation not only reflects a change in monarchs (new rulers tended either to reiterate earlier laws or to enact new ones), but it may also suggest that vestimentary rules were not being routinely observed or enforced. At the Cortes of Madrigal in 1476, the Catholic Monarchs complained that Jews and Muslims customarily ignored the rules about distinctive signs and clothing, so that "it is not possible to tell if the Jews are Jews, or if they are clerics or *letrados* of great estate and authority, or if the Moors are Moors, or if they are gently bred courtiers [*gentiles honbres del palaçio*]." Moreover, they noted that some of these Jews and Muslims had documents (*cartas*) certifying that they were allowed to dispense with distinctive signs or permitted to wear luxurious clothes. To correct this laxity and liberty, Fernando and Isabel reaffirmed earlier vestimentary legislation.[100]

Parallel to these efforts to prevent Muslims from looking like Christians were the laws that required them to look like Muslims (at least insofar as Christians perceived "Muslim" appearance). We see this in legislation that required them to let their beards grow long, in accordance with Islamic law and to wear the *aljuba*, *albornoz*, and other articles of traditional clothing. These garments are mentioned in laws from the Crown of Aragon and from Portugal, including a ruling by Afonso V of Portugal from the middle of the fifteenth century that required Muslims to wear "Moorish costume" (*traje de mouro*), namely, the *aljuba* and *albornoz*, and that these long-sleeved enveloping garments be worn closed in front. In 1454, the Muslim community of Lisbon successfully appealed this law, and they were allowed to wear their robes open, as was more traditional. Meanwhile, another Muslim, from Setúbal, was permitted to wear silk garments so long as these were completely covered by his outer Muslim-style clothing.[101] There were no such laws in Castile. In 1480, a local law in Murcia allowed Muslims to wear silk *aljubas* and head coverings during the public festivities celebrating Corpus Christi, but this was a special exemption to mark the holiday (just as all people in the town were permitted to wear fancy clothes on Holy Thursday, including items that would normally be forbidden) not a general everyday requirement.[102]

There is almost no evidence regarding views about dress and visual distinction from the Islamic perspective, and it is very hard to know whether Muslims in Christian Spain either dressed or wished to dress like their Christian neighbors. What is clear is that they strongly objected to the imposition of new, burdensome, and often confusing regulations about dress and hairstyles, and the concurrent costs of paying fines and purchasing exemptions. In a number of cases they won their appeal and the law was rolled back, sometimes for a significant period, as in Huesca in 1387. But overall, it was a long-fought and losing struggle, and one in which we do not hear direct Mudejar voices.

Codes of Islamic law written by and for Mudejars in late medieval Spain have little to say about dressing in Christian garments, presumably because standard Islamic legal thought, including the Pact of 'Umar, assumed that the populations in question were living within the Dār al-Islām.[103] Only the *Breviario sunni*, written by the jurist of Yça Gidelli (Īsa ibn Jābir) in Segovia in the middle of the fifteenth century, mentioned the matter, stating that "it is abhorrent to wear clothing in Christian styles [llebar bestidos á la usança de los christianos] for prayer."[104] Unlike standard books of Islamic law, Yça Gidelli wrote this text explicitly for Muslims living under Christian rule. His comment not only rejects Christian clothing in the context of Muslim worship, but it also implies both a recognition that there was something recognizably distinct about Christian styles and the possibility that some Muslims living in Castile might adopt these fashions.

Even within Muslim borders there may have been some degree of similarity between late medieval Muslim and Christian Iberian dress. According to Arabic authors familiar with both Granada and the Maghrib, Muslims in Granada had adopted a number of fashions that were perceived as "Christian." Both Ibn Sa'īd (d. 1286) and Ibn al-Khaṭīb (d. 1374) claimed that Naṣrid styles of clothing and weaponry imitated those of their Christian neighbors.[105] Ibn Khaldūn (d. 1406) analyzed this tendency, explaining that "a nation dominated by another, neighboring nation will show a great deal of assimilation and imitation. At this time, this is the case in Spain [al-Andalus]. The Spaniards [Andalusīs] are found to assimilate themselves to the Galician nations [*umam al-Jalāliqah*] in their dress, their emblems, and most of their customs and conditions."[106] Although many garments typical of Granada, such as the *burnūs* and the *aljuba*, were shared with Maghribi fashions, they may well have developed characteristically Iberian variants.[107]

Yet at the same time that Ibn Khaldūn described the natives of Granada as adopting northern ("Galician") fashions (and it is noteworthy that he chooses regional rather than religious terminology), a chronicler in Aragon described the traditionally "Moorish" items of clothing worn by ambassadors from the Naṣrid sultan at the coronation of Fernando de Antequera in Zaragoza in 1412 ("todos vestidos con albornoces e capuces e aljuvas moriscas").[108] Perhaps these ambassadors were wearing distinctively regional dress in their diplomatic role on a ceremonial occasion. But it is also possible that the garments this Aragonese author saw as so typically Moorish were the same items that appeared to be inflected by northern fashions from the point of view of the Maghribi observer. Ultimately, the interpretation of style is in the eye of the beholder.

The story of medieval Christian legislation concerning Muslim dress, from the Fourth Lateran Council in the early thirteenth century until the edicts of forced Muslim conversion in the early sixteenth century, makes clear that the issue was never fully resolved. Rulers and churchmen experimented with a number of different strategies relating to hair, clothing, and distinctive signs, but none of these dealt conclusively with the ongoing problem of visual identity. At the Cortes of Madrigal in 1476, just as at the council in 1215, the legal record continued to lament the persistent confusion of Christian and non-Christian appearance.

Although Fernando and Isabel worried about the misidentification of social status, the sexual hazards of ambiguous identity also remained an issue—in line with Innocent III's original warning. In most respects, Christian law codes were categorical in their condemnation of sexual relations between Christians and non-Christians (even Christian prostitutes were not permitted to accept non-Christian clients, although Muslim prostitutes could sleep with Christians), and some cases that ended up in court rested on excuses of uncertain identity. In 1304 and 1334, a court in Zaragoza heard of two Muslim men who had tried to pass as Christians in order to have sex with a Christian prostitute.[109] Another incident came before the bailiff of Valencia in 1359, regarding a Christian prostitute who sometimes dressed as a Christian and sometimes as a Muslim ("nunc in christiano, nunc agarenorum habitu")[110] depending on her client. Her case is an excellent example of the ways in which people may have both understood and manipulated expectations of visual identity. And either way, whether the problem of identity was social or sexual, the basic difficulties remained essentially unchanged. In the later fifteenth century, Christian legislators were still deeply concerned that Muslims looked too much like Christians.

At the same time, visual identity was becoming more complex, as fashions changed and increasing numbers of Christians sometimes chose to wear certain elements of Muslim dress, especially the *toca* (a turban-like head covering or hat), *marlota*, and other garments that had long been characteristic of styles in al-Andalus and the Maghrib. This conscious fascination with Moorish fashions (*vestidos moriscos*) among Spanish Christians, particularly

the elite who wore them for festivities and special events (especially the popular *juego de cañas*), was a trend that appeared in the later Middle Ages and
extended well into the sixteenth century. Kings and nobles, such as Enrique
IV of Castile and his constable, Miguel Lucas de Iranzo, were known for wearing Moorish garb. A letter sent from the sultan of Granada to Alfonso V of
Aragon in 1418 described an accompanying gift of richly adorned garments,
included a gilded *aljuba*, a *burnūs*, two silk *tocas*, and a *marlota* embroidered
with gold.[111] This Christian delight in "Moorish" clothing has been amply discussed by Carmen Bernis, Barbara Fuchs, and others as a facet of the maurophilia that was so prevalent in the fifteenth and sixteenth century.[112] But
although late medieval Christian kings, queens, and their courtiers may
have enjoyed dressing up in the luxurious and exotic *alharemes*, *almaizares*,
*quiçotes*, and *albornoces* described in their chronicles, inventories, and account
books, it is highly unlikely that anybody would actually have mistaken these
prominent public figures for Muslims.[113] Certainly, there was no sudden legal
or clerical outcry denouncing this fashion trend.

Overall, there were very few complaints about Christians being mistaken
for Muslims before 1500, although Christians had certainly worn many similar styles, including versions of the *toca*, *aljuba*, and *almejía*, at least since the
thirteenth century.[114] According to Iñigo López de Mendoza y Quiñones, who
was writing in 1514 to object to new ordinances against Muslim clothing and
hairstyles, it had been perfectly normal for Christians to dress in *vestidos moriscos* and to wear their hair in Muslim styles until the middle of the fourteenth
century (he dated the change to the accession of Enrique II in 1369).[115] It has
already been noted that medieval Christians in Spain had long valued Islamic
luxury textiles, and these items have been found in church treasures and royal
tombs dating back to the twelfth century. Ramon Llull commented favorably
on the fact that loose-fitting "Saracen" clothes were cool and healthful.[116] Even
more ordinary people seem to have appreciated their worth, taking them as
booty in war and loot from theft.[117]

For the most part, the choice of medieval Christians to wear these styles
passed without comment, a fact that raises significant questions about how
such clothes were perceived, and how they fitted within a broader dialogue
about religious visual identity. Even though medieval sources persistently
tagged certain styles as "Christian" or "Muslim" (and this tendency has been
mirrored by modern scholars), the realities of day-to-day appearance were
surely more complex. But it is difficult to see beyond the centuries of com-

plaint about confusion of identity and consequent legislation, to get an idea
of why people dressed in certain ways, how they perceived the appearance of
themselves and others, and what they intended to look like. On the one hand,
there is the ongoing evidence of muddled visual identity; on the other
hand, there is the relentless rhetoric (probably reflected to some degree in
reality) that there was—or at least it was possible to create—something that
was recognized as a "Muslim" or a "Christian" appearance.

One factor here is that many clothing items widely worn by medieval
Christians were simply seen as ordinary "Christian" styles, even if they had
names clearly derived from Arabic, or were a type of textile or garment known
to have been originally created or worn by non-Christians. Some of these styles
may have been genuinely shared, effectively removing their religious valence and
making visual distinction impossible—hence the ongoing legal concerns. This
was very different from the situation in which fifteenth- and sixteenth-century
Christians consciously donned exotic *vestidos moriscos* as fancy dress (although
this had probably happened in earlier periods too). If appearance was not always easily differentiated by clothing, which could in any case be easily changed,
this may explain the ongoing attempts to define "Muslim" appearance through
more lasting hairstyles, such as the *garceta* in the Crown of Aragon.

But there are also other ways to explain the fact that medieval Christians
were rarely censured for wearing "Muslim" clothes. Perhaps they simply never
wore them, but the evidence is against this conclusion. Alternately, and perhaps more likely, garments of similar names and styles actually had subtle but
recognizable differences depending on the religious identity of the wearer, differences that would have been familiar to medieval contemporaries but which
have been erased by time. Fashions have long had the ability to project aspects
of social and economic identity, but these meanings—though well understood
at the time—leave little long-term imprint in a world of changing aesthetic
tastes. It is likely, also, that sumptuary laws about "Muslim" dress were often
ignored and that periods of enforcement tended to focus on non-Christian
violators rather than Christian infractions.

Overall, it appears that the legal burden of differentiation was generally
placed on Muslims rather than Christians. This tendency even extended to
new converts from Islam, who were ordered to cease dressing as Muslims and
strongly urged not to attend Muslim weddings or other festivities that might
tempt them to don Muslim clothing and ornaments.[118] Laws requiring that
New Christians must dress in the same manner as Old Christians can be found

in the thirteenth and fourteenth centuries, but they became strident in the sixteenth century, after the promulgation of edicts demanding conversion or expulsion.

The conversion of entire populations from Islam to Christianity, from *moro* to *morisco*, fundamentally changed the language of legislation about identity in sixteenth-century Spain, but without shifting any of the underlying assumptions about the proper relationship between appearance and religion. New Christians should now look the same as Old Christians, and if they did not, the burden was on them to change their appearance just as their faith had been changed by baptism. The fact that this did not happen, and that many Moriscos (and especially Morisca women) continued to dress as they had before conversion, presented a huge problem. Castilian administrators and inquisitors demanded that there be a rupture with the past, and they interpreted the continuity of appearance as representing active resistance by Moriscos to their new religious condition. In many cases, they were probably perfectly correct in this assumption. But in others, the persistence of earlier clothing traditions was surely also due to the varying pressures of inertia, familiarity, comfort, convenience, aesthetic preference, and economy.

Inquisition records indicate that a perception of non-Christian appearance was one among many indicators of imperfect faith. An accusation that somebody either routinely or occasionally donned Morisco clothing immediately generated suspicions of heresy, and in concert with other evidence it could land the accused in court, in jail, or on the scaffold. As early as 1498, even before the official edicts of conversion, a letter from King Fernando indicates that the Inquisition in Valencia was already paying close attention to Moorish dress.[119] In 1526, when the Moriscos of Granada purchased their forty-year exemption from laws requiring that they abandon their traditional dress, it came along with a promise that they would also not be subject to inquisitorial attention during that grace period. After this expired, however, inquisitorial attention again included appearance among its measures of unbelief, and Moriscos were well aware of the dangers of continuing to wear clothing that did not distinctively mark them as Christian. When inquisitors visited Morisco communities in the region of Málaga in 1568–69, they inspired such fear that "they found all the women dressed in Castilian costume" (por este temor de la Inquisición hallaba vestidas las mujeres a la castellana).[120] Likewise, in the Aragonese village of Gea de Albarracín, where the Morisco community would come under intense inquisitorial scrutiny and persecution, local officials insisted to the inquisitor general in 1566 that the inhabitants never used Moorish dress or language any more, and that they did whatever else was necessary to be good Christians ("los deste lugar jamas usaron el habito de moros ni la lengua . . . hizieron lo demas que es necesario para qualquier pefecto christiano").[121] Both reports reflect an assumption, on the part of the inquisitorial recorders, that *moriscos* did not normally dress like Old Christians, and they only put on Christian clothing in order to avoid inquisitorial attention. This may have been the case, but it is also possible that by the 1560s some Moriscos had genuinely made the switch to wearing Christian fashions.

## A New Focus on Women: Female Veiling and the *Almalafa*

There is no question, however, that in the early sixteenth century, New Christians continued to dress differently from Old Christians, and this was especially the case in Granada, where the population had only recently come under the rule of Fernando and Isabel.[122] Comments from Christian administrators, inquisitors, visiting travelers and artists, and the Moriscos themselves all testified that Granadan fashions were completely unlike those of Castile, though they might disagree as to whether this was a factor of religion, region, or culture. A famous series of illustrations by the German artist Christoph Weiditz, who traveled in Spain in 1528–29, includes depictions of Moriscos and Moriscas in Granada, with special attention to their costume and its differences from other contemporary Iberian dress (see Figures 4 and 5).[123]

These detailed descriptions of women in Granada draw our attention to a striking difference, in terms of gender, between medieval comments on Muslim appearance and sixteenth-century descriptions of Moriscas. Whereas almost all medieval legislation about Mudejar hair and dress was directed toward male appearance, with only passing comments on female dress, early modern attention was very strongly focused on women. Sixteenth-century Christian authors were fascinated by the Moriscas' voluminous white veils (*almalafas*), baggy trousers (*zaragüelles*; from Arabic *sarāwīl*), *marlotas*, distinctive shoes, and hennaed fingers. Legislative and inquisitorial attention to clothing was also mainly directed toward women, requiring that they give up these earlier styles in favor of decent Christian skirts and mantles (*sayas* and *mantos*), no matter what it cost to replace an entire wardrobe. Yet even after years of such legislation, Morisca dowry documents from 1565 still listed *almalafas*, *marlotas*, and other items of characteristically Granadan clothing.[124]

Figure 4. Christoph Weiditz, *Trachtenbuch* (1529). Germanisches National-museum Hs. 22474, fols. 97–98. Visiting German artist's illustration of a Morisca woman in *almalafa*.

Figure 5. Christoph Weiditz, *Trachtenbuch* (1529). Germanisches National-museum Hs. 22474, fols. 99–100. Depiction of Morisco casual home wear; note child's *sábana*.

The reasons for this relatively sudden switch in attention from male to female fashions are unclear, and they were undoubtedly multiple. If we follow the arguments of Francisco Núñez Muley, women held on to traditional garb much longer than did men, thus creating the greater problem with female dress. Since Morisco men were more likely than women to be out and about, pursuing the work and public activities of daily life and mixing with Old Christians, it was likely that their appearance would assimilate more quickly. Women, meanwhile, were more often shielded within the privacy of the home, away from Old Christian sight—a fact that, in itself, tended to direct inquisitorial attention toward female practices. It is also possible that both Moriscos and Moriscas felt more protective of the traditions of female clothing than they did of male attire, and thus held on to them for longer. Differences in cost may also have presented a more burdensome issue as regards female attire. Writing in 1513, Iñigo López de Mendoza, the Count of Tendilla, explained that basic Morisca garments were very simple and inexpensive, consisting only of a shirt (*camisa*), *zaragüelles*, and a face veil, plus almost any kind of all-encompassing cloth—even a bedsheet (*sábana de la cama*)—that she could throw over herself when she left the house. In contrast, the purchase of multiple Christian female garments ("faldillas y mantos y sayas y abitos de christianas") would represent a real financial burden, especially for households with multiple women.[125]

This line of economic argument had been a factor in negotiations from the first years after the edicts of conversion, when New Christians were promised that they "would not be pressured to buy and wear new clothes until those that they and their wives currently owned had worn out."[126] Later, it would be pursued by a number of other authors sympathetic to the Morisco cause, including Francisco Núñez Muley himself. To offset the costs of procuring new clothes, Fernando and Isabel went so far as to distribute vast quantities of cloth, of various different kinds and lengths, to Muslim notables who presented themselves in Granada for conversion.[127] At the same time, as we have seen above, Hernando de Talavera made a point of distributing articles of Christian attire to poor Morisco men and women, in order to help them to dress in Castilian styles ("que se vistiessen a lo Castellano").[128]

New attention directed toward female Muslim styles in the early sixteenth century brought special attention to the issue of female veiling, whether women covered themselves with the all-encompassing white *almalafa* or a more multipurpose cloth often simply referred to as a sheet (*sábana*).[129] Both terms begin to appear in Christian legislation in the sixteenth century as these articles of Morisca attire were banned along with other clothing styles associated with Islam. The *almalafa* seems to have been especially characteristic of Granada, where the analogous *milḥafa* was worn in the Naṣrid period, but similar enveloping garments were common elsewhere throughout the Muslim world.[130] Moriscas elsewhere in Spain also covered their faces, as did a woman in Zaragoza who "was covered by a mantle so that nobody would know her" when she visited a Morisco jailed by the Inquisition in 1586.[131]

Legislation on the *almalafa* was closely related to regulations regarding the full exposure of women's faces in public, something that was frequently required by sixteenth-century mandates in Granada. Clerics and administrators had an interest in enforcing overt visual identity, as well as suppressing clandestine behavior and residual Islamic practice, and these goals might in themselves explain their focus on the *almalafa*. But there were deeper implications to the *almalafa*, in terms of female honor and Muslim tradition, that raised the stakes in this debate beyond mere clothing styles and made it a passionately felt issue for the Morisco community in Granada. One of the first complaints voiced in a Morisco appeal to the Ottoman sultan, sent in the first decade of the sixteenth century, sought his aid "on behalf of some faces that have been bared to the company of non-Arabs after having been veiled."[132] The depth of Morisco feeling is what makes regulations on *almalafas* and the covering (or uncovering) of Moriscas' faces stand out from other legislation on clothing in sixteenth-century Granada.

In contrast to this early modern emphasis, there is very little data on veiling before the later fifteenth century, either in al-Andalus or in Christian Spain. This silence not only reflects the emphasis on male dress in medieval legislation, but it probably also stems from the view that female appearance was an internal matter to be handled by the Mudejar community. The few earlier references that survive suggest that veiling was common and expected for Mudejar women in the thirteenth and fourteenth centuries, as for their Andalusi counterparts.[133] A surrender treaty in Minorca in 1287 promised that Muslim women would not be insulted, "nor would their faces be unveiled."[134] In 1373, legislation from Valencia mandated that Mudejar women should cover their faces.[135] Thirteenth- and fourteenth-century images, from manuscripts such as the Alfonsine *Libro de ajedrez* or the ceiling paintings in Teruel Cathedral, also depict women with covered heads and partially veiled faces, although it is not always clear whether these women are intended to be understood as Muslims or Christians. As will be addressed in more detail below, there is some evidence that medieval Castilian women also may have covered their faces when out in public, a trend that would continue in early modern Spain.[136]

Nevertheless, the prevalence of the *almalafa* was a visually distinctive element in newly Christian Granada. As noted earlier in this chapter, Fernando and Isabel had been greeted by what must have looked like a sea of white, a scene created by thousands of women wearing *almalafas*, when they returned to Granada in 1499.[137] European travelers who visited Granada in the 1490s and early 1500s were impressed by this style, which they clearly viewed as exotic. They described these garments in their journals and letters and made sketches of veiled Moriscas. Antoine de Lalaing, a Burgundian nobleman traveling to Spain in 1501–2 with Philip the Fair, husband of Juana, remarked that he "found the clothing of women in Granada very strange [*fort estranges*], for they wear nothing but a white cloth which reaches all the way down to the ground, covering them up to the middle of their faces when they go out in the streets, so that one can see only one eye . . . they look like ghosts [*semblent espris*] if one meets them at night."[138] An Italian visitor received a very similar impression a couple of decades later (visiting in 1516–19), reporting that "the Moorish women wear a very strange type of clothing [*uno habito molto strano*], namely, a length of white cloth over their heads that covers their limbs . . . and they cover their faces so that one cannot see more than their eyes."[139] Another Italian, the Venetian diplomat Andrea Navagero, arrived in Granada in 1526 and described Morisca dress as "fantastical" (*abito molto fantastico*), with various strange fashions including a long white covering that allowed them to go incognita when they wished.[140] Johannes Lange, visiting Granada with the court of Charles V in 1526, likewise commented that Moorish women and girls in the city covered their heads and bodies with a white mantle, half covering the face, and in order for Moriscos in Granada to be allowed to wear such clothes, they paid one ducat each year to the emperor.[141] The German artist Christoph Weiditz, as mentioned above, created visual records of the *almalafa* that were based on observations during his visit to Granada in 1528–29, and his drawings of this voluminous garment exactly reflect the written descriptions of other travelers.[142]

Given the distinctive character of the *almalafa*, it is not surprising that this fashion would receive special attention in Christian legislation that sought to prohibit anything perceived as Muslim dress. Of two decrees issued in the name of Queen Juana on July 29, 1513, one condemned the fact that Moriscas "still wear *almalafas* and go about with covered faces" despite the fact that New Christians may no longer wear Moorish dress. The other drew attention to a related problem, noting that the queen "had been informed that some Old Christian women who live and reside in the said city of Granada [and in other parts of that kingdom], pay no attention to the fact that we have generally ordered and decided that New Christians must abandon Moorish fashions and clothing and adopt the manners and clothing of Christians. These [Old Christian] women dress themselves like Moriscas, cover themselves with *almalafas*, and in other ways set a bad example to the newly converted, with the result that because they think that they are covered and anonymous they indulge in various excesses and bad deeds" that cause harm and detriment to the Christian faith. As a result, the queen ordered that Old Christians were not allowed to dress *a la morisca*.[143] In the next summer (June 1514), New Christian women in Huéscar and Castilléjar (both towns in the region of Granada) were instructed that they must fully expose their faces when they were in church.[144]

Queen Juana's ordinances in 1513 against *almalafas* were part of the same royal effort (discussed earlier) to ban Morisco clothing generally and to prevent tailors from mending worn garments. We find a sharp reflection of these royal ordinances in the letters of Iñigo López de Mendoza y Quiñones, the second Count of Tendilla, who—more than many of his fellow Castilians—was sympathetic to the plight of Moriscos and understood the difficulties that they faced in abandoning their traditional forms of dress. In August 1513 (shortly after Juana's legislation issued in late July), he had responded by explaining the economic inconveniences that Moriscas would face in buying a whole new wardrobe of Castilian skirts, mantles, and other items. In this same letter, he also mentioned "another major problem" (otro inconveniente mayor) in that the reason that Morisca women covered their faces is because their menfolk were not willing to have other men see the faces of their women, "and therefore, if they go unveiled [*descubiertas*], this will quickly result in quarrels, murders, and feuds with those who saw them uncovered." Furthermore, he points out yet another inconvenience (while at the same time confirming Juana's accusation that veiling facilitated impropriety): that new converts could justifiably rail against the hypocrisy of such laws, arguing

> that Old Christian women in all of the major cities in the kingdom
> of Castile go about with mantles covering their heads, and hats
> over these mantles, and in this manner they go hidden
> [*disimuladas*] and people neither see them nor know who they are.
> And [yet] they take away our fashions with which we guard our
> wives, daughters, and sisters so that they will neither be seen nor

coveted. But this is not a fashion imposed by [religious] law, it neither removes faith nor imposes faith [*pues esto no es abito de ley, que quita fe ni pone fe*], and they are requiring us to give up almost all of the wardrobes that our women possess.[145]

The matter did not resolve itself, and over the next two years López de Mendoza's letters still alluded to the increasingly incendiary atmosphere that surrounded the question of Morisca veiling and the refurbishing of traditional clothing in Granada. In February 1515, he wrote that he had recently received a delegation of Moriscos brimming with rumors about secret deals made with the makers (*texedores*) of *almalafas* and payments to the crown in return for continuing to wear Morisco clothing.[146] Two months later, after several related communications, he described another meeting in April with a group of New Christians who had come to talk to him about the issue of *almalafas*, during which "one honorable man among them said to me: 'We are loyal to the king, he may ask us for all that we have and we will give it to him, so long as he does not order that we uncover the faces of our women.' I do not remember what reply I made to him, but then he said: 'Remember, señor, that there are twenty of us for every one of you.'" After reporting this thinly veiled threat, Tendilla added that "it is a dangerous thing to begin such a game."[147] But later in the year, he still reported fruitless negotiations over *almalafas* and other issues of Morisco clothing, although there had been no outright rebellion over these matters.[148]

Christians continued to suspect that women veiled for nefarious purposes, even while many Moriscos passionately held to their traditions. A decade later the town council of Baza issued three separate ordinances in 1524 and 1525, all prohibiting women from veiling—whether single, married, or widowed (and apparently both New Christian and Old Christian)—and citing the shameful, dishonest, harmful, and disorderly consequences that resulted from women covering their faces.[149] Shortly thereafter, Charles V's general mandate in 1526 regarding Morisco clothing and other customs dedicated a whole paragraph to the *almalafa*, making clear that the main issue was concerned with face covering, and secondarily with the distinctive white color of these garments.

It is of the greatest inconvenience that women who are newly converted continue to wear *almalafas* and to go about with their faces covered. We order that from now on none of them, nor any of their children of whatever age, may wear *almalafas* or sheets [*sábanas*], and if they wish to wear them, then they must dye them in whatever color they wish, and they must keep their faces uncovered. And in order that there shall not be any fraud in connection with this, we likewise order that no Old Christian woman may go hatted or veiled [*ensombrerada ni atapada*] unless she leaves her face uncovered, even if she is wearing a hat. And if this is not complied with, our justices [have the authority] to take off the *almalafa* or sheet that was being used as a veil.[150]

These rules about the *almalafa* (along with other regulations in the 1526 ordinances) met with great resistance from Granada's Morisco community, and they were put on hold in return for payments made to the crown (as reflected in the comments by Johannes Lange). A few years later, in 1529 and 1530, letters from the empress Isabella of Portugal to the archbishop of Granada particularly noted that "for many good reasons" the king had not implemented the ban on *almalafas*, and thus the church in Granada could not condemn their use.[151] Isabella's intervention may have been sparked by hard-liners within the archdiocese, especially after the appointment of Antonio de Guevara as bishop of Guadix in 1528. Guevara not only opposed Morisca veiling, but he even threatened further humiliations by expressing the intention to shave the heads of Morisca women because they styled and braided their hair in African fashion ("según la costumbre del Africa").[152] As a result of Isabella's timely reminder that the king had permitted the *almalafa*, New Christian women were still wearing these garments when the empress's body was brought to Granada for burial in 1539.

Nevertheless, Christian clerics and administrators continued to express concerns about veiling. In 1554, the Synod of Guadix insisted that New Christian brides could not be veiled and that they must keep their faces uncovered during their wedding ceremonies.[153] Similarly ineffective edicts demanding that brides and grooms be *vestidos a la Castellana* were issued by the Synod of Granada in 1565 and confirmed by the Junta of Madrid in 1566.[154] The comprehensive Granada ordinances in 1567 prohibited the *almalafa*, along with other Morisco clothing but granted a brief period before the ban would go into effect. But even during this grace period, women wearing the *almalafa* were instructed to keep their faces exposed ("queremos que desde luego las dichas moriscas y nuevamente convertidas, que traxeren las dichas almalafas trayan sus rostros descubiertos").[155] This repressive 1567 legislation sparked a serious Morisco uprising in the region of Granada. In his history of the wars of Granada, which lasted from 1568 to 1570, Diego Hurtado de Mendoza (the youngest son of Iñigo López de Mendoza y Quiñones) would explain that, among other insults and indignities driving the Moriscos to rebellion, "the king . . . obliged them to dress, at much expense, in the Castilian manner. He ordered that the women's faces should be uncovered. . . . For a proud people these were terrible things to bear [*tan grave de sufrir entre gente zelosa*]."[156]

Francisco Núñez Muley's memorandum in response to the 1567 decrees likewise included arguments in defense of the *almalafa*, nested within his broader defense of traditional Morisco fashions. But unlike his other arguments about clothing, which largely rested on points about the cost, comfort, practicality, and familiarity of local styles, his discussion of veiling tellingly brought up issues of modesty, privacy, and the strong emotions that these evoked. As he points out, "issues such as covering and uncovering one's face have caused great disturbances and suffering," much like the requirement that Morisco doors remain open, which also assaulted traditions of privacy.[157] He argued that this insulting and impractical law would encourage public disorder and the abuse of women:

> In order to insult native women even more, it has been ordered that from the moment the decree is proclaimed these women uncover their faces in public so as to be targets of jokes and ridicule. In the end, all confidence will be lost in informants, constables, and law enforcement officials, as these will take advantage of the punishments allowed by the decree that suit them; and even before this the women will be harassed by the attacks of the constables who lift their veils and force them to go uncovered. Due to all the aforementioned points, this decree will cause great suffering, aggravation, as well as financial and personal losses.[158]

As elsewhere in his memorandum, Núñez Muley pointedly deflects his arguments about female covering away from issues of religion, instead emphasizing commonly accepted requirements of modesty and decorum. Like others before him, he points out that both New Christian and Old Christian women veil themselves in order to avoid the insults and improprieties of exposure to the male gaze. He posits the question of

> whether the women of this kingdom who cover their faces do so as part of their supposed adherence to the Muslim faith. We might

then ask, why do the majority of Old Christian women cover their
faces? They do so in order that people not recognize them at times
when they do not wish to be recognized, and New Christian
women do so for the same reason, and so that men might not fall
into the mortal sin of seeing the beautiful face of a woman they
admire and pursuing her, by licit or illicit means, in order to marry
her. That a woman covers her face is nothing but a matter of
modesty meant to prevent these events from occurring.[159]

Ultimately, the question of female veiling became an issue that had as
much to do with concerns about female virtue, generally, as with anxieties
about residual Muslim customs. It was widely recognized that Muslim women,
and Moriscas also, preferred to cover their faces when in public, and that this
habit was also widely practiced by Christian women in Castile (and perhaps
elsewhere in Spain). Some people saw the veil as a protection from male lust
(even if the temptations of female beauty were often deemed the true culprit),
while others suspected that women veiled themselves in order to pass unno-
ticed while pursuing illicit errands and assignations. Either way, the focus had
shifted toward the implications of female appearance.

Covering the head was very different from veiling the face. In his late
fifteenth-century treatise of sumptuary law, Hernando de Talavera had traced
the traditions of female head covering back to biblical examples and saw it as
something "natural" (es cosa natural) that women should cover their heads
while men did not.[160] Yet it is clear that Christian women also obscured their
faces in early modern Spain, even after the succession of edicts issued throughout the sixteenth century. An Italian papal nuncio who visited the court of
Felipe II in 1594 described how women in Madrid covered their heads and
veiled part of their faces, and that they would have been completely covered
("as had been the case just a few years earlier") were it not for a royal mandate
prohibiting this.[161]

Early modern observers assumed that face veiling had been adopted from
Andalusi custom, and this certainly seems a reasonable supposition, although
we actually know very little about earlier Christian veiling in Spain or its origins. A treatise on veiling by Antonio de León Pinelo, published in Madrid in
1641, discussed the use of veils in the ancient and biblical worlds and in early
medieval Spain and claimed that half-veiling ("el tapado de medio ojo") was
an Arab usage that came to Spain, or was further introduced, by Arab women
(las árabes) and later adopted by the Mozarabs (assimilated Iberian dhimmī

Christians) and "from them, Spanish women [*las españolas*] have it to this day, now as so much their own, that no women wear it with greater liking, grace, and tidiness."[162] Furthermore, León Pinelo explained that Moriscas had ceased to wear their traditional veils and Arab dress (*traje árabe*) in response to sixteenth-century prohibitions, instead clothing themselves in Castilian-style mantles and hats (*mantos y sombreros*), and "from that point they began to half-veil using their Castilian mantles, just as they had done before [with their Arab clothes], and because this style is graceful, easygoing, pleasing and (as we have already remarked) charming, and because the Moriscas, as all could see, walked about in a more spirited and elegant manner than the Spanish ladies, the latter also began . . . to veil themselves, and because of this common style it was easy to confuse one group with the other."[163] Perhaps one might conclude from this that the problem of visual identity had finally been resolved, insofar as all Christian women now looked alike, but female veiling (going about *a tapada*) continued to be a contested fashion in early modern Spain.

## Marks of Distinction: Henna Use as a Locus of Difference

The use of henna was another aspect of appearance that originated in Muslim tradition and that focused sixteenth-century inquisitorial and administrative attention on female attire. The colorful staining of fingernails was noticed and commented on by Christian travelers in the early sixteenth century, though they put little thought into whether it was a religious or a cultural practice. One Milanese merchant, visiting the region circa 1516–19, wrote with some disgust that the region's "Moorish women [*femine moresche*] tinted their nails red [*di uno certto colore rosso*]," presumably with henna, and thought it a "beautiful thing" (*bella cosa*).[164] A few years later, the Venetian Andrea Navagero also described Granadan women's reddened nails ("di colore come incarnato") and use of a malodorous hair dye (presumably henna, "che no ha molto buon odore").[165] Different colors may have been favored for different complexions, and the use of cosmetic dyes was not necessarily restricted to the New Christian populace. Navagero's contemporary Johannes Lange observed that the "white moors and ladies of Castile" painted their nails yellow.[166] For these visitors, such exotic beauty regimes were not explicitly connected to Islam and warranted no more than passing comment but clearly remained part of their overall sense of Morisco difference.

Henna served as a traditional dye and medicinal plant extract for many centuries before the emergence of Islam.[167] It was widely used among Arab tribes at the time of Muhammad, but—unlike veiling—it is not even obliquely mentioned in the Qur'ān. It appears in *ḥadīth* literature as a permissible hair and beard dye (for men) or as a hand or nail coloring (for women), but in no way was its use considered obligatory for Muslims. In one *ḥadīth* the prophet's wife Aisha actually mentions that she preferred not to wear it because Muhammad did not care for the smell; however another from the same collection suggests that he considered unhennaed fingernails to be unfeminine.[168] Islamic law in Spain dictated that henna should be forbidden to women in times of mourning (or other somber occasions, such as after a divorce, during a mandated period of *'iddah*), presumably because it was considered an unseemly display of feminine adornment at such times.[169]

Throughout the medieval period, henna remained a mundane cosmetic for both women and men of all religions. Its widespread use among Muslim men is attested in the chronicle of Juan II, where the striking red beards and hair of the opposing army are described as giving them the appearance of cows: "barbas y cabellos alfeñados, parecian que eran vacas."[170] Application of henna to the fingernails was evidently known among Christian women too. *Uñas alheñadas* is just one of many vain beauty treatments listed in 1438 by the Arcipreste de Talavera (Alfonso Martínez de Toledo) in his *Corbacho*, a satirical treatise on the vanity of women that was inspired by Boccaccio's work of the same title.[171]

Beyond its aesthetic qualities, however, henna could also have ritual functions that, while not essentially Islamic, were considered distinctive to Mudejar and later Morisco communities. Traditional patterned dying of brides' hands and feet—a far more ornate process than simply painting the nails—was identified as a sign of continued allegiance to Islamic ways in a Castilian Inquisition report from the Extremaduran town of Magacela in 1510, and such *ritos de alfeña* were condemned in the 1514 Ordenanzas of Fernando de Toledo for Huéscar and Castilléjar.[172] A ban on henna use in general, on hands or feet or anywhere else whether publicly or in secret throughout Granada ("no se alheñe las manos ni pies ni otra cosa alguna, pública ni secretamente"), was among the reforms proposed but not enacted by royal order in December of 1526, and Bishop Antonio de Guevara of Guadix tried unsuccessfully to repeat this ban in 1530.[173]

Morisco customs involving the application of henna to newborn infants' foreheads or faces, sometimes in a talismanic star shape, also troubled Christian

authorities. In an *instrucción* of December 10, 1526, the newly elected archbishop of Granada, Pedro de Alba, was warned that "children raised up
for baptism should not have henna on their foreheads," since chrism could
not be properly applied over "stars or henna" ("no se lleven los niños a bauti-
zar pintados con estrellas ni alheña en la frente ni en la cara, porque la crisma
no se ha de poner sobre el alheña").[174] Such practices smacked of both super-
stition and a deficit of respect for the church's own protective rites, and henna
use on both brides and babies was thus explicitly forbidden by the Synod of
Guadix and Baza in 1554.[175]

Still, not everyone saw these sorts of temporary festive adornments as a
serious threat to the faith, and bans on henna remained a relatively minor part
of the campaign to suppress Morisco signifiers. According to Mármol Carvajal the Granadan Audiencia's decree of 1567 did mention in passing that *women*
were no longer to use henna, but Núñez Muley did not raise it in his counter-
arguments and it appears in no other accounts of the legislation.[176] Moriscas
such as Mari Gomez la Sazeda insisted to inquisitors that henna had nothing
to do with Islam and that Christian women also frequently used it on their
nails and hair.[177] Others were uncertain just what henna was really for. In one
trial document from Daimiel, Pedro de Agreda and the Morisco Gonzalo de
la Pintada's dispute over the matter was recorded for posterity: "You put henna
on your hands," Pedro demanded. "What is it for, why do you do it?" Gonzalo replied that using henna was "nothing," especially when compared to the
real theological importance of his Muslim ancestors' rejection of the virgin
birth.[178] Inquisitorial prosecutions for henna use did occur from time to time
throughout the sixteenth century, but some cases were dismissed as trifling
matters worthy of only minor punishments.[179]

Decorative use of henna, then, was quite different from veiling in that it
never became a central aspect of the struggle to eliminate Islamic elements
from the visual appearance of converted New Christians. But while henna (unlike the veil) had no formal religious significance to Islam itself, it also clearly
functioned as a marker of difference. Christian (and Jewish) women may have
used henna from time to time on their hair and nails, but in Granada especially it was associated above all with members of the Morisco community.
Furthermore, like the veil, it was targeted as a particularly female practice. By
the sixteenth century, there is little evidence that men continued to use henna
in their hair and beards. Women's ongoing appreciation of its cosmetic appearance, however, and even more of its ceremonial contribution to important moments in the female life cycle (marriage, birth), led them to cling to

traditional henna usage. In doing so they attracted the attention of Christian authorities who were increasingly determined to eliminate any form of visual difference that could mark them out from their new coreligionists.

## Conclusion

In a series of large canvases, commissioned by King Felipe III and commemorating some of the waves of Morisco expulsions that he personally authorized in 1609, vestimentary difference is displayed both prominently and somewhat ambiguously. Lined up on the beach to await their destiny, facing the last hours of their time as citizens of Christian Spain, these descendants of Muslims are still presented as maintaining their own distinctive habits of dress despite decades of persecutory measures (Figure 6). The women in particular stand out with their white head coverings (though with faces exposed) and colorful long skirts, singing and dancing, almost as if engaging in a final act of defiance and assertion of cultural—if not religious—pride.[180]

Perhaps they were indeed making a statement to their Christian oppressors. Perhaps they were preparing to indicate their allegiance to the North African Islamic regimes they would soon be forced to live under. In their previous appeals to Muslim rulers the Moriscos had often made reference to the indignity they suffered in Spain as a result of having to remove their women's veils, and they clearly hoped that their desperate efforts to continue such traditions would engender feelings of solidarity in Islamic court circles.[181] But the painter Vicent Mestre reveals a final irony in his depiction of the Moriscos' arrival in North Africa, entitled *Desembarco de los moriscos en el Puerto de Orán* (Figure 7): when the dapper Moriscos arrive on the Algerian shore they are met not by similarly dressed compatriots but rather by turbaned and cloaked (and/or partially naked) savages who quickly proceed to rob and kill the newcomers. From a Maghribi viewpoint, the painting seems to acknowledge, these immigrants were Spanish, and they were dressed in Iberian fashions. Francisco Núñez Muley's argument is here at least partially vindicated: Morisco clothing was evidently not in itself a definitive indicator of Islamic identity, and it would do little to connect them with Muslims living in other parts of the world.

At the same time clothing did matter, and resistance to assimilative demands was stubborn for a reason. Ironically, the very imposition of Christian legislation about appearance itself may have exacerbated the problem by bringing

Figure 6. Vicent Mestre, *Embarque de los moriscos en el Puerto de Denia* (1613). Collección Fundación Bancaja. Spanish artist's rendition of expulsion scene, with Morisca women at left, separated from Morisco men wrestling at right.

Figure 7. Vicent Mestre, *Desembarco de los moriscos en el Puerto de Orán* (1613). Collección Fundación Bancaja. Spanish artist's rendition of exiled Moriscos landing in North Africa; note central scene of local Muslims (at right) attacking distinctively-attired newcomers (at left).

fashion into the spotlight as a focus for resistance and rebellion. Just as Mudejars had objected to the imposition of new laws about the *garceta* in the fourteenth century, so too Moriscos opposed laws requiring that they abandon their traditional clothing. But for many Moriscos, over the course of the sixteenth century, this increasingly became a desire to maintain difference rather than efface it.

It is easy to believe that early in the century, when Moriscos in Granada appealed the ruling on clothing in 1526 and purchased a long-standing exemption from Charles V, many people in the Morisco community still had a wide variety of reasons for preferring their familiar clothing styles that had been perfectly licit until two decades ago. Likewise, both their appeal and their exemption echoed patterns of thought and modes of operation that would have been well understood two centuries earlier. Forty years later, however, their persistent adherence to traditional Granadan styles in 1567 looks more like an active and organized opposition to assimilation, an assumption borne out by the well-organized Morisco revolts in the Alpujarras in the later 1560s. The fact that clothing differences remained so noticeable among Morisco exiles on the Valencian docks in 1609, despite yet another half century of concentrated assimilative pressure, seems equally telling.

CHAPTER 3

# Bathing and Hygiene

Modern popular lore tells us that medieval people did not bathe regularly. While there may be a small kernel of truth to this idea, at least as regards northern Europe during the winter, the opposite was true in Iberia, where public bathhouses were a normal feature of medieval urban life. Muslims, Christians, and Jews visited bathhouses on a regular basis, probably at least once a week, both in al-Andalus and in Christian Spain, from the tenth century through the fifteenth. Bathhouses were familiar facilities in medieval cities, where they provided a desirable service to the population, were closely regulated by urban statutes and delivered considerable revenues to their owners and administrators. But Iberian bathing habits changed in the sixteenth century, in the wake of expulsions, conversions, and inquisitions, as bathhouses were increasingly suspected of being sites for sexual vice and vicarious Islamic practice. Thus, in contrast to their relatively clean medieval predecessors, Old and New Christians in early modern Spain no longer bathed regularly, while bathhouses had become associated with immorality and heresy.

In January 1567, along with other prohibitions relating to local Morisco life, legislation in Granada ordered the immediate closure of public bathhouses. "From this day forward," the mandate stated, "there may no longer be manmade baths [*vaños (baños) artificiales*] in the kingdom of Granada, and all those currently in existence must be abandoned, demolished, and cease their function. No person, whatever their condition or estate may use these baths, or bathe in them." New Christians, especially, were warned that they could not have bathhouses and were not allowed to use them, nor might they bathe either inside or outside their own homes, on pain of imprisonment, monetary fines, and—for repeat offenders—five years of galley service and the loss of all their possessions.[1]

This statement was a dramatic shift from earlier policies and must have severely impacted the routines of daily life and personal cleanliness in Granada, but Christian sentiments against bathhouses had been growing for decades. Clerical and secular administrators had long been concerned that Moriscos were using bathhouses for ritual washing before prayer and for purification (either partial ablution, *al-wuḍū'*, or full immersion, *al-ghusl*) and perhaps for other Muslim ceremonies.[2] Christians were well aware that these ablutions ranked high among Islamic religious requirements.[3] At the time of the first edicts requiring conversion, circa 1500, a memorandum written by Hernando de Talavera to the inhabitants of the Albaicín, a neighborhood in Granada, urged that the first and most important step in the process of becoming Christian was to forget "all ceremonies and Moorish things" (toda cerimonia y toda cosa morisca), particularly Muslim prayers, fasts, festivals, births, weddings, funerals, and bathing.[4]

Later, however, Moriscos were suspected of preserving Muslim habits and mingling them with Christian practices, including performing ritual ablutions before going to mass. In consequence, ordinances began to appear that prohibited visits to bathhouses before going to church on Sundays and other religious holidays. In 1532, a letter from Charles V to the New Christians in Granada cited rumors that they were going to bathhouses along with their children on Sundays and ruled that nobody (*persona ninguna*, presumably neither New Christians nor Old Christians) was to bathe on feast days before mass. Additionally, for good measure, nobody was allowed to repair a bathhouse or to build a new one without procuring a license from the crown.[5] Two decades later, in 1554, the Synod of Guadix cited this imperial decree and repeated its rulings. It also went on to list visits to bathhouses among many other Moorish *supersticiones y ritos*, with the comment that although there was no clear regulation of these facilities, Morisco visits to bathhouses were highly suspect, especially when they bathed on Thursday and Friday nights before prayer, or after having sex, or in connection with other "harmful ceremonies."[6] Morisco communities in Valencia were subject to similar legislation, in 1564 and 1565, when ordinances prohibited bathing on Thursdays and major holidays.[7]

Alongside regulations forbidding bathing on certain days, lest visits to the bathhouse conceal ritual ablutions before prayer, other ordinances took a different tack toward a similar end. The Synod of Guadix also ruled that ovens and bathhouse furnaces were not to be lit on Sundays and holidays, nor during the final days of Holy Week.[8] Earlier, in 1514, a proclamation to the Moriscos in Huéscar (northeast of Granada) had ordered that the bathhouses not be heated

on Fridays, Sundays, or feast days, and it imposed fines on any bathhouse keepers who violated this rule and any bathers who visited on these days.[9] Presumably, the prospect of bathing in unheated water would have discouraged many
visitors, but the ruling may also have been intended to address the issue of
preventing work and recreation on holy days. Rules against heating bathhouses
on Sundays were much older than those restricting New Christians from bathing on that day. Already in the twelfth century, long before there were any
concerns about residual Islamic practices among Moriscos, the *fuero* of Teruel
(dated 1177) had ruled that nobody among the town's Christian, Muslim, or
Jewish inhabitants was to bathe in the community bathhouse (*bannyo comunal*)
on Sundays, and the facility was not to be heated on that day.[10]

Restrictions on bathing and on the heating of bathhouses probably also
stemmed from associations between bathhouses and sexual improprieties. The
Synod of Guadix also recommended that bathhouses should be closed at night
and not heated in order to prevent "offenses and abominations."[11] These had
been long-standing concerns, and bathhouse regulations in medieval Iberia
had always stressed the importance of gender segregation, either setting aside
different days or times on which men and women could bathe or establishing
separate facilities for men and women. Similar rules continued after 1492, but
concerns with the sexual activities of New Christian bathers (especially women)
became much more explicit during the sixteenth century, when they would
be cited among rationales for restricting and closing bathhouses. The sweep-
ing Granada ordinances of 1526, which were never fully implemented but
which in many ways previewed the more effective restrictions in 1567, established a two-tiered system of oversight, requiring not only gender segregation
but also that New Christian bathers were to be supervised by Old Christian
bathhouse staff. The text noted "the things that cause great harm, impropriety, and set a bad example that continue to happen in the artificial bathhouses
of this realm. In order to stop these, and to prevent them from happening in
the future, we order that from here onward, all persons who work in these
bathhouses must be Old Christian men [for male bathers], and Old Christian women for female [bathers], and that no New Christian man or woman
may work [in the bathhouses] or have anything to do with them."[12] These rules,
implying the monitoring of both suspected religious and sexual activities in
bathhouses, would be repeated in later legislation.[13]

Francisco Núñez Muley's memorandum protesting the ordinances of 1567
contained several pages arguing against the closure of bathhouses in Granada.
He organized his defense with particular attention to refuting accusations that

Moriscos were using bathhouses for Islamic practices and illicit sexual encounters. This is noteworthy, because the wording of the ordinance itself mentioned neither of these things. Nevertheless, Núñez Muley clearly felt it necessary to counter popular rumors that he believed had given rise to the prohibition of bathhouses, both the idea "that it is possible to practice Muslim ceremonies and rites in them," and the belief "that mortal sins occur there . . . I'm speaking here about the women who supposedly go to the baths to meet their lovers and have sex with them."[14] In this section on bathhouses, as throughout his memorandum, Núñez Muley was forced to emphasize the purely utilitarian and customary aspects of the practices that he was defending. It would have done no good to admit any connection to Islam. However, this tricky circumstance created several contradictions in his argument, revealing not only the difficulties of his brief but also, it seems likely, his own personal suspicions that some bathhouses were indeed sites for impropriety.

In answer to the charge that Islamic rituals were taking place in bathhouses, Núñez Muley drew attention to the fact that both Old and New Christian bathers frequented these facilities, and that some baths in Granada employed both Old and New Christian workers (*bañeros*). Because of this extensive and mixed group of patrons and staff, "it is impossible to carry out Muslim ceremonies or rites, as these require a degree of solitude and are not carried out in public."[15] Also, taking a new line of argument, "these ceremonies and rites require a clean place in which there is not even the suspicion of dirtiness . . . [but] the baths themselves are pools of filth and other such things, for the sick go to them with their various maladies and sores, as well as those who have dirty occupations," such as fishermen, butchers, blacksmiths, skinners, garbage and dung collectors, coal suppliers, sewer cleaners, and others. "All these people come to the baths, particularly when they have need to clean themselves of the aforementioned forms of filth and relieve themselves. In the baths they take buckets or make depressions in the ground and urinate in them, so that . . . it is impossible to cleanse the bath of all of the aforementioned things."[16] Because of all this, he explains, bathhouses can provide neither the privacy nor the cleanliness required for religious purification. These arguments suited the purpose of Núñez Muley's memorandum, especially the need to downplay any religious content in bathhouse activities, but he was also reviving a much older Muslim debate, drawing on long-standing concerns that bathhouses were not clean enough for ritual washing.[17]

Apparently continuing his discussion of dirt, Núñez Muley provides further information that sheds light on actual bathhouse practices in Granada and medical beliefs about the benefits of washing in a steamy environment. He reports that "the baths themselves were instituted in order to provide a place to cleanse oneself with hot water and a hot environment, for when one sweats the body releases all form of dirtiness and bad humors. And the bath workers wash the patrons by scrubbing them with their fingernails and other instruments made of wool with hard centers that are known as *almoçahas*. They also use their palms and stones from the sea with which they wash the soles of their feet and their heels."[18]

From this discussion of scrubbing, Núñez Muley then turns to his second line of argument, regarding charges that women are visiting bathhouses for illicit sexual encounters. This claim, he writes, "is wholly without merit and cannot be substantiated in any way, for while the women—whether Old Christians or New Christians—are in the baths they are surrounded by many other women and the female bath workers that bathe them, and not a single man enters the bath. This being the situation, I fail to see how it's possible to claim that men and women meet in the baths to commit such sins."[19] This line of reasoning might seem sufficient, especially because it was confirmed by legal materials requiring gender segregation in bathhouses. However, it was well known that such rules were sometimes ignored.[20] So Núñez Muley felt the need to add a further bit of logic to his refutation: "Let us say for the sake of argument that such women—Old and New Christians—get the awful idea to meet their lovers for sex. It would be much easier for them to do so while going on visits, or visiting churches, or attending jubilees and plays where men and women regularly interact with one another; and it also seems a better plan for them simply to reserve a room in an inn to have sex."[21]

From here, Núñez Muley goes on to discuss other aspects of bathing, then turns to his defense of female veiling (previously discussed in Chapter 2), on the grounds that wearing a veil prevents men from falling "into the mortal sin of seeing the beautiful face of the woman they admire and pursuing her, by licit or illicit means . . . [so] that a woman covering her face is nothing but a matter of modesty meant to prevent these events from occurring." Then, immediately following this, he returns back to the issue of female bathing, with the observation that, after all, "one cannot deny that if Bathsheba had not been bathing herself, David would not have sinned."[22] Although this sudden comment about David and Bathsheba might appear to be a non sequitur, it is nothing of the sort. Instead, this telling transition in the text reflects the strong connections perceived between bathing and female sexuality, apparently also held by Núñez Muley himself and despite his earlier arguments attempting to refute such links. He believed, as did many of his contemporaries, that the sexual temptations presented by a woman bathing, or uncovering her face, were a danger to society.

This is not the only point at which Núñez Muley appears to contradict his own assertions. Despite his efforts to portray bathhouses as filthy and crowded places, and thus unsuitable for religious ablutions, he still needed to argue for their utility and the necessity of their remaining open to the public. His arguments in support of these facilities are illuminating in what they reveal about bathhouse use in Granada and about beliefs regarding cleanliness and health. First, he asks "if the public baths are done away with . . . what will the sick do or those [workers such as butchers and blacksmiths] who have to cleanse themselves of the forms of filth that I have described above?"[23] Since Moriscos were not allowed to bathe at home (as legislation had been enacted to avoid the possibility of secret ritual ablutions), where could they go to clean themselves? One option might be to visit natural hot springs (such as those in Alhama de Granada), since these did not fall within the condemned category of *baños artificiales*. However, as Núñez Muley points out, the fees charged to bathe in natural springs were much higher than those charged at public bathhouses, making them unaffordable for most Moriscos ("only one person out of a hundred can afford to go to the natural spring baths").[24] Also, in spite of his earlier comments about bathhouse filth, he adds that the public baths "leave a person much cleaner than the natural spring baths do."[25] Another option for sick people wishing to visit a public bath for health reasons was to obtain special permission from a doctor. But this took time, waiting for consultations first with a doctor, then with a priest and a notary, and it cost money.

Núñez Muley's arguments in favor of bathhouses also cited divisions in sixteenth-century Granada between Castilians (*los de Castilla*) and the local Morisco population (*los naturales deste reyno*) and their different bathing traditions. Whereas "Castilians have the freedom to bathe wherever they like, and so they have no need of public baths, the natives of this kingdom, however, do not in any way enjoy such freedoms."[26] So if the public bathhouses were closed, where would New Christians bathe? Beyond this—and here Núñez Muley indulges in comparative judgment—people in Granada (unlike in other kingdoms) had always enjoyed "public waterworks to handle both clean water and sewage, [and] we, unlike Castile, have long had public baths." Indeed, public baths were even mentioned in scripture, "and yet Castilians never desired to have any."[27]

In order to explain this antipathy to bathhouses, Núñez Muley cites a widely held Castilian belief "that going to the baths can weaken the limbs and veins of a man in times of war."[28] Many other sixteenth-century authors, both Castilians and Moriscos, repeated this dictum, often tracing the idea back to a brief passage in the late thirteenth-century compilation of Castilian history the *Primera crónica general de España*, which mentioned that when Alfonso VI learned that his armies had been defeated at the Battle of Uclés in 1108 because his soldiers had been enervated by too much bathing, he ordered that bathhouses in his kingdom should be destroyed.[29] This story also appears earlier in the thirteenth century, in the *Chronicon mundi* of Lucas of Tuy, but there seems to be no twelfth-century record of the event.[30] And except for its narration in these thirteenth-century chronicles, the story appears to have been largely forgotten until the fifteenth and sixteenth centuries, when, as well as being noted by Francisco Núñez Muley, the anecdote appears in the work of Rodrigo Sánchez de Arévalo in 1470, Alonso López de Corella in 1547, Luis de Escobar in 1552, Miguel de Luna in 1592, and Sebastián de Covarrubias Orozco in 1611.[31] Other contemporaries noted similar links between bathing and male weakness, though without mentioning the anecdote about Alfonso VI.[32] Clearly, the idea that bathing caused a loss of energy, and especially impotence, had real traction in the sixteenth century, and the example of Alfonso VI, whose capture of Toledo in 1085 was seen as turning the tide of the Christian Reconquista, had resonance in an age of ongoing Christian-Muslim tensions, both within Spain and in the wider Mediterranean context. By rejecting all practices that were perceived as Muslim, including bathing, Christian spiritual, military, physical, and moral victory could be achieved.

Yet as characteristic as these beliefs were for sixteenth-century Christians in Spain, they would have been strikingly uncharacteristic among their medieval predecessors. Whether or not the story about Alfonso VI had any truth to it (possibly he spoke against bathhouses in a moment of anger and frustration), he never actually closed bathhouses and probably never wished to.[33] Later, when this very brief anecdote (told in a mere three sentences) appeared in thirteenth-century chronicles, it was included without any further comment or value judgment, since at the time bathhouses were common and widely accepted. One imagines that some later researcher must have been reading very closely in order to find this reference that would hold such resonance for the fifteenth century, even if not, in fact, for the earlier period.

Núñez Muley had no grounds for claiming that Castilians had never used or desired public bathhouses, even though this disinterest may have characterized his sixteenth-century Old Christian neighbors. In fact, bath-houses were a perfectly normal feature of Iberian urban life in Christian and Muslim cities during the period of Alfonso VI's reign (1065–1109), and the tradition had much older roots.[34] Alfonso would have been familiar with Andalusi bathhouses (*ḥammāmāt*) from living at the Dhu'l Nūnid court in Toledo, but there were also plenty of public bathhouses in northern cities, including Oviedo, Lugo, Zamora, and León, that had been in existence since the ninth and tenth centuries, and they would have been common in Castile and elsewhere by the eleventh century.[35] A document issued by Alfonso VI in 1091 mentioned bathhouses in Burgos, and in the neighboring kingdom of Aragon King Sancho Ramírez had made a gift of the bathhouses in Jaca to his son in 1086.[36] In cities that shifted from Muslim to Christian rule, like Toledo after its conquest by Alfonso VI in 1085, bathhouses were merely one among a bundle of revenue-producing urban amenities (markets, houses, mills, ovens, *fanādiq*, olive presses, and so on) that usually survived the transfer more or less intact.

Christians were perfectly aware that they were perpetuating a tradition that had been common in al-Andalus, and this Muslim precedent did not hinder adoption or use. Thus, a grant from Alfonso VIII of Castile in 1179 authorized a new bathhouse to be built in Toledo with the explicit remark that this was to be constructed "just as had been done in the time of the Moors" (tamen facta fuerunt tempore maurorum).[37] Because of this conscious association with Muslim traditions of bathing, it is helpful to examine bathhouse culture in al-Andalus in order to trace later continuities and changes in medieval Castile and Aragon (where Muslims, Christians, and Jews all visited bathhouses on a regular basis), in Naṣrid Granada, and in early modern Spain.

## Bathing and Bathhouses in Muslim Spain

When Fernando and Isabel campaigned against the kingdom of Granada in the 1480s and early 1490s, they conquered cities with bathhouses and a bathing culture that were very similar to those that had been in operation in Andalusi cities since the Umayyad period. Archaeological and documentary evidence suggests that the basic layout of Andalusi bathhouses and Islamic traditions of bathing did not change significantly between the tenth and the fifteenth centuries (although there were stylistic differences in the architectural design over time).[38] Thus, in the first decades after the conquest of Granada, expectations and arrangements for the continuity of bathhouses were not unlike those reflected in earlier postconquest contexts. Bathhouses remained open for business, while their physical, administrative, legal, and fiscal oversight came under Christian control. The details of this transfer will be discussed in detail later in this chapter, but for the moment, the important point is that Muslims living in Spain in the early sixteenth century, like their counterparts in earlier centuries, expected to be able to bathe and there were plenty of bathhouses available to meet their needs.

Cleanliness is a requirement of Islamic law, but *ḥammāmāt* also served social, recreational, and cultural functions in al-Andalus.[39] As well as serving for bodily cleansing and religious purification, visits to a bathhouse provided an opportunity to talk with friends, to relax, to promote health, to beautify oneself, and to prepare for special occasions such as weddings. Although it is generally assumed that Islamic bathhouses derived their existence from Roman bathing traditions, there were a number of important differences from that earlier period. Muslim bathhouses did not serve the broad range of recreational and athletic functions that were expected for Roman bathhouses, and they were smaller, without deep pools for swimming or the many different rooms and spaces characteristic of Roman facilities. Instead, archaeological evidence and existing structures show that most baths in al-Andalus were relatively simple, with a room for changing and three basic bathing spaces equivalent to the Roman cold room (*frigidarium*), warm room (*tepidarium*), and hot room (*caldarium*). In Arabic, these spaces were called, respectively, *bayt al-bārid*, *bayt al-wasṭānī*, and *bayt al-sakhūn*. Bathhouses also had an area near the hot room for a furnace to heat water and create steam.[40] These spaces are not only attested in the archaeological record and existing buildings, but also in Andalusi poetry, where much is made of the deliciously contrasting sensations of cold water and hot vapor experienced by bathers.[41] Most bathhouses were of modest size, such as the well-preserved and restored Ḥammām al-Jawza (Bath of the Walnut Tree, now known as the Bañuelo) in Granada, though there were also more lavish examples, notably the elegant bath complex Baño de Comares in the Alhambra Palace.[42]

Individual bathhouses might be small, but there were often many of them in any given city, and their presence was important to urban life. Medieval Arabic geographers routinely described even modestly sized towns as having "mosques, markets, bathhouses, and hostelries," creating a collective trope that recognized bathing among a cluster of other markers of urban identity. The twelfth-century geographer al-Idrīsī cited this constellation of baths, markets, and *fanādiq* not only in major cities, such as Córdoba, Almería, and Málaga, but also in several smaller Andalusi towns.[43] A century later, al-Shaqundī (d. 1231) remarked on the houses, baths, markets, and mills along the river in Granada.[44] Some authors cited large numbers of baths. In the fifteenth century, al-Himyarī noted eight thousand villages in the region of Seville, each with a bathhouse.[45] Ibn ʿIdhārī (d. circa 1295) claimed that there had been three hundred baths in tenth-century Córdoba, while al-Maqqārī (d. 1632) later upped the count to six hundred.[46] Real numbers were probably not so high, but archaeology has shown that in late medieval Granada, the Alhambra complex alone contained a dozen different bathing facilities, with at least four more bathhouses in the lower town and Albaicín.[47]

Some of the *ḥammāmāt* would have been open to the public, while others were built for the use of a particular family or group. Some were privately owned, while others belonged to the state or ruler (who collected revenues by leasing the bathhouse to an individual who would administer it). In the fifteenth century, al-Himyarī listed bathhouses in many Andalusi towns, including six in Jaén, two that he noted as "belonging to the ruler" (or to the state; *lil-sulṭān*) and four others bearing the names of individuals.[48] Earlier, in the twelfth century, Ibn ʿAbdūn had listed *ḥammāmāt* among a group of urban and revenue-generating facilities (along with mills and shops) that belonged to the ruler (*min al-sulṭān*).[49] This official status is noteworthy because it would also be the case in Christian Spain, where bathhouses were often designated as property of the crown, even including some facilities in Granada after the conquest of 1492.

One of the most intriguing descriptions of a private bathhouse in Umayyad Córdoba appears in an *aljamiado* tale about a rich husband who built a sumptuous bathhouse for his wife, after she complained that she was not getting sufficient attention from the staff of the public bathhouse. This new privately built *ḥammām*, called the Baño de Zaryeb, was to be open to all men and women in the city, free of charge. The bath was immediately popular and attracted so many male patrons that a special period had to be set aside for women to bathe.[50] Although set in the tenth century, this story was recorded by Mudejars in fifteenth-century Aragon, and it probably reflects both its later context and an imagined vision of a celebrated past. Either way, it reveals realities and expectations of Muslim bathing in both periods that are confirmed in other sources, including the facts that some bathhouses were built by wealthy individuals, but open to the public; that some bathhouses charged fees while others did not (they may have been supported by an endowment, or *waqf*); and that separate bathing times were needed for men and women.

Andalusi legal materials make clear that an establishment should either be entirely devoted to bathers of one sex, or that men and women should bathe on different days and at different times (women were often assigned the afternoons, while men bathed in the morning).[51] This segregation is confirmed in other Muslim sources, as when an Egyptian visitor to Granada in 1465 mentioned that there were two separate buildings, one for men and the other for women, at the thermal baths outside of the city.[52] The gendered segregation of bathhouses was required by propriety and Islamic law, in part because bathhouses were often suspected as being potential sites for illicit sexual encounters. The kind of rumors that Francisco Núñez Muley addressed in the sixteenth century had also circulated about Andalusi bathhouses, along with concerns about rape, voyeurism, and prostitution. In the early twelfth century, both Ibn ʿAbdūn (in Seville) and Ibn al-Ḥājj (in Córdoba) prohibited men from loitering near the entrances of bathhouses at the times when women were bathing in order to prevent them from ogling or propositioning the female bathers as they went by.[53]

Nudity in the bathhouse provided fodder for suspicions of improper activities. After entering a bathhouse, bathers left their clothes in the changing room, then either went into the bathing spaces nude or wrapped in a towel or loincloth (see Figure 8).[54] In twelfth-century Seville, Ibn ʿAbdūn recommended that patrons and staff should wear shoes and a short covering while in the bathhouse—not surprising, since as a *muḥtasib*, his primary concern was with public decency and decorum.[55] A century later, al-Saqaṭī discussed the odd case of a man who was found naked in the courtyard of a bathhouse, dousing himself with water on a very cold day.[56] On a lighter note, disrobing is attested in a line of poetry from verses written to be inscribed over the door of the royal bathhouse of the Alhambra, constructed for the Naṣrid sultan Yūsuf I (1333–54), comparing the clothing a bather takes off with the cares that he lays aside upon entering the bath.[57] Other Andalusi poets also addressed the sensual and sexual pleasures of bathing.[58]

Concern for the body was primary in the experience of bathing, even while cleanliness was also required for religious reasons. An inscription recorded as being over the door of another bathhouse in Granada proclaimed that "God created water so that people may purify themselves. Bathing is both healthful and pleasurable, and anybody who would have a spotless soul must also have a clean body."[59] Many people visited the bathhouse in search of better

Figure 8. Mīrak Khurasānī and Bihzād (attr.), *Hārūn al-Rashīd and the Barber* (ca. 1490). British Library Or. 6810 (*Khamsah*), fol. 27v. Persian depiction of Muslim men in various states of undress at a bathhouse. © The British Library Board

health, since hot steam and bracing cold water were both recommended by doctors and in medical writings.[60] But most bathhouse patrons sought relaxation, hygiene, and beautification. Bathhouse workers included barbers and masseurs for male bathers and a variety of female staff to attend to the needs of female clients for washing, shaving, and plucking hair, soaping, oiling, massaging, and sponging skin, and putting on cosmetics. The application of henna to the hair, face, hands, feet, and fingernails was an especially popular bathhouse ritual for women.[61] In his early thirteenth-century *ḥisba* text, al-Saqaṭī recommended scrubbing a newly purchased slave with borax and vinegar in a bathhouse and mentioned bathhouse attendants using a pumice stone to smooth the rough skin on clients' feet.[62] Even aside from the fact of nudity in bathhouses, this emphasis on the body—and the ways in which it could be stroked, salved, smoothed, sponged, and shaved in the bathhouse—reinforced the connection between bathing and other sensual pleasures, such as eating and sex.

## Bathing and Bathhouses in Christian Spain

When Alfonso VI of León-Castile conquered Toledo in 1085, he would have found a city filled with bathhouses that were frequented by the Muslims, Christians, and Jews already living there.[63] Incoming Christians would also have been familiar with such facilities, which had long been a feature in northern towns, though in less profusion than in Andalusi cities. Although no bathhouses were mentioned in the early *fueros* granted to Toledo, their importance to urban life is attested in other early documents from Christian cities, whether newly conquered or not.[64] For example, in a grant to the inhabitants of Tudela (which was conquered by Alfonso I of Aragon in 1119), the king promised them rights over the bathhouses and ovens in their city, while the roughly contemporary *fuero* from Pamplona (long in Christian hands) also granted the city rights over its local churches, mills, ovens, and bathhouses.[65] Later, in the thirteenth century, *repartimiento* texts often listed existing bathhouses that were to be distributed into Christian hands. In Valencia, the *repartimiento* listed at least ten bathhouses, and while some of these buildings would have been demolished or used for other purposes, others continued their earlier function.[66] The lucrative nature of bathhouses as revenue-producing assets encouraged the preservation of some facilities and assured their mention in grants, charters, and other Christian fiscal records.

Christians from all walks of life regularly visited bathhouses, as is evident from legislation about bathing, in records distributing the bathhouse revenues, and more casual references to the activity. Most of these citations refer to public bathhouses, which were shared by all inhabitants of the city, or to bathhouses located within *morerías* and *juderías*, and reserved for use by the local Muslim and Jewish communities. There were also private bathhouses in palace complexes, enjoyed by Christian kings, their wives, and members of the court.[67] In December 1315, the bailiff of Valencia received an order to prepare the bathhouse in the royal palace for the arrival of King Jaume II and his queen, and a similar order had earlier been sent to Zaragoza concerning the royal baths in the Aljafería palace.[68] In 1336, Pere IV bathed in the Aljafería on the night before his coronation.[69] Evidence for royal bathing survives in archaeological data as well as texts. Just as there was a bathhouse in the royal complex of the Alhambra, so too there were private baths of a very similar design in the contemporary royal palaces in Córdoba (built by Alfonso XI of Castile in 1328) and in Tordesillas, near Valladolid, which was constructed in the 1340s for Alfonso XI's longtime mistress Leonor de Guzmán.[70]

Bathing was seen as promoting health as well as cleanliness, and both natural hot springs and artificial steam baths were valued for their salubrious qualities. In 1318, Jaume II made arrangements for his daughter Violante to visit the hot springs at Caldes de Montbui.[71] This was just one among a great number of thermal spas in the Crown of Aragon and elsewhere in the Peninsula, many of which had been known since Roman times.[72] Despite the story about Alfonso VI and the bad effects of bathing on virility, there is no evidence that this was a pervasive or long-standing concern. Other medieval Iberian monarchs, and their medical advisers, clearly believed in the value of bathing. Medical treatises in both Arabic and Latin, written by physicians serving at royal courts, discussed the benefits of bathing. It is likely that there was an exchange of ideas between the two traditions, and certainly they all cited the earlier works of Greek and Arabic medical authorities (Galen, Hippocrates, Avicenna, Razi, and others).[73] Arnau de Vilanova, who served as royal doctor at the court of Jaume II, wrote his *Regimen sanitatis ad regem Aragonum* in about 1307, a text that included advice on the benefits of bathing both in cold water and in steam baths.[74] Another treatise, *Sevillana medicina* (composed in Castilian in the early fifteenth century by the physician Juan de Aviñón, a convert from Judaism), included a detailed description of the various circumstances and advantages to bathing in Seville, whether in artificial baths, natural pools, or in the Guadalquivir River.[75] Interest in the benefits of bathing continued into the middle of the fifteenth century, when at least three luxury manuscripts were produced at the court of Alfonso V of Aragon, based in Naples after 1442, reproducing the early thirteenth-century treatise *De balneis Puteolanis*, by Peter of Eboli. These manuscripts are noteworthy not only for their extensive information on hot springs and health, but for the numerous illustrations of men and women taking the waters in tubs and pools as will be further discussed below.[76]

Manuscript illuminations and other material data provide compelling evidence of the similarities and continuities in bathhouse culture and usage in Christian and Muslim regions. Former Andalusi baths that came into Christian hands after military conquest were very similar in their basic architecture and layout to those that were later built by Christians (see Figure 9). In most cases, the layout continued to be simple, with three rooms of different temperatures and a vestibule for disrobing and storing clothes. Ceilings were usually fairly low, to hold in heat, with rounded vaults supported on pillars. Ornament was provided by glazed tiles and decorative brickwork, with illumination coming from the star-shaped openings serving as skylights in the roof that were characteristic of both Andalusi and Christian bathhouse structures. Some baths had shallow pools of water, deep enough to splash or wade, but patrons usually used buckets to wash and rinse themselves. The twelfth-century bathhouse in Girona was unusual for its high and elegant Gothic arches and for the raised pool in its cold room that was large and deep enough for immersion. The baths in Girona were first mentioned in a grant conceded by Alfonso II of Aragon in 1194, and they would have been patronized by the Christian and Jewish inhabitants of the city. Yet today they are usually referred to as the "Arab Baths" (Banys Àrabs), despite the fact that there was never a significant Muslim population in Girona.[77] This misleading name is understandable in light of the general similarities in style and design between Muslim and Christian bathhouses.

Artistic images of bathing provide visual evidence about bath usage beyond what is revealed by the bathhouse buildings themselves. Late medieval French artists and readers appear to have been fascinated with depictions of bathing, to judge from the considerable numbers of illuminations of bathers in French manuscripts produced between the thirteenth and the sixteenth centuries. In most cases, these either illustrate the story of David and Bathsheba or the chapter on Luxuria from Valerius Maximus's *Facta et dicta memorabilia*.[78] These images emphasize the sensuality of bathing scenes, especially in manuscripts from the fifteenth and sixteenth centuries, reflecting growing associations between bathing and sex in this period, in tandem, perhaps, with

Figure 9. Arab Baths, Jaén (eleventh century). Note star-shaped openings in
ceiling. José Ignacio Soto/Shutterstock.com.

the increase in private reading.[79] Such associations were also true in Spain,
but the growing sexualization of bathing was more reflected in Spanish literature than in Spanish art. In fact, in contrast to French production, there are
almost no depictions of bathing in medieval Spanish manuscripts. This is striking, given that all evidence suggests that public bathhouses were much more
common in Iberia than they were in northern Europe.

I know of only three medieval Spanish images of bathing, only one of
which is clearly situated in a bathhouse. These are distinct from the many images (especially in the famous thirteenth-century *Cantigas de Santa María*)
that show naked figures sitting in tubs and being doused with water during
baptism. The earliest manuscript depictions of David and Bathsheba actually
come from Spain rather than from France and are found in a pair of illuminated Bibles from Pamplona, commissioned by Sancho VII of Navarre (1194–
1234).[80] In one of the images (in Amiens 108, fol. 94r), David watches from an
upper window while a maid washes Bathsheba's feet below (see Figure 10). The
latter is seated on a chair, but it is not clear whether the scene takes place inside or outside a building (many medieval depictions of Bathsheba place her
in the open air, often in a garden). The other Pamplona volume (now Har-

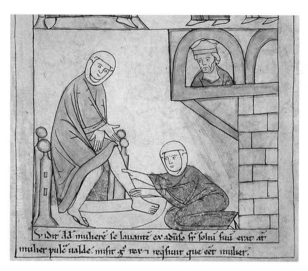

Figure 10. Pamplona Bible (ca. 1230). Amiens 108, fol. 94r. Navarrese depiction of Bathsheba washing (fully clothed).

burg 1, 2, Lat. 4°, 15, on fol. 110v) clearly places Bathsheba within an arched and pillared structure, possibly a bathhouse, and she bends to wash her own feet while David views her from outside the building. Since bathhouses were common in Navarre by the later twelfth century, it is reasonable that a local artist might have set this scene in one.[81] Yet aside from the attentive gaze of David, hinting at passion to come, both images are relatively modest, with Bathsheba entirely clothed and showing only her bare lower legs and feet. Neither suggests that she is planning full-scale ablutions or further disrobing.[82]

In contrast, a small image illustrating the *Lapidario*, a manuscript on the magical properties of stones commissioned by Alfonso X of Castile in about 1250, shows a nude male bather, evidently in a bathhouse (see Figure 11).[83] The figure has his bare back to the viewer, and with his right hand he clutches a towel to cover his front from the waist down. This towel would have been provided by the bathhouse, along with hot water and soap, as part of his entrance fee.[84] His left hand reaches into an arched alcove in the wall, possibly where his clothes are kept or—more likely—where he will find the "bath stone" (*piedra del banno*) that the image illustrates. This stone, described as drab brown (*parda*), porous, lightweight, and easy to crumble, was presumably pumice, and used for smoothing rough skin.[85] Or perhaps he is in search of a sponge, since elsewhere the *Lapidario* describes stones that were called "sea

De la piedra del banno:

El LVIII. grado del signo de sagitario: es la piedra aq̃ dizen del banno. Et este nombre a por que la fallan en las entradas de los vannos. ca se cuajan del agua en fondo del las: por escalentamiento que reciben en muy grand tiempo de las calenturas. Porosa es y liuiana de peso y ligera de quebrantar. De natura es caliente y seca: y de color purpura. Et si la muelen y la echan sobre la cancer que se faz a las mugieres en las naturas: sanan luego. Et la estrella q̃ es en la mano con q̃ tiene apretado el arco la figura del sagitario a poder en esta piedra della recibe su uertud. Et quando es en medio cielo: muestra esta piedra mas manifiesta miente sus obras:—

Figure 11. *Lapidario* (ca. 1250). Escorial MS H.l.15, fol. 69v. Castilian image of nude man in bathhouse. © Patrimonio Nacional

foam" (*espuma de mar*) or sponges (*sponia*) "that women use to wash their bodies, because they are very good at forceful scrubbing" (despite the fact that they smelled of fish).[86] Whatever our bather is reaching for in the alcove, there are other more revealing aspects of this image. On a shelf under the alcove sits a wooden cup with a handle for dipping and pouring water; at the bather's feet are six wooden buckets for holding water, perhaps of different temperatures, for washing and rinsing. The architecture of the space itself is also noteworthy: not only the low interior room with pillars, capitals, and arches, but also the vaulted roof, with its circular windows to let in light. One more ornamental element, the three stepped merlons along the roof line (ziggurat-like decorations that are often seen as characteristic of Andalusi, Mudejar, and Maghribi architecture), suggests the ubiquitous nature of Iberian bathhouse architecture.

Stories told by Juan Manuel, Alfonso X's nephew, confirm contemporary expectations about bathhouse practices, including group bathing, the use of water buckets, and nudity. In one tale, a bathhouse owner fears that his income will decline precipitously after a madman begins to frequent his establishment, throwing around buckets of scalding water at the other naked bathers.[87] Fears of such behavior may explain urban ordinances that required patrons of bathhouses to wash without causing inconvenience to their fellow bathers.[88] In another story, Juan Manuel describes a haughty Christian king who left his palace one day to visit the bathhouse, where he disrobed and left his splendid garments in the changing room. While he was in the bath, God decided to teach him a lesson, sending an angel who took on his form, put on his clothes, and returned home with all his attendants, leaving the king naked, penniless, alone, and anonymous when he emerged from the bath.[89] Tales of female bathers also attest to expectations of nudity while bathing and undergoing beautification, but these stories tend to focus more overtly on bodily charms and flaws and on the sensual and lascivious possibilities of the bathhouse. This becomes especially true in fourteenth- and fifteenth-century literature, including stories about the bath of La Cava, in the misogynistic writings of Jaume Roig and Alfonso Martínez de Toledo, and even in the *aljamiado* tale of the Baño de Zaryeb as will be further discussed below.[90]

As attested by Juan Manuel, the disappearance of a bather's clothes or belongings was a recognized problem. Another late thirteenth-century story, from the *Cantigas de Santa María*, turned on a similar loss, when a woman in Toledo left a valuable necklace with her clothes in the changing room and later came out of the bath to discover that it had been stolen.[91] Perhaps, given these tales, it is not surprising that many urban law codes strongly condemned anybody who stole clothes or other items from a bathhouse. Among these, the influential late twelfth-century *fuero* of Cuenca ordered that if a man harmed a woman in the bathhouse on the women's bathing days, or took her clothing, he should be hurled from the city cliffs. The same penalty was stated, a bit later, for a thief who stole any bather's property that was worth more than a certain amount, whereas stealing bathhouse equipment resulted in the loss of an ear.[92]

Christian lawmakers, like their Muslim counterparts, were concerned about the harm that could result from men trespassing in bathhouses when women were bathing, as well as other legal issues relating to these facilities, their fees, and their staff. Despite its prescriptive nature, this legal evidence is revealing, especially when it is confirmed in other types of sources. On the one hand, the fact that urban law codes (*fueros*) so frequently included clauses regulating public bathhouses indicates their normality as part of everyday life in Spanish medieval cities.[93] But on the other, although all public urban spaces needed oversight, bathhouses presented special concerns. Naked patrons were vulnerable and separated from their belongings, and there were always suspicions (sometimes backed up by actual cases) that bathhouses provided a conducive setting for sexual crimes, including rape, prostitution, and adultery.[94] *Fueros* were therefore especially concerned with issues of access—dictating who could use the bathhouse and when—along with more general legislation about security and revenue. Not only were male and female bathers strictly segregated, but most *fueros* also established particular days on which Christians, Muslims, and Jews were permitted to bathe.

The appreciation and use of bathhouses was shared across religious boundaries, but Christian administrators were concerned to ensure that the facilities themselves were not sites for interaction between Christian, Muslim, and Jewish bathers. A synod in Lérida in 1280 promised excommunication to any Christian who shared the bathhouse with a Muslim bather, and the *Siete Partidas* (commissioned by Alfonso X in about the same period) ordered "that no Jews shall dare to bathe in company with Christians."[95] Later laws reiterated the importance of religiously segregated bathing.[96] To avoid such conjunctions, urban statutes normally reserved two or three days a week for Christian women to bathe (the exact days varied), three days for Christian men, and one or two days (usually including Fridays) were allotted to non-Christians. This division by day was notably different from bathhouse scheduling in Andalusi cities, where men and women bathed at different times (usually morning and afternoon, unless a bathhouse was entirely devoted to one sex) rather than on different days, and there was no official segregation of Muslim and non-Muslim bathers. In Christian Spain, schedules for bathing differed slightly according to the region in which a *fuero* was issued, but they followed the same general plan.[97] In Cuenca (and in other towns with similar *fueros*), men were to bathe on Tuesdays, Thursdays, and Saturdays; women bathed on Mondays and Wednesdays; Jews on Fridays and Sundays.[98] We find a similar allocation for Christian men and women in Teruel, in 1177, but Muslims and Jews in this city could only bathe on Fridays. Nobody was to bathe on Sundays, when the bathhouse was not heated.[99] In the thirteenth century, the *fuero* of Usagre allotted Sundays, Tuesdays, and Thursdays to women, and all other days to men; the *fuero* of Plasencia assigned Tuesdays, Wednesdays, and Saturdays to men; Mondays, Thursdays, and Sundays to women; and Fridays to Jews.[100] This list could be prolonged, but it is sufficient as it stands to emphasize general patterns, especially the fact that where Jews and Muslims are mentioned, the allocation of Fridays for their use suggests a recognition of non-Christian religious schedules and bathing requirements.

Some scholars have argued that the religious segregation of bathhouses applied only to male bathers, whose contrasting identities would have been inscribed by circumcision, while women of all three religions could bathe together.[101] This is conceivable, since early *fueros* do not specifically address this issue, but it seems unlikely given prevailing religious and legal attitudes toward interreligious bathing.[102] Certainly, by the fourteenth century it is clear that Christian women normally bathed together on the days reserved for women (though perhaps in the company of Muslim slave women, or in the care of non-Christian female bathhouse attendants), while Muslim and Jewish women bathed on the same days as their male coreligionists (though presumably at different times). A law from Tortosa, in June of 1346, stated that Jewish and Muslim women (*juhies* and *sarrahines*) could only use the bathhouses on Mondays and Fridays respectively. A month later, the law was emended to clarify that Jewish men and women (*juheus e juhies*) were only allowed to use the bathhouse on Mondays, and that Muslim men and women (*sarrahins e sarrahines*) could visit the bathhouse on Fridays.[103] Presumably each community established different bathing hours for men and women in order to prevent cases, such as one from Valencia in 1317, in which a Jewish man was accused of raping a Jewish woman in a bathhouse.[104] The fact that both parties were from the same religious community makes it likely that the crime occurred on a day assigned for Jewish bathing.

Occasionally, cities permitted less restricted access to bathhouses, probably spurred by the lucrative revenues from rents, leases, fees, and other

income generated by these urban facilities. In Tortosa, for instance, legislation from 1279 stated that "the baths in which one pays, and which charge a
fee for washing oneself, are for all of the people in Tortosa. All of the citizens
and inhabitants of the city and its surroundings, including Muslims, Jews, as
well as Christians . . . must pay the fees to bathe [here] and not in other bathhouses."[105] A later version of these urban statutes (dating from 1309), added that
the bathhouses of Tortosa were for the use of all citizens, and that "all men and
women could bathe when they chose, whether by day or by night" (tot hom e
tota femna que aquis vulla baynar de nit e de dia).[106] Night bathing was unusual, although a late medieval bathhouse in Seville allotted daylight hours
for female bathers and nighttime hours for men.[107] More normally, bathhouses
were open only during the day ("from sunrise to sunset"), and nocturnal
bathers—especially women—were often suspected of having immoral intent.

The most effective way to preserve religiously segregated bathing was to
establish different bathhouses for Muslims, Christians, and Jews. This model
seems to have become common by the end of the thirteenth century, when
non-Christians increasingly gathered in their own separate religious and residential communities (morerías and juderías), with their own bathhouses, ovens, butcher shops, and other facilities. Over time, this separation may have
fostered the perception that bathhouses were closely linked to a non-Christian
lifestyle, especially as Christian use of bathhouses began to decline in the later
Middle Ages. Meanwhile, the system helped Muslims and Jews to preserve
the urban institutions that were important to their religious communities,
while it also benefited the Christian administration that collected taxes and
rents on these facilities. Bathhouses in morerías were generally considered to
be property of the king, who leased these properties to either Christian or Muslim operators. This proprietary pattern is especially well documented for the
Crown of Aragon, but also existed in Castile and Portugal.[108] In their fiscal
capacity, bathhouses in Christian cities were routinely grouped together with
other revenue-producing facilities such as mills, shops, and ovens. This bun-
dling in Christian sources was directly comparable to the economic and
institutional grouping in Andalusi Arabic texts of the "baths, mosques, markets, and hostelries" that characterized a flourishing town in Muslim Spain.
Indeed, in an accord made with the Mudejars of Morón, in 1255, Alfonso X
granted them the same fiscal rights that they had enjoyed under the Almohad
caliph (en tiempo de Almiramolin), along with baths, shops, ovens, mills, and
alfondegas that they held "according to the custom of the Moors" (fagan esto
a la costumbre de los moros).[109]

The financial side of bathhouse administration, and the baths' importance as a source of income for the crown, for the city, for the church, and for private individuals, is the most broadly documented aspect of their existence. Bathhouse revenues went to royal treasuries, religious houses, private coffers, and to meet urban expenses such as maintaining bridges and walls.[110] Charters, *fueros*, grants, *repartimientos*, and other sources all confirm that bathhouses were common, respectable, and lucrative properties in medieval Christian cities. They generated considerable sums of money, mainly from fees paid by bathers, and this revenue was collected by bathhouse administrators who, in turn, would lease the facility from the owner of the property (whether the king, a city, a religious order, or a member of the nobility). Fines, such as those imposed for entering a bathhouse on the wrong day, may also have produced a certain amount of income. Bathhouse fees and fines were carefully set down in urban statutes, and a paying bather was usually allowed to bring in children or servants for free or at a reduced price. Endowed public bathhouses—those that were funded by a *waqf* and could therefore offer free entrance to patrons— existed in Andalusi cites but not in Christian Spain. It is noteworthy that among its many lavish wonders, the privately funded Baño de Zaryeb (supposedly built in tenth-century Córdoba but described in the fifteenth-century *aljamiado* tale) offered free entrance to all comers. This detail may reflect a nostalgic contrast between the money-grubbing present and the generous past, since *ḥammāmāt* in late medieval *morerías*, just like other bathhouses in Christian cities, were expected to deliver profits to their owners and administrators.

Even outside the *morerías* of many Christian cities, bathhouses and other seigneurial assets (ovens, mills, shops, and so on) were explicitly reserved as royal property, just as Andalusi bathhouses were often described as belonging to the ruler or state (*lil-sulṭān*). This was already common in the twelfth century, when kings like Ramiro II of Aragon and Alfonso VII of León and Castile controlled the revenues from royal bathhouses, and it became standard in the thirteenth century, especially in newly acquired territories.[111] After Jaume I's conquests in the region of Valencia, there followed a long documentary trail of references to bathhouses designated as royal property (*balneis nostris*).[112] In 1251, after the conquest of Játiva, Jaume granted various rights and privileges to the city's Muslim inhabitants, with the exception that "we perpetually retain, for us and for our heirs, the butcher shop, dye works, bathhouses, ovens, workshops, and all other revenue-bearing assets [*derechos censuales*]."[113] We find a similar pattern of seigneurial claims to baths in Castile and Aragon, as in both thirteenth-century Toledo and Seville where "todos los baños que son en las villas y en las cibdades deven ser del rey" (all baths which are in towns and cities should belong to the king), while in Zaragoza by 1291, records noted "el bannyo del Senyor Rey . . . et las otras cosas trehuderas que son del Senyor Rey" (the bath of the lord king . . . and other tributary properties pertaining to the lord king).[114] Royal interest in these urban assets continued through the fourteenth and fifteenth centuries, and even after their conquest of Granada in 1492, Fernando and Isabel took over the revenues from bathhouses in the newly Christian city. There is no sense, in any of these claims to crown property, that bathhouses were anything other than normal and lucrative urban facilities, and the only mention of crime or immorality in bathhouses arose in the context of its possible negative impact on royal revenues.

Bathhouses might be designated as belonging to the king, but he certainly did not intend to run these facilities himself. Instead, the buildings were normally leased by the year as a tax farm. We see this in 1257 and 1258, when Jaume I "sold" (vendimus) the right to collect all crown revenues in Alcira—including taxes on bathhouses, mills, ovens, bridges, slaughterhouses, and salt pans—in return for an annual payment.[115] Later, in 1273, Jaume granted revenues from the king's bathhouse in Murviedro, along with its sweat room and other appurtenances ("cum caldaria et aliis apparamentis ipsorum balnorum"), to a Jewish tax farmer.[116] Thus, in Murviedro, the award of a rental contract was not limited by religious affiliation, and the royal bathhouse could be leased to both Christian and Jewish tax farmers. In the middle of the fourteenth century, a public bathhouse in Madrid (noted as belonging to the consejo) was rented and run by a Muslim woman (una mora), Doña Xançi, although by 1399, when the property was investigated, the bath was no longer functioning and the building had been leased to a Jewish tanner.[117]

Other rental contracts were religiously circumscribed, at least at first, as in Játiva in 1258, where Jaume I promised local Muslims that no Christian or Jew would ever be allowed to collect rents on the ovens or bathhouses in the morería.[118] Surrender documents and charters granted to other Mudejar communities also suggest a strong Mudejar preference for Muslim bathhouse administrators in morerías, as in Chelva in 1277, where the bathhouses were confirmed in the continued possession of a local faqih, who had held these properties in the past.[119] In Eslida, also, the Muslim population was promised in 1276 that nobody would pressure them to use the bathhouse in any way other than as they chose.[120] But these promises of communal control were neither perpetual nor universal. In 1283, Pere III gave the concession for bathhouses in Játiva to a Christian leaseholder, and a new bathhouse in the morería of

Valencia, constructed with public funds, was leased to a Christian tax farmer in 1272.[121] In 1338, Pere IV would also assign a Christian collector for the rents on this Valencia bathhouse and its "buildings, sweat rooms, and other apparatus," and he reconfirmed this grant to the same lessee in 1346.[122]

Although some bathhouses in Christian cities were holdovers from an earlier Muslim period, like those mentioned in *repartimiento* texts, many others were built in the period of Christian rule or in cities that had always been in Christian hands. Some of these new facilities were crown property, while others delivered a portion of their revenues to the ruler. Bathhouse buildings were considered to be unitary and indivisible property, but their income might be divided between several recipients.[123] In 1160, Count Ramon Berenguer IV of Barcelona allowed a man named Abram to build a bathhouse (*balnea*) on a parcel of land in Barcelona that belonged to the count, with the stipulation that future revenues from this facility were to be divided between them: two parts going to the count and one part to Abram. Four decades later, in 1199, this same bathhouse was sold to a Christian buyer by a Jewish woman and her two sons, and King Pere II released the New Christian owner from paying any percentage of its revenues to the crown.[124] Later, in 1269, Prince Pere (later King Pere III) granted Soriana, the widow of Fernando Pérez, the right "to construct and build a public bathhouse [*balnea*]" in buildings that she owned in a village near Játiva, with the understanding that if she would "hold the baths for Us [i.e., the king], and give Us [an annual] rent of one gold Alfonsine *morabatin* . . . [she] may have, hold, and possess this bathhouse in perpetuity, with its entrances and exits, and all of its appurtenances" under royal overlordship.[125]

But royal permission to build or sell a bathhouse may not always have directly profited the crown. In 1270, King Jaume granted Astruc Jacob Shishon, a Jewish bailiff in Valencia, the right to build a bathhouse on his (Shishon's) own personal property near the city. This facility was to be open to anybody wishing to bathe, and the contract included no explicit requirement of any payment to the crown for this license.[126] Three years later, in 1273, the king confirmed the sale, by three Christians, of a bathhouse, oven, and mills in Valencia to this same Astruc Jacob Shishon.[127] Again, no royal profit was stated, although the nature of the facilities and Jaume's oversight of the transaction suggest that this may actually have been a transfer of lease rights rather than a sale of freehold property.

Despite royal claims, too, many bathhouses were owned by people and institutions other than the king, including members of the royal family and the nobility, military orders, religious houses, and private people, both men and women. These facilities crop up frequently in a range of urban documents recording sales, grants, gifts, and other transactions. In 1194, for example, Alfonso López sold a bathhouse in Toledo that had belonged to his grandfather, Count Pedro Ansúrez. This may be the same property that was later given by the master of the Order of Calatrava to the *almojarife* of Toledo in 1249.[128] After the conquest of Córdoba, Fernando III granted the Baths of Santa Catarina to Don Gonzalo, prior of the city, in 1241 to be his permanent property, free and unencumbered ("heredat para siempre, quito et libre").[129] In Seville, after taking the city in 1248, Fernando granted a bathhouse to his wife, Queen Juana, and there are records of at least a dozen other Sevillian bathhouses held by various individuals and institutions.[130]

Juana was not the only Castilian queen to profit from such facilities; María de Molina, wife of Sancho IV of Castile, also received revenues from a bathhouse, a building that may have previously been the property of her mother-in-law, Queen Violante.[131] In the neighboring kingdom of Valencia, Ines Zapata, the mistress of King Pere III, owned (or held lease rights to) bathhouses in Valencia City in 1279.[132] A number of other more ordinary Christian women also appear owning bathhouses in thirteenth- and fourteenth-century sources from both the Crown of Aragon and the Crown of Castile.[133] There is also evidence of Mudejar women owning or administering bathhouses, both in Mallorca (where Na Marsella, from Granada, ran a bathhouse in 1302) and in Madrid (where there was a bathhouse rented by Doña Xançi a few decades later).[134] The fact that women from across the social spectrum owned and profited from bathhouses confirms the perception of these facilities as ordinary, respectable, and lucrative aspects of Christian urban life during the thirteenth and fourteenth centuries.

The same point holds true for the many bathhouses owned and administered by the churches and religious orders, or from which the church received revenues. As early as 905, Alfonso III of León had given income from the bathhouse in Zamora to the church of Oviedo, and there are other tenth-century references to the baths of Zamora.[135] Such grants became commonplace by the twelfth century, as when Queen Urraca gave a tenth of bathhouse rents to the church in Burgos in 1120, or when the cathedral chapter in Sigüenza received half of all rents on the local bathhouse in 1144 (the same year that Alfonso VII of Castile granted bathhouse revenues to the church in Salamanca). Baths in Guadalajara were given to the archbishop of Toledo by Alfonso VIII of Castile in 1173, and Alfonso II of Aragon ceded part of the royal income from Girona's bathhouse to the church of Santa María in that city in

1194 (a century later, however, when the Girona bathhouse needed major re-
pairs in 1294, Jaume II made a permanent grant of its revenues to a citizen of
the city, Ramón de Toylano, on the condition that Ramón renovate the
building and administer the baths).[136] Ecclesiastical grants did not cease in
the thirteenth century; Alfonso X of Castile would give several bathhouses in
Seville to the cathedral chapter.[137] Iberian monastic houses in both the
Crown of Castile and the Crown of Aragon, such as Santa Cristina de Som-
port, San Zoilo in Valladolid, and Santas Creus in Montblanch, likewise profited
from bathhouse revenues, as did the military orders.[138] In 1170, Elvira, daughter
of count Pedro Alfonso, donated a bathhouse in Toledo to the Order of Santiago, and Count Nuño Sánchez of Roussillon gave the public baths that he
owned in Valencia to the Hospitallers in 1241.[139] Profits even extended beyond
Spain, since part of a grant to Cluny in 1142 from Alfonso VII of Castile included a portion of the annual rents from the public bathhouses in Burgos
(earlier, in 1128, he had granted a tenth of these same rents to the cathedral of
Burgos).[140]

Female religious houses also benefited from bathhouses, enjoying the use
of both their revenues and their facilities.[141] The Cistercian convent of Las Huelgas in Burgos was granted all income from the city's bathhouses in 1187 by King
Alfonso VIII (apparently superseding the earlier concession to Cluny), and the
abbess later constructed a new bathhouse on property given by the king; these
privileges would be renewed by King Alfonso X.[142] When Alfonso VII founded
the convent of San Clemente, just outside of Toledo, in 1131, he endowed it with
a bathhouse that had earlier belonged to the Jews of the city.[143] Presumably this
was the same bathhouse later confirmed as the convent's property in a grant
from Alfonso X, in 1254, along with instructions that the nuns should run the
bathhouse, bathe in the baths, and otherwise do in and with it as they wished
("que bannen e que fagan del e en el como ellas quisieren").[144] This uncompli-
cated acknowledgment that nuns might wish to use the baths themselves stands
in sharp contrast to later assertions, so common by the fifteenth and sixteenth
centuries, that bathhouses were associated with prostitutes, adulteresses, and
other immoral females, and especially with Muslim women. Evidently this negative perception was not widespread in the twelfth and thirteenth centuries.

If the nuns of San Clemente were to use the bathhouse themselves, it was
presumably located within the walls of their convent, or nearby, and its value as
a source of revenue is unclear. Perhaps it was open to the public at certain
times, or on certain days, following the model of bathhouse scheduling outlined in contemporary *fueros*. The lucrative nature of bathhouses is more

evident elsewhere, and in some cases actual figures can be tracked. These lend support to the assumptions we can draw from the frequent appearance of bathhouses in grants and leases, or from Jaume I's apparent obsession with royal control over these facilities. David Alegría Suescun has mined urban records to track the income and expenses of public bathhouses in Tudela and Estella (now in modern Navarre) from the 1260s into the middle of the fourteenth century, demonstrating considerable variation from year to year, but net profits in most years.[145] Robert Burns has estimated that in Valencia in 1310 annual income from the bathhouse in the *morería* of Valencia City totaled 1,200 solidi (falling very slightly to 1,150 solidi in 1315), a sum that was "almost as much as the quarter's other revenues" all put together.[146] Further to the south, in Elche, many of the records of annual bathhouse rents and expenses survive from the two decades between 1399 and 1419. As in Estella and Tudela, costs and revenues in Elche varied significantly from year to year, although the reasons for this instability are unclear.[147]

It is also evident that most patrons of later medieval bathhouses, like the facility in Elche, were Muslim. Although there may have once been bathhouses frequented by Christians in that city, by the early fourteenth century only the bathhouse in the *morería* survived.[148] This was a common pattern in the later medieval period, as Muslim communities were increasingly segregated and Christians bathed less regularly. Because of this shift, public bathhouses had virtually disappeared in northern cities with very few Muslim inhabitants by the later fourteenth century.[149] At the same time, in cities where there was a Muslim community, Christians were not supposed to use Muslim bathhouses (although some may have done so).[150] Laws established in 1412 by Queen Catalina, regent for Juan II of Castile, prohibited Christians from bathing in Muslim or Jewish facilities.[151]

Meanwhile, records of taxes and rents on Mudejar communities continued to routinely list bathhouse revenues along with income due from ovens, butchers, shops, mills, and other seigneurial rights. It was difficult for Mudejars to avoid payment for these urban services, as suggested in a 1371 contract issued by Enrique II of Castile for the lease of the *morería* of Palma del Rio to an Italian tax farmer (Ambrosio Bocanegra), specifying that the Muslim community was not allowed to use any other bathhouse or oven than those that paid seigneurial rents.[152]

Despite Burns's evidence from Valencia, baths were not necessarily the largest sources of revenue produced by a *morería*. In Játiva in 1382, the *morería* bathhouse was assessed at 79 sous per month (for an annual total of 948 sous), while the two ovens in the *morería* paid a combined annual rent of 186 sous. But bathhouse revenues were much lower in Crevillent, in 1399, where the bathhouse was required to pay just over 60 sous annually, while the Muslim community's oven was assessed at 121 sous and change. In Paterna, in 1412, the two ovens yielded 1,910 sous together, while the bath was assessed at a mere 44 sous. This same pattern continued later in the century, a trend that suggests declining revenues from bathhouses in the later medieval period.[153]

Lower-assessed rents may also indicate the declining relative importance of bathhouses in Mudejar communities, although there is evidence against this assumption. Although many urban bathhouses fell into disuse in the fifteenth century, those in *morerías* continued to operate, and some were even built anew. In Gandia, for instance, King Joan II authorized the construction of a new bathhouse in the *morería* in 1459.[154] Declining income may instead suggest decreased usage, as the cost of bathing—in contrast to the payment for using public ovens—became a discretionary expense that fewer people could afford on a regular basis. It is probably in this context that we should understand the nostalgic reference in the *aljamiado* tale, told in fifteenth-century Aragon, that the Baño de Zaryeb had once been open to all men and women in Umayyad Córdoba, free of charge.

By the fifteenth century then, the geography of bathhouses in Christian Iberian cities had shifted, their usage had declined, and attitudes toward bathing were changing. In contrast to the situation in the twelfth and thirteenth centuries, it was no longer common for respectable Christians to visit public bathhouses, and many of these once-shared buildings had fallen into disuse and ruin.[155] Instead, washing became a private activity within the home, especially for those Christians wealthy enough to have servants heat and carry the water. Over time, bathing may also gradually have become a less regular and expected activity in Mudejar communities. Ritual washing for prayer would undoubtedly have continued, but the deeply rooted and convivial culture of earlier Muslim bathhouses, still so vividly described in the story of the Baño de Zaryeb, may have become largely a thing of the past in the *morerías* of Castilian and Aragonese cities.

## Bathing in Conquered Granada

The situation was different in late medieval Granada, where bathhouses continued to flourish under Muslim rule until the conquest of 1492. There were public bathhouses throughout the city, both in the lower town and in the Albaicín, and there were multiple bathhouses in the Alhambra, the late medieval fortress-palace, with different facilities for soldiers, servants, administrators, and officials, and one—the lavish Baño de Comares in the central palace—for the men and women connected to the ruling family.[156] As in al-Andalus, many bathhouses in Muslim Granada returned revenues to a pious endowment (*waqf*) or to individual proprietors. This can be seen in the initial surrender negotiations for the city of Granada, in November 1491, where special mention was made of the bathhouses, mills, gardens, and similar properties that belonged to the sultan's mother, wife, and related royal women.[157] Other bathhouses, especially thermal spas, were themselves supported by charitable endowments. This was probably the case in Alhama de Granada, where an Egyptian visitor in 1465 reported that there was no fee for bathing in the bathhouse and hot spring (which was renowned for its healing qualities).[158]

Bathhouses continued to be registered as assets in the 1480s and 1490s, after cities in the kingdom of Granada came under Christian rule. In Málaga, the *repartimiento* (drawn up between 1487 and 1495) claimed—rather surprisingly—that there was only one bathhouse in the city, a facility that was promptly granted to a Christian proprietor ("baños no ay ninguno en la çibdad, syno el que esta en la casa de Fernando de Çafra"). This bathhouse appears several times in the text, but there is actually another bathhouse also mentioned in passing ("los baños del señor don Françisco Enrríques").[159] This suggests, as had been the case in Valencia and other repartitioned cities in the thirteenth century, that there may have been many more bathhouses in operation before the conquest, and their numbers were reduced under Christian rule.

Bathhouses may have declined in number, but they certainly did not disappear under the rule of Fernando and Isabel. The situation in Málaga points to the fact that arrangements for the surrender of cities, the submission of Muslim communities, and the transfer of real property (including bathhouses) in the final two decades of the fifteenth century were very similar to the treaties and *repartimientos* made after the conquests of Fernando III of Castile and Jaume I of Aragon in the thirteenth century. It is clear that initial thinking was that baths and other Muslim institutions in newly conquered territories would function as did their counterparts in *morerías* throughout Christian Spain. Documents promulgated by the Catholic Monarchs suggest that they assumed, as did their new Muslim subjects, that the organization of Mudejar life would continue much the same as it had been for centuries, and that fiscal arrangements for Muslim urban institutions—such as bathhouses, butchers, and ovens—would follow long-standing and well-understood patterns. Purpose-built urban bathhouses (*baños artificiales*) were run for profit, in contrast to thermal baths and natural hot springs (like those in Alhama de Granada) where the sick were sometimes allowed to bathe free of charge under both Muslim and Christian administrations.[160] These charitable facilities may have disappeared by the middle of the sixteenth century, however, given Francisco Núñez Muley's complaints about the high cost of thermal baths.

Many bathhouses remained seigneurial property after the conquest, to be controlled, leased, or given by the crown. Fees were under royal oversight, and a royal license was required for building or repairing such a facility. A detailed study of the bathhouse in La Peza, a small town between Granada and Guadix, reveals numerous appeals to the crown and royal interventions concerning the bathhouse, its lease, repair, cleaning, water rights, access, and fees in the years between 1494 and 1514.[161] Meanwhile, an edict given by Fernando and Isabel in 1495 relating to a bathhouse in Graena, another small town northeast of La Peza, ordered that this facility be closed and locked, so that it could be cleaned and repaired, during which time nobody could use it. After this renovation was accomplished, it was to be reopened and leased to a proprietor who would be responsible for its running and upkeep, and bathers would be required to pay established fees. These were to be waived, however, in the case of anybody who had a certificate from their doctor stating that bathing was necessary for medical reasons. Strict segregation of male and female bathers, both Muslims and Christians, was also mandatory.[162] Maintaining gender segregation remained a perennial concern for all bathhouses. In 1501, the urban council of Granada reported to the crown that many men were entering the city's bathhouses at times reserved for women, a circumstance that was jeopardizing royal income from these facilities ("es mucho perjuicio de la renta de Sus Altezas").[163]

The turn of the sixteenth century marked a critical change, as treaties negotiated with Mudejar communities were displaced by new edicts requiring conversion. This profound shift brought with it understandable concerns about bathing and its long association with Islamic practice, and yet regulations from the early 1500s indicate an attempt to assure continuity. Even though Hernando de Talavera would list bathing among the Muslim practices that must immediately be abandoned by converts, royal capitulation agreements with several New Christian communities in 1500 and 1501 explicitly promised that bathing would not be forbidden and that anybody who wished to could visit the bathhouse.[164] This apparent indulgence could be explained by fiscal motivations, since this is the same year in which the threat to royal rents was noted in Granada. Evidence for the economic importance of bathhouses in that city would continue for at least two more decades.[165]

But in spite of these ongoing interests in the fiscal productivity of bathhouses, profound contemporary changes in broader attitudes toward bathing exerted strong pressures against their survival. Christians in the sixteenth century increasingly viewed bathhouses as unsanitary sites for immoral and un-Christian behavior, intimately linked with prostitution and Islam. Respectable Christians should therefore not visit such places (although, in fact, a number of Christians probably did). Adding to this atmosphere of distaste and disapproval were the consequences of forced conversion on the Muslim population, which was now required to abandon all of the long-established protections for the institutions of Muslim life. Conversion not only destroyed all previous assumptions about the continuity of Mudejar bathhouses, but it added a new rationale for their suppression as suspected sites for residual Islamic rituals. In 1526 bathhouses became the target of Christian prohibitions, along with a number of other elements of Morisco daily life, and the increasingly stringent regulations against them, culminating in their complete suppression in 1567, have already been outlined at the start of this chapter.

Because of suspicions that New Christians were practicing ritual cleansing in connection with Muslim prayer and marriage ceremonies, bathing also became a target of the Inquisition.[166] Moriscas, more than Moriscos, faced inquisitorial accusations and suspicions regarding their bathing practices, especially when these took place behind the closed doors of the private home. Records of an inquisitorial visit to Morisco communities in the region around Málaga in 1560 named thirty-three people who were accused of bathing; six of these were men and twenty-seven were women. In several of these cases, it was explicitly stated that bathing took place in private baths at home (*baños particulares en sus casas*), not in a public bathhouse.[167] One record discussed the accusation against "Isabel Hernández, a Morisca, who had bathed herself in a private bath. The Moriscas all have these baths and washrooms [*lavatorios*] in their houses, and they wash their entire bodies, in effect performing the *guadoc* [from Arabic, *wuḍū'*], an act that is punishable by the Inquisition."[168] This circumstance was restated by inquisitors in Granada in 1562, where—they claimed—"there were private baths in every house" used by

Morisco men and women.[169] In Cuenca, New Christian men and women both were censured for bathing, likewise within the home. In one report, from 1572, a Morisca slave from Granada, María Mendoza, was reported by another servant girl to have brought a container of water from the fountain in the garden to an upstairs room warmed with a brazier, where María took off her clothes and shoes and "naked as her mother bore her" (desnuda en cueros como su madre la pario) she crouched down and washed her hair.[170]

These inquisitorial cases make clear that Christian suspicions of residual Islamic practice in the later sixteenth century largely focused on accusations of clandestine washing in the home, not in public bathhouses. This may lend weight to Francisco Núñez Muley's claim that bathhouses were too dirty and crowded to be used for Muslim ablutions or prayer. Nevertheless, Christian clerics and administrators remained uncomfortable with the possibility of ritual washing in bathhouses, passing legislation to prevent Morisco visits to these facilities on Thursday and Friday nights, or before mass on Sundays and Christian holidays.[171] Whether or not actual Muslim practices were taking place in these spaces, it is likely that bathhouses were too closely aligned with a residual Islamic identity, in the perception of both Old and New Christians in the sixteenth century, for them to continue in operation.

At the same time, public bathhouses were no longer viewed as the respectable and reputable places that had once offered relaxing steam and a good scrubbing to all comers in medieval cities. Instead, they now mainly served the working class (including the grimy Morisco fishermen, butchers, and blacksmiths mentioned by Francisco Núñez Muley), and they were increasingly associated with crime, female sexuality, and sin. Although illicit gender mixing and sexual misconduct had long concerned bathhouse administrators, these issues came to dominate the discourse about bathhouses in the fifteenth and sixteenth centuries, alongside their reputation as sites for residual Islamic practice.

Rather than merely being possible sites for trouble, bathing and bathhouses were increasingly seen as a definite venue for indecent and immoral behavior, especially among women. Starting in the fifteenth century, there was a new fascination with images of the naked Bathsheba in her bath and with descriptions of amorous bathing in Latin classics, whether Ovid or Valerius Maximus. As has already been noted, fifteenth-century French illustrations of Valerius Maximus depicted men and women sitting in bathtubs before going to bed together (Figure 12), while the images of men and women bathing in the manuscripts of Peter of Eboli's *De balneis Puteolanis* (Figure 13), produced

Figure 12. Valerius Maximus, *Facta et dicta memorabilia* (ca. 1470). French illumination of mixed nude bathers feasting. Staatsbibliothek zu Berlin—Preussischer Kulturbesitz, Manuscript Department, Dep. Breslau 2, vol. 2, fol. 244r.

Figure 13. Peter of Eboli, *De balneis Puteolanis* (ca. 1400). Morgan Library
MS G. 74, fol. 18r. Italian image of nude group bathing. Courtesy of The
Pierpont Morgan Library, New York.

at the Neapolitan court of Alfonso V of Aragon, seem likely to have appealed to prurient as well as medicinal interests.[172]

The image of bathing in the Iberian imagination, and especially the image of the female bather, had indeed taken a striking sexual turn during the fifteenth century. This is evident in the ever popular story of La Cava, the young woman whose seduction by Roderic, the last Visigothic king of Spain, was said to have caused the Muslim invasion of 711.[173] Although early accounts portrayed La Cava as an innocent victim, by the middle of the fifteenth century she was seen as the agent of her own seduction by bathing naked in front of Roderic. This new plot twist—in which the king glimpsed La Cava while she was bathing—first appeared in a chronicle written circa 1440 by an anonymous converso author in Toledo, in an explicit comparison with the story of David and Bathsheba (whose typically erotic late medieval depiction can be seen in Figure 14). King Roderic looked out a window of his palace and caught sight of La Cava and another girl bathing in a pool (*alberca*) in the garden, "naked as they were born and dousing themselves in the water. . . . [La Cava] had such a graceful body, with skin as white as snow, that the king was immediately overcome with love for her, to the point that he wanted to die for her."[174] As a result of this provocative bathing incident, Muslim armies invaded Spain. According to the Catalan poet and doctor Jaume Roig, writing in about 1460, "all of Spain was trampled and dissipated by very evil people, Moriscos and foreign people [in the 711 invasions]. La Cava did it, whom King Roderic was bringing up."[175]

The links between female bathing and sin (lust, pride, envy, sloth, and gluttony) had become a trope in Iberian writing by the fifteenth century, following the similar pattern found in European literature more generally. La Cava was not the only bathing woman to become a target of censure in Jaume Roig's misogynistic poem the *Llibre de les Dones*. Elsewhere in the work he described the sensual delights of a woman's nocturnal visit to the new bathhouse in Valencia, where, after taking off her clothes, she bathed, danced, and dined on partridges, eggs, and Malmsey wine (all three known as aphrodisiacs).[176] A similar scene takes place in the Catalan novel *Tirant lo Blanc*, written by Joanot Martorell in the early 1460s, in which the hero spies on his lover as she bathes, eats partridges and eggs, and drinks sweet Greek wine before heading for bed.[177] Alfonso Martínez de Toledo had also lampooned female vices in the *Corbacho*, with his depiction of a wicked woman's envy on encountering a more comely lady in the bathhouse; the tale concludes with a lively account of spiteful things women are alleged to commonly say about

Figure 14. Book of Hours (1495–1503). Morgan Library MS M. 261, fol. 61v.
French depiction of Bathsheba bathing nude before King David. Courtesy
of The Pierpont Morgan Library, New York.

each other's naked bodies and beauty routines.[178] The roughly contemporary *aljamiado* tale of the Baño de Zaryeb also turned on the themes of female envy and luxurious beatification in the bathhouse.[179] Later, the prostitutes in Francisco Delicado's picaresque Castilian novel *Retrato de la Lozana Andaluza* (set in Rome and published in 1528) mentioned frequent visits to local public steam baths.[180] The erotic poem "Estando en los baños," composed by Cristóbal de Castillejo in the 1530s, spoke of the delights of the bathhouse, where different people came together, mingling and bathing in the nude.[181] This lascivious image of bathing and sexual indulgence was exactly the kind of thing that Núñez Muley attempted to refute in 1567, though by so doing (and by adding his comment about Bathsheba) he actually revealed the degree to which he himself subscribed to the popular trope.

Fifteenth- and sixteenth-century Christian writers, in parallel with contemporary inquisitors, cherished a special fascination for the bathing habits of Muslim and Morisca women.[182] Critiques of female bathing often cited beauty routines strongly associated with Muslim bathhouses, such as the use of henna on hair and fingernails, along with other vices. The chronicler Alfonso de Palencia took time out of his description of Fernando and Isabel's campaigns in the 1480s to mention that the thermal baths near Granada were much frequented by local women, "who all gave themselves up to vices and pleasures, regardless of any caution."[183] Foreign visitors to Granada after 1492 were taken to see the baths in the Alhambra, and their accounts reflect not only their own observations but also the exotic tales that they heard.[184] Andrea Navagero, a Venetian ambassador to the court of Charles V in 1526, described the luxurious marble decoration of the Baño de Comares and also commented on the bathing habits of Morisca women who anointed their hair, painted their nails with henna, and enjoyed the bathhouses even more than men did.[185] Two separate German visitors to Granada, Hieronymus Münzer (who came in the 1490s) and Johannes Lange (in the 1520s), both reported being told the same titillating tale about Muslim use of the Baño de Comares before the conquest. Here—it was said—the wives and concubines of the Naṣrid ruler were accustomed to bathe in the nude, while the sultan looked down on them from a balcony above. He would then throw down an apple to one of the ladies, signaling that she was the one chosen for his bed that night.[186] A visitor from Milan was probably told the same story as he traveled in Spain between 1516 and 1519, for he wrote of the subterranean baths in the Alhambra Palace that had been "built for the delights of the Moorish king."[187]

Attention to Morisca bathing continued in the later sixteenth century, even after the prohibition of bathhouses in the 1560s. In a treatise against Islam printed in 1586, Pedro Guerra de Lorca, a theologian in Granada, criticized Moriscas for the amount of time that they spent luxuriating in the baths while eating and using cosmetics.[188] Even more sympathetic writers could not resist the image. Diego Hurtado de Mendoza's account of the Morisco rebellions, completed circa 1568 (first published in 1610, though written well before the author's death in 1575) also included mention of Morisca women's devotion to bathing.[189] Clearly, associations in the popular mind between Islam, femininity, and bathing were quite enduring—and generally negative—in early modern Iberia.

## Bathing and Public Health

By the end of the sixteenth century, bathhouses all over Granada had been closed and a whole generation had grown up living under the decrees of 1567. Of course, people continued to bathe from time to time, and a certain degree of cleanliness was understood to be desirable for purposes of hygiene. But opinions varied as to the moral and health benefits of different bathing practices, especially in light of the epidemic spread of syphilis across Europe in this period. In one of the earliest treatises on the subject, Heidelberg professor Conrad Schellig warns against excessive bathing as detrimental to overall health and so to the management of syphilis, but otherwise he accepted it in moderation and only briefly hinted at concern that it could become a mode of transmission.[190] Others, however, saw public bathhouses as positively beneficial therapeutic venues and did their best to mitigate popular mistrust.[191]

For the Venetian doctor Nicolò Massa, in an influential treatise probably first published in 1527, therapeutic bathing in both natural and manmade facilities ("balnea termarum vel artificialia") was an option worthy of consideration in the treatment of syphilis, though not one that he personally favored. Bathing could produce temporary relief, he argued, but its more impressive benefits likely derived from sulfur content in special water sources rather than the act of immersion itself. Perhaps unconsciously echoing the old tales of Alfonso VI, Massa also suggested that extended baths could deplete one's vigor, "as it is said that strength is dissipated by frequent and lengthy periods in the bath" (ut dictum est quod virtus resolvitur a frequenti et longa

mora in balneo).[192] His Spanish colleague, the royal physician Luis Lobera de
Ávila, agreed in 1542 that while therapeutic baths could be useful for some
patients they were not really suited to the "men of Spain, who have never
used them" (señores de España, que nunca lo han usado).[193] Still, concerns
over bathing as an actual vehicle for contagion seem not to have been very
widespread, while washing and sweating were recognized (by the celebrated
humanist doctor Francisco López de Villalobos, among others) as potentially
beneficial means of purging the syphilitic body.[194] Earlier medieval, Greek,
and Arabic treatises on therapeutic (and especially thermal) bathing were
read with new interest by some in the medical community, and their growing
demand for this sort of information resulted in Tommaso Giunti's decision
to publish a major compilation *De balneis omnia quae extant apud Graecos,
Latinos et Arabas* at Venice in 1553.[195]

There was even a proposal, advanced in 1592, to once more fill Spain with
royally appointed hot-and-cold bathing facilities for the sake of public health.
Miguel de Luna, a well-known Morisco translator, had been assigned in 1588
to help decipher a cryptic Arabic parchment discovered at the Torre Turpi-
ana. His value as a medical specialist was also recognized by 1596 at least, when
he was called upon to translate an Arabic manual on gout.[196] His short treatise
on the revival of bathing makes explicit reference to the Sacromonte prophecies, citing a passage (in Arabic) on the curative properties of running water, but
he was careful not to raise the issue of Islamic practice. In a refutation of
claims that bathing could sap away martial energy, he somewhat sardonically
noted that Spain's Turkish enemies did not seem to suffer from this problem
and that their use of baths stemmed from a desire to preserve health rather
than from religious devotion.[197] Throughout, Luna advanced the public utility
of regular bathing as a purely pragmatic matter, with no questionable aspects
or potential for negative repercussions.

Given his belief that diseases such as syphilis (*bubas*) required an expulsion of malign humors, and that this could be done most cheaply and effectively by means of perspiration, Miguel de Luna's main argument was that
only greedy and self-interested physicians would advocate for more invasive
treatments such as bleeding or administration of costly chemical purgatives
as a first resort. A far better and more cost-effective general health-care system would involve the provision of affordable and adequately resourced bathhouse facilities for all, both on account of the prophylactic effects of regular
bathing and for curative purposes. More drastic measures could be taken if
necessary on a case-by-case basis, but for many health problems (including

syphilis) Luna felt that baths and sweat treatments, with application of herbal formulas when necessary, were by far the best way to go. His missive concludes with an outline of how the construction of new baths could be financed by farming out their revenues, effectively rendering them cost neutral to the king within two years. This earnest and ambitious brief thus provides at least some indication that bathing was still not perceived as an irredeemably "Islamic," or otherwise distasteful, practice at the end of the sixteenth century.

## Conclusion

For all the sophistication of Miguel de Luna's policy proposal, grounded in the very latest scientific thinking, it seems to have fallen on deaf ears and may never have reached the king at all. Both the fact that Luna needed to argue for a wholesale reestablishment of the once ubiquitous Moorish bathhouses and the fact that he failed to be given a serious hearing demonstrate just how much Spanish culture had changed in its attitudes toward baths and bathing since the conquest of Granada: such facilities were, quite simply, no longer part of the landscape. When the Aragonese doctor Pedro de Torres (personal physician to the dowager empress María at Madrid) published his own observations on the effective use of sweating cures for syphilis in 1600, he took it for granted that the operation was to be performed entirely in one's bedchamber, with the aid of medicinal preparations and heavy bedclothes.[198] The possibility of sending patients to a public hot bath or steam room apparently never occurred to him. Five years later his Granadan colleague Andrés de León was of a similar opinion: therapeutic sweating and baths should be part of an overall treatment regime, but there is no suggestion that these activities could be carried out in public bathhouses.[199]

Miguel de Luna's plea had been to no avail, like Francisco Núñez Muley's, and public bathing had indeed become a foreign experience for most Spaniards by the turn of the seventeenth century.[200] It was now a private affair, and one generally to be gotten over with as quickly as possible, rather than a sensual indulgence of everyday life. The ubiquitous heated bathhouses of al-Andalus and their lucrative equivalents throughout medieval Spain had become things of the past, taking with them a significant aspect of Mudejar and Morisco culture.

# Food and Foodways

In 1547, a Morisca woman from Toledo, Jerónima la Franca, was brought before the Inquisition and accused (among other things) of eating like a Muslim. The case against her stressed not only the particular food that she ate—couscous—but also that she ate in a Muslim manner, "sitting with her relatives, together with other Morisca women, squatting around a tray on which they served couscous, and eating the couscous with their hands, pinching it into little balls, as the Moors used to do according to the tradition and custom of the sect of Muhammad."[1] This case encapsulates the ways in which certain foods and foodways had become inextricably entwined with perceptions of Muslim identity in sixteenth-century Spain, just as particular forms of dressing and bathing were likewise linked to residual and illicit Islamic practice. And as with traditions of clothing and bathhouses, we find distinct changes over time in the perception of these eating traditions between the medieval and early modern periods. Many foods and foodways that had been seen as unremarkable and acceptable (and in some cases delicious and luxurious) in the thirteenth century were perceived as disgusting, un-Christian, and unacceptable three centuries later.

Although the restrictions imposed on Granadan Moriscos in 1567 did not mention food or foodways, and thus Francisco Núñez Muley did not discuss these in his response (except to note that Old and New Christians often ate and drank together at weddings), he was nonetheless well aware of cross-cultural alimentary concerns.[2] Nearly half a century earlier, in 1523, Núñez Muley had sent a petition to Charles V, drawing the emperor's attention to the intolerable inconveniences that recent laws about butchering imposed on the Morisco community in Granada. Because Old Christian authorities feared that New Christians might continue to observe Islamic practices for slaughtering animals, new rules established under Fernando and Isabel insisted that Moriscos must only buy meat from Old Christian butcher shops and they must bring animals to Old Christian butchers to be killed. And if no Old Christian butchers were available, then Moriscos might only kill animals in the presence of a Christian cleric.[3] In his already characteristically pragmatic style, Núñez Muley pointed out how difficult this law was for farmers, whose beasts might be ailing and untransportable, or for hunters who would need to keep game animals alive until they could get them to a butcher, and how aggravating it was—if there were no Old Christian butcher available—to have to find an abbot or a sacristan (*abad e sacristán*) every time one needed to kill an animal for meat.[4]

Differential religious expectations for butchering were a perennial issue of concern in Iberia, not only in the Middle Ages wherever and whenever Christians, Muslims, and Jews lived side by side, but also after conversion in the sixteenth century as New and Old Christians negotiated their assimilation. As will be discussed below, medieval and early modern Iberian legislation had a good deal to say about Christian and non-Christian butchers, while Old Christians would pay intense attention to Morisco attitudes about meat during the sixteenth century.

Meat was not the only aspect of food culture that merited scrutiny—as evident in the case of Jerónima la Franca. What one ate and how one ate it were seen as critical markers of social and religious identity in the eyes of both Old and New Christians.[5] In about 1500 (as previously noted in Chapter 1 above), when Muslims in Granada were required to convert to Christianity, the city's first archbishop, Hernando de Talavera, wrote of the importance not only of Morisco religious practice and belief but also of their appearance and actions as New Christians: "So that no one might think that you still adhere to the sect of Muhammad in your heart, it is necessary that you conform in all things to the good and honest ways of good and honest Christian men and women, including their manner of dressing, wearing shoes, doing their hair, eating at tables, and cooking their food."[6] According to the later chronicler Francisco Bermúdez de Pedraza, Hernando de Talavera was also in the habit of inviting New Christian nobles to dine with him so as to teach them civilized ways (tellingly, the word used here is *domesticarles*) and to instill an appreciation of Christian customs (*costumbres Christianas*) such as "sitting in chairs and eating according to our manners." He even went so far as to give tables and benches to poor Moriscos "so that they would not eat on the floor."[7] Half a century later, at the Synod of Guadix in 1554, residual Muslim foodways were still seen as a significant impediment to proper Christian practice. First on the synod's list of prohibited "superstitions and rites" was the instruction that New Christians "must not eat *en ataifor*"—in other words, they must not sit on the ground around a slightly raised tray of food (*tayfūr*).[8]

As is apparent in even these few examples, Christian perceptions of Morisco foodways combined two strands of thought. First, that their foods and eating habits were tainted by Islam and unsuited to correct Christian practice. For this reason, butchering came under scrutiny for any residual Muslim rituals, while an accusation that one ate (or did not eat) certain foods in certain ways could land one in front of the Inquisition, as happened to Jerónima la Franca and many others. Efforts at Christianization not only required that Moriscos abandon Islamic dietary laws, but also that they actively adopt Christian foods (most notably pork products) and observe all Christian fast days, especially avoiding the consumption of meat on Fridays.[9] Second, Morisco foodways, such as sitting or squatting on the floor around a common bowl or tray of food, without a table or tablecloth, using one's hands to eat, and licking one's fingers, were described as uncouth, even bestial and disgusting, by early modern Christian observers. This distaste for Morisco foods and foodways stood in contrast to earlier medieval Christian perceptions, which were often more positive about the spices, foods, and cooking traditions that came to Europe from the Muslim world, even while disapproving of Islam.[10]

These two strands of thought were combined and reinforced by medieval and early modern Christian views of Islam as a carnal religion that focused on bodily pleasures (there was a prurient fascination with the life of Muhammad and with descriptions of a Muslim paradise with rivers flowing with milk and honey and filled with beautiful young women),[11] while Muslims were commonly derided as "dogs" in Christian writings.[12] These ideas were supported in Christian thinking by New Testament passages in which Jesus compared Gentiles to dogs eating crumbs off the floor under the table.[13] In the late thirteenth century, King Sancho IV had described the delicious and sensual delights of Muslim paradise, where Muslims feasted on honey, milk, butter, and fritters (*bunnuelos*), followed by the opinion that "Muslims are nothing but dogs."[14] By the sixteenth century, inquisitors perceived Morisco food habits as un-Christian, while humanists saw them as uncivilized, and both groups believed that these Morisco manners must change before New Christians could be fully assimilated within the Christian fold.

When this change did not happen, and Moriscos continued to preserve their traditions of eating, the incompatibility of foodways would become a target for inquisitors and would be cited as one of the rationales for the expulsion of Moriscos in the first decades of the seventeenth century.[15] Apologists, such as Pedro de Valencia, would cite the ways in which the Moriscos persisted in "setting themselves apart from Old Christians in their language, clothing, and foodways [*comidas*]."[16] Other writers condemned Morisco foods and table manners as disgusting and uncivilized.

Some of the condemned food traditions were truly linked with Islam, as when Moriscos continued to follow Qur'ānic requirements that they fast during the month of Ramadan, avoid wine and pork, and eat only properly killed (halal) meat.[17] But other foodways, such as eating a diet that relied heavily on vegetables, fruits, and grains (including couscous), reflected regional and cultural preferences rather than religious dictates. Nevertheless, it was common for the religious and regional aspects of food culture to be conflated in Christian minds, as was also the case with traditions of bathing and dressing. For example, in 1612, Pedro Aznar Cardona wrote a lengthy treatise denouncing the Morisco way of life in Valencia, including a description of Morisco foodways that seamlessly combined cultural and economic choices with Qur'ānic injunctions:

> They ate vile things . . . such as potages made from various grains, vegetables, lentils, sorghum, broad beans, millet, and bread made of the same. Along with this bread, those that are able [to afford it] ate raisins, figs, honey, syrup, milk, and seasonal fruits such as melons (although these were green and no bigger than a fist), cucumbers, peaches, and whatever else, even if it was not completely ripe, so long as it was fruit. . . . Throughout the year, they maintained themselves on fresh and dried fruit (sometimes stored until it was almost rotten) and bread, with only water [to drink] because they drank no wine, and they would not buy meat or any animals killed by dogs while hunting, or trapped, shot, or caught in a net; they would not eat meat unless they had killed it themselves according to the rite of Muhammad.[18]

A change in foodways, especially the ingestion of pork and non-halal meat, was one of the signs of Christianization most ardently sought by inquisitors and most bitterly resisted by New Christians. Moriscos (like converted Jews, or conversos) lived in fear of Christian inquisitors, who scrutinized their eating habits and probed to see if they were now cooking with lard and salt pork (*tocino*) rather than olive oil.[19] In other cases, Moriscos were confronted with pork or bacon to test whether they could eat it and, if they did, to see whether they could keep it down or would vomit afterward (either spontaneously or by induction).[20] A fatwa issued in North Africa in 1504, shortly after the edict of conversion, by a mufti clearly sympathetic to the Morisco dilemma, advised that "if they force pork on you, eat it, but reject it in your heart."[21]    Inquisitorial accusations of cooking without pork products were common, especially for women, and difficult to escape. One trial text from Cuenca in 1572 recorded the words of María de Mendoza, a Morisca recently resettled from Granada, who tried to justify her cooking habits on regional rather than religious grounds, in much the same way that Francisco Núñez Muley had defended Morisco lifeways five years earlier. She argued that although people in Castile did "not know how to cook a stew without using *tocino*, in her land [i.e., Granada] they made these dishes with olive oil."[22]

The avoidance of pork was only one among many food traditions that came to define Morisco identity in early modern Spain. And unlike the strict regulations concerning pork and halal meat, most of the other foodstuffs closely associated with Muslim and Morisco cuisine were not delineated by the requirements of religion. Couscous falls into this category, as did raisins, figs, milk, butter, honey, rice, fruits, eggplants, tripe, goat, fritters (*buñuelos*), and other items. Many of these were produced in the region of Granada, which was especially famous for raisins and figs.[23] These foodstuffs would later be targeted by critics such as Pedro Aznar Cardona and Jaime Bleda, while other early seventeenth-century writings also indicate that these foods were perceived as characteristic of Morisco identity. In his play *Los Porceles de Murcia* (first published in 1617), Lope de Vega has one character ask another, "Are you familiar with the Moors?" (¿Conoces los moros?), and the person questioned responds that he does know them and that "they are a people who eat rice, raisins, figs, and couscous."[24] Meanwhile, contemporary Spanish ballads portrayed Morisca women as selling figs and raisins.[25]

Despite their associations with Islam, none of the fruits and other foodstuffs mentioned by Aznar Cardona and others were actually illicit for Christians to eat, and, in fact, we know that many of these items were enjoyed by both Old and New Christians. In contrast to Muslim and Jewish dietary laws, there were few specifically Christian requirements for laypeople concerning food, other than fast days, particularly avoiding meat on Fridays. In practice, foodstuffs and culinary techniques were easily transferred and assimilated across the borders of religion, region, and culture in medieval and early modern Iberia, as is clear in the evidence of cookbooks and other sources. Even couscous, widely seen as one of the most indicative items among "Muslim" foods, was also eaten and enjoyed by Christians in late medieval and early modern Spain. A recipe book written by the head chef to King Felipe II (who was crowned in 1554, only a few years after the conviction of Jerónima la Franca for eating couscous) contained recipes for making and cooking this dish.[26] Because of such overlap, in many ways it seems unproductive for historians to identify certain foods and cooking techniques as either "Muslim" or "Christian," since they were widely used by people of both religions. Thus, a regional argument may be more compelling, and these could better be seen as local cuisines enjoyed in Granada, Valencia, Castile, or elsewhere. On the other hand, contemporary sources make it abundantly clear that certain foods—like styles of dress and bathing—were often understood as signs of religious distinction, even if they were in fact commonly shared in daily life.

Foodways and personal tastes were difficult to control through legislation. The existence of a shared culinary culture in medieval and early modern Spain made it virtually impossible for clerics or secular administrators to craft or enforce laws restricting or requiring particular foods in the ways that they had tried, even if ineffectually, to legislate clothing and bathing. A ban on figs, raisins, milk, butter, or honey would surely have been equally resisted by both Old and New Christians. At the same time, because most meals took place within the relative privacy of the home rather than in the public street or the bathhouse, it was difficult to observe and control foodways, despite reports to inquisitors and laws requiring that Moriscos keep their doors open. The most successful attempts at the legal control of food came through regulations on buying and selling, especially laws concerning butcher shops and meat sales. Because butcheries were often regalian or seigneurial properties, along with mills, baths, and ovens, people were used to legal controls on these facilities. But even so, as Francisco Núñez Muley's 1523 petition demonstrates, people resisted restrictions on access to butchers.

Christian attitudes also changed over time. Foodways really only became an issue of concern to Christian legislators after 1500, when the edicts of conversion created a new focus on food as a critical aspect of residual Muslim identity. Before 1500, Christian law had paid little attention to Muslim food, generally considering it as a matter internal to the Mudejar community except in a few areas—such as the marketplace—where Christians and Muslims might interact over food, or in the regulation of fiscal assets such as Muslim butcher shops and community ovens. Like bathhouses, meat stalls and ovens produced revenues through rents, fees, and sales. They were often distributed by the crown as seigneurial properties or tax farms, assuring their appearance in the documentary record, and they were necessary (though sometimes contested) concessions granted to Mudejar communities in Christian cities during the thirteenth, fourteenth, and fifteenth centuries.

## Sharing Food Before and After 1500

The most common food concern expressed by Christian legislators in medieval Spain was that Christians might buy and eat food that had been sold or prepared by Muslims or Jews (or share a meal with them). Debates and regulations regarding interreligious commensality were integral to all three religions, and each group closely linked food with identity. Thus, there was already an extensive legal tradition in Judaism, Christianity, and Islam about sharing food long before this became an issue in the medieval Iberian context.[27] In Christian Spain, the issue took two linked but separate forms as it related to Christian and Muslim relations over food, one created by coexistence and the other by conversion. The first was characteristic of the period before 1500, while the latter prevailed in the sixteenth century.

First, in a context in which Christians and Muslims lived side by side, there were the issues arising over eating, buying, selling, cooking, serving, or in any way sharing food across religious lines. Could Christians eat meat slaughtered by a Muslim butcher? Could Muslims eat meat killed by a Christian butcher? On the face of it, most Christian legal opinion disapproved the first question, and all Muslim opinion rejected the second. And yet, there is plentiful evidence that many Iberian Christians were perfectly comfortable obtaining their meat from Muslim butchers (especially if they charged cheaper prices), while in some late medieval *morerías*, the concession for the community's butcher shop was held by a Christian. Beyond meat, the lines of demarcation would have become much vaguer for less religiously charged foodstuffs, such as grains, fruits, and vegetables. For many Christians in medieval Spain, it may have been almost impossible to avoid food that had passed through Muslim hands, in an economy that employed so many Mudejars in agriculture, transportation, and service industries such as baking—not to mention Muslim slaves working in the kitchens and gardens of elite households.[28] Perhaps for reasons of practicality, medieval Iberian legislation devoted relatively little attention to restricting commensality for its own sake. Some canon lawyers addressed the issue, but most medieval rules about shared foodways focused on buying and selling and the locations in which these actions took place, usually with an eye to fiscal concerns. Aside from these questions of profit and sharing, Christians had little interest in what or how their Muslim neighbors ate in the privacy of their own community.

This relative inattention to matters of food and foodways changed dramatically with the introduction of the second issue: conversion. The presence of New Christians generated fears about sharing food and religious backsliding, especially after 1500. Christian inquisitors and administrators were well aware that eating familiar foods in a familiar fashion, for instance, enjoying a dish of couscous while sitting on the floor together with friends, could reinforce powerful Morisco bonds both with each other and with their common Muslim heritage. Equally problematic, in Old Christian eyes, was for New Christians to mingle and share food with their previous coreligionists, lest eating with Muslims encourage converts to return to their old religion and its routines.

Festive and family occasions were seen as especially dangerous in this regard, whether these events brought Moriscos together or drew a mixed crowd of Muslims and New Christians, since these festivities often featured traditional foods, costumes, and music. In 1567, Francisco Núñez Muley had noted that Old and New Christians often shared food and drink at weddings, and these gatherings had certainly become a target of inquisitorial attention during the sixteenth century. Old Christians suspected that Morisca brides returned home after a proper Christian church wedding, then changed into different clothes in order to eat and celebrate the rest of the day in Muslim style with Morisco guests.[29] In 1575, the Inquisition in Granada recorded the case of Isabel, a Morisca who confessed that she had attended a wedding "as a Muslim" (como mora), eaten couscous, and sung "Moorish songs." A year later, another Morisca, Juana, made a similar confession.[30] But the danger of exposing new converts to mixed eating at festive events had already been noticed much earlier. Already in the 1270s, there had been concerns about New Christian converts in Seville attending Muslim weddings and other holiday celebrations that would have included food.[31]

In fact, these concerns about mixing and eating together were relatively rare for the thirteenth century, and they arose from the context of conversion.

Aside from this, the issue of Christian and Muslim commensality was generally unproblematic. Although a few canon lawyers might object, Iberian Christians in the initial period of territorial conquest (twelfth and thirteenth centuries) apparently had few quálms about sharing a dinner table with Muslims or accepting food from them, even during times of war.[32] Both Alfonso X of Castile (1252–84) and Jaume I of Aragon (1213–76) had extensive interaction with Muslims and had Muslims serving at their courts. On at least one occasion Jaume I ate with Muslim guests, when he invited a group of Muslims from Murcia to dine with him in 1266, promising a meal of chicken and goat cooked in new pots (lest his guests be concerned that the dishes had previously been in contact with pork).[33] While chronicling Jaume's reign, the Catalan historian Bernat Desclot mentioned that one of the king's leading nobles, Count Nuño Sánchez, was invited to attend a Muslim feast in 1229, during the Christian siege of (Muslim) Mallorca City. The count accepted the invitation and prepared to depart, telling Jaume that he would return in four days. However, he quickly changed his plans when the king expressed displeasure at his departure in the middle of a critical military action (Desclot indicates that Jaume was not bothered by the idea that the count had planned to be a guest at a Muslim banquet).[34]

Christian armies often relied on food provided by Muslims. Desclot reported that in 1280 King Pere III accepted "fresh bread, meat and chickens, eggs, cheese, and butter" from the Muslim governor of Minorca when he stopped in Mahón with his navy on the way to North Africa.[35] Two years later, according to Ramon Muntaner, Muslims in Collo sent ten oxen and twenty sheep, together with bread, honey, butter, and fish to Pere's troops.[36] Closer to home, in 1300 Jaume II ordered that the citizens of Tarazona and Borja, both Muslims and Christians, must provide supplies of meat, grain, and wine to his armies.[37] Later, the semi-fictional account of the exploits of the Castilian count Pero Niño (1378–1453) described how his troops were offered food in Gibraltar and Málaga during a truce between Castile and the Naṣrids. These gifts included "cows, sheep, chickens, plenty of baked bread, great flat trays filled with couscous [atayferes llenos de alcuzcuz], and other cooked dishes."[38]

In contrast to this apparent openness to sharing food across religious lines in the thirteenth century, prohibitions against eating with Muslims and buying their food gained traction over the next two centuries. Clerics, legislators, and inquisitors in the fourteenth and fifteenth centuries became increasingly worried about their Christian flock sharing food with non-Christians or buying comestibles from Muslims and Jews. The *Siete Partidas*, completed in the early fourteenth century, stated that Christians should not eat or drink with Jews, but (perhaps merely an oversight) said nothing of Muslims.[39] However, ordinances enacted by the bishop of Calahorra in 1324 ruled that Christians should not enter the houses of Jews or Muslims, or eat their foods (*comen de sus viandas*), and similar segregation strictures were issued in Valladolid in 1322 and Tarragona in 1329.[40] Later in the century, the fiery preacher Vincent Ferrer advised that Christians should not buy food (*conprar d'ells vitualles*) from Muslims or Jews, nor should they accept slaughtered meat (live animals were permissible).[41] Influenced by these admonitions, Queen Catalina of Castile, acting as regent for her son Juan II, issued groundbreaking new regulations in 1412 that included laws restricting the sharing of food across religious lines. Not only were Muslims forbidden from selling bread, butter, or anything else edible to Christians, they were also prohibited from having public shops or stalls for dealing in any kind of foodstuffs. Especially, they could not sell olive oil, honey, or rice to Christian buyers. Nor should Muslims visit Christians or send them gifts of "spices, baked bread, wine, poultry, nor any other killed meat, or dead fish, or fruits, or . . . anything else to eat."[42] After reaching his majority, Juan II himself would also rule against eating or drinking with Muslims or Jews.[43] Later, in 1465, ordinances enacted under Enrique IV repeated similar strictures, including a rule that Muslims and Jews should not "sell dead meat [*carne muerta*], nor baked bread, nor wine, nor fish, nor any other cooked food for the sustenance of Christians."[44] The Franciscan scholar Alfonso de Espina made similar recommendations in his *Fortalitium fidei*, begun around 1459, ruling that Christians should not eat together with Muslims or Jews.[45] Cities also restricted Mudejar food sellers, as happened in Burgos in 1484.[46]

Whether this fifteenth-century royal, clerical, and urban legislation was enforced is another question. Although these new condemnations against eating together with Muslims must have reflected one emerging strand of Christian thinking, other Christians ignored such strictures by hosting Muslim guests. Miguel Lucas de Iranzo, the constable of Castile under Enrique IV, was famous for dressing in Morisco costumes and for entertaining Muslim guests at his court. In 1463, he organized a feast to please a group of visiting *cavalleros moros*, serving them a lavish dinner of chickens, partridges, goat, cakes, and cheeses.[47] An *aljamiado* account described how a Carmelite friar invited a Muslim friend to visit him in 1500 ("the year of our conversion"), and served him a meal of pomegranates, Valencian conserves, and roasted meat. Notably, the friar himself did not eat, because it was a Christian fast day.[48] Even Hernando de Talavera was said to dine with Muslim and Morisco guests.

## Butchers and Halal Meat in Medieval and Early Modern Spain

Whether at the court of Jaume I in the thirteenth century or in the fifteenth-century cases just mentioned, we see Muslim guests accepting meat from Christian hosts, and such interactions mattered. Meat, more than any other food, became a special focus for discussion and legislation concerning sharing and buying food across religious lines. The profound religious significance of meat, in tandem with the importance of meat as a taxable commodity, generated abundant records concerning butcher shops, butchers, and the regulation of Muslim and Christian meat sales. These data demonstrate a complex overlay of religious, fiscal, and commercial interests that sometimes blurred strict distinctions between Muslim and Christian butchers and buyers. At other times, it drew this contrast into sharper focus.

Iberian Christian kings such as Jaume I, who found themselves ruling over large numbers of recently conquered Muslims, made special provisions in order to ensure their new subjects' continued ability to practice Islam. Christians in Spain were well aware that Muslim law imposed strict regulations regarding food—and especially meat—that had been intended from the earliest days of Islam to distinguish Muslims from non-Muslims and continued to do so over the centuries. The Qur'ān (5:3) prohibits consumption of "anything that dies by itself, and blood and pork, as well as whatever has been consecrated to something other than God. Also any animal that has been strangled, beaten to death, trapped in a pit, gored, or what some beast of prey has begun to eat, unless you give it the final blow."[49] The well-known prohibition against pork is stated here, but the main emphasis is that the manner of an animal's death is critical in determining whether its meat is licit (halal) or illicit (ḥarām) for Muslim consumption. Jaume himself certainly understood Muslim dietary laws, at least to some degree, since when he presented a captured crane as a gift to Muslims in the castle of Almenara in 1238, he made a point of the fact that he had "sent it alive because we knew their custom, and they would not want it dead."[50]

Agreements with Mudejar communities in conquered territories emphasized promises that they were allowed to live under their own law (sharī'ah and *sunnah*), to pray, fast, give alms, and go on pilgrimage. They were likewise guaranteed access to Muslim butcher shops, schools, mosques, cemeteries, bathhouses, and other spaces and institutions necessary for living a Muslim life.[51] In return, Muslim communities promised subservience and the regular payment of taxes and rents to their Christian overlords. Access to properly trained butchers, who were familiar with ritual methods for cutting an animal's throat and draining the blood, was critical to maintaining Islamic dietary laws, so there were halal butcheries (*carnicerías*) and meat stalls in most towns that had a Mudejar community.[52] This remained the case for as long as there were Mudejar communities in Spain, and the summary of Muslim law written by Yça Gidelli in about 1450 still included strictures against "eating any meat which has been improperly slaughtered [*mal degollada*]."[53]

Fifty years later, the edicts of conversion would prohibit Muslim dietary practices and ban halal butchers. In 1500 and 1501, charters of capitulation for newly converted Morisco communities in the kingdom of Granada all specified that New Christians might continue to have their own separate butcher shops, as they had in the past, but the butchers must now "butcher the meat according to the order and manner in which Christians butcher meat, and in no other manner."[54] These new laws were deeply resented, and a Morisco plea sent to the Ottoman sultan in the first decade of the sixteenth century especially begged for his aid on behalf of "old women who have been compelled to eat pork and flesh not killed according to ritual prescriptions."[55] These laws were also resisted, and there is evidence that some New Christian butchers continued to kill and prepare meat according to halal prescriptions for Morisco communities in Granada, Valencia, and elsewhere. Throughout the sixteenth century, inquisitors would pay special attention to New Christian dietary practices, especially with regard to butchering rituals and eating pork, and such accusations are common in trial records.[56] Yet even aside from inquisitorial data, there are also less biased indications of continuing differences in Old and New Christian meat preferences and butchering practice. As late as 1597, a notarial contract for the rental of a butcher shop in Elche (where a third of the population was Morisco) provides suggestive evidence that this shop catered to a New Christian clientele, with stipulations about what meats were to be sold (only beef and mutton are mentioned), that the butcher must be properly trained in killing and cutting, and that animals must be brought alive to the butcher.[57]

In contrast to the sixteenth-century restrictions resulting from conversion, during the Middle Ages there was little thought of closing Muslim butcheries or forbidding Islamic dietary practices. Nonetheless, medieval butcher shops were closely regulated and thus well documented. Not only were these facilities recognized as necessary to the Mudejar community, but they were also highly profitable to the Christian administration. Revenue-producing facilities such as meat stalls and communal ovens (along with bathhouses) were of special interest to rulers and their treasurers and appear frequently in records of leases, concessions, tax farms, grants, appeals, and legal cases. The latter indicate that disputes over butcher shops were common, with arguments focusing on who could buy and sell meat to whom, where, when, and for how much. Butchers were at the center of these cases, but rulers and cities also had strong vested interests in resolving such disputes in order to preserve the smooth functioning of these lucrative concessions, to maintain urban peace, and to regulate relations between religious communities.

There were separate Christian, Muslim, and Jewish butcheries in most larger towns in the Crowns of Aragon and Castile in the period from the twelfth through the fifteenth century. In smaller communities, or in other circumstances when there was no Muslim butcher available, Mudejars sometimes shared a butcher with the Jewish community or obtained meat from a Christian butcher who would prepare it according to halal standards. In 1169, Alfonso II of Aragon granted a license to a Muslim bailiff in Lérida to operate a Muslim butcher shop (*carnizeria Sarracenorum*) in the city in return for a payment of two pounds of meat per week.[58] This may have replaced an earlier shared facility, since another charter from Lérida dated in the same year refers to a location as being near "the butchery of the Muslims and the Jews" (mazel sarracenorum et iudeorum).[59]

References to Muslim butcher shops proliferated in the thirteenth century, especially in the Crown of Aragon. In 1249, a decade after the capture of Valencia City, there was a stall for cutting and selling meat by the gate of the *morería*, with a monopoly granted by Jaume I with the stipulation that "no other Christian, Jew, or Saracen can set up stalls for selling meat elsewhere in the said *morería* except at the said stall, ever at any time."[60] Despite this declaration, within twenty years there were several royally controlled Muslim butcher shops operating in the city (though perhaps not in that particular area), since chancery records cited income from "our Saracen butcheries in Valencia" (nostris carnicerie sarracenorum Valentie) in 1267.[61] In Játiva, Jaume I's otherwise very generous concessions to the city's Muslims in 1252 reserved royal possession of the *morería*'s slaughterhouse (*carniceriam*), bath, ovens, workshops, and other income-generating real estate.[62] Similar fiscal policies were in place in the Crown of Castile, where ordinances from Seville in 1279, during the reign of Alfonso X, regulated Muslim and Jewish butchers and collected fees on sales of meat and hides.[63]

Regalian and urban taxes on butcher shops could be collected directly on butcher shops and their sales, or the property could be leased out as a tax farm. Meanwhile, separate fees were levied on the animals that were slaughtered.[64] Sometimes leases were granted to individual Christian, Muslim, or Jewish tax farmers, while in other cases a whole community was granted the farm and became responsible for paying an annual fee to the crown, receiving all profits from the farmed facility in return.[65] During the later Middle Ages, this income would be a substantial asset for many Muslim communities.[66] Rulers and urban authorities also regulated whether one religious community could claim a monopoly on butchering and selling meat in a certain location, either to buyers from their own community or more widely. Some kings, such as Jaume I, maintained close oversight of butcher shops in his realm (*nostris carnicerie*) along with other revenue-producing facilities, but royal control was not always so direct. During the fourteenth and fifteenth centuries, monarchs continued to intervene in butchering matters, both to preserve regalian income and to resolve communal disputes, but cities, local lords, and Muslim communities also took an interest in butcheries.[67] In 1398, King Martí I saw fit to chastise the city of Huesca for taxing and regulating the Muslim butchery, since these matters pertained to the crown.[68]

Direct royal oversight could provide considerable freedom and independence for Muslim butcheries. A grant from Pere IV to the Muslim community in Valencia City in 1376 allowed the *aljama* "to build, make, and maintain a butchery within the boundaries of the said quarter [the *morería*], wherever you prefer, and to cut and sell in it any kind of meat you want to anyone at all; and likewise to impose and regulate the price you want not only for buyers among themselves but any others [buying] the said meat, [and] to farm and administer [the tax] as you decide best, for as long as it pleases us."[69] Even in the late fifteenth century, expectations that Mudejar communities would maintain their own religious traditions and butcheries were still firmly in place. In 1481, Fernando II confirmed the privileges of the *morería* of Valencia, including the rights of its inhabitants to be judged according to Islamic law and to have a butcher shop where they could butcher all kinds of meats except pork ("tallar tota natura de carns exceptat porch").[70] A decade later, in 1492, Fernando and his wife Isabel would still promise Muslims in newly conquered Granada that Christian butcher shops would be kept separate from

Muslim butcher shops ("las carnecerías de los cristianos sean apartadas de las de los moros").[71] It is noteworthy that the capitulation documents issued a few years later, after the edicts of conversion, reaffirmed this continued separation of butcher shops despite the fact that all butchers were henceforth required to kill and cut meat in a Christian manner.

The religious valence of food (and especially meat) always created special complexities for legislators and administrators when dealing with Muslim communities and their butcher shops. Unlike bathhouses or fabric shops, where Muslims, Christians, and Jews could share the same spaces and services, though usually at different times, places for selling food were not so easy to partition or regulate. Food shopping was an almost daily necessity, making it impossible for urban administrators to assign one or two days a week during which food stalls and butcher shops were open to minority communities. Sharing was also complicated by the fact that religious communities, food providers, and consumers did not all necessarily agree or cooperate with any one policy. Some people believed that food should only be purchased from a coreligionist, and that meat, particularly, could be rendered unclean by contact with nonbelievers or improper methods of butchering. Meanwhile, other consumers appear to have been perfectly happy to buy meat and other foods from any vendor, of whatever religion, provided that they sold quality goods at competitive prices in a convenient location.

The interpretation of evidence about butcher shops in medieval Spain is complicated by overlapping religious and commercial interests. While disputes over butchers entailed real and deeply felt religious differences in dietary practices, they often came to the attention of medieval legislators for economic reasons rather than because of strictly religious concerns. For example, questions about whether a Christian butcher might kill and cut meat for Muslims, or whether Christians could purchase meat at a Muslim butchery, often had their origin in competition for customers between Muslim and Christian butchers, and rivalries stemmed from the fact that the two groups paid different rates of tax and thus often charged different prices. In August 1308, when local officials in Onda ordered that Muslim butchers located outside the walls must sell their meat for the same prices as Christian butchers selling inside the town, it is probable that Muslim meat had previously been cheaper and had drawn Christian buyers away from the more centrally located Christian shops. The hypothesis that the new law responded to a complaint from Christian butchers is supported by a second ordinance, issued two days later, that flatly prohibited Muslim butchers from selling meat to Christians.[72] Although the latter ruling, on its own, could look like a purely religiously inspired mandate, the two in combination suggest that the problem was fundamentally based on commercial rivalry (though possibly also influenced by religious prejudices). A year later, in Huesca, Jaume II prevented a move by the city to put Muslim and Jewish butchers under the same laws as Christian butchers (thus equalizing prices), by arguing that Muslim and Jewish butchers were different from Christian butchers in that they owed special tribute to the crown.[73] Evidently, it was in the royal interest that these minority community butcher shops flourished, even at the expense of Christian butchers.

Similar conflations of religious and commercial motivation continued in the fifteenth century, as shown in two cases from Teruel in 1454, in which the city put financial pressure on both the Christian and the Muslim communities to prevent Christians from shopping at Muslim butchers'. In the first, dated September 5, Christians are warned that they will be subject to a fine if they buy meat from any Jewish or Muslim meat stalls in the city. In the second, issued two days later on September 7, it was noted that because some Christians persisted in buying beef and mutton from Muslim butchers in the *morería*, the Muslim community would be held responsible for collecting taxes on these sales and turning them over to the city.[74] Although couched in the language of religious separation, Teruel seems to have been hedging its bets in order to ensure a profit from probable violations.[75] Similarly complicated disputes about who could buy meat and where arose in Toledo during the next decade (1455–62), triggered by efforts to collect fees from Christian and Muslim butcher shops in order to fund building work on a royal chapel.[76] In Zaragoza in 1475, Muslims were required to buy their meat exclusively from the butchery in the *morería* and to pay a tax (*sisa*) on their purchases (the butcher was to make sure that all meat of all kinds was weighed for taxation before it was cut and sold). Even a Muslim who was working in the house of a Jew or Christian was not permitted to eat any meat on which the *sisa* had not been levied. Meanwhile, Jews and Christians were not allowed to buy meat in the *morería*.[77]

Local butchers sometimes came up with ingenious strategies that involved cross-religious cooperation and prioritized the profitable deployment of tax loopholes over any concerns about religious difference. One such strategy is revealed in an edict from Queen Leonor de Sicilia (Pere IV of Aragon's influential third wife), issued to Elche and Crevillent in 1368, ordering that Christian butchers could no longer sell meat that had been killed by Muslim butchers to Mudejar buyers, since this practice defrauded the crown by avoiding the tax normally charged on each animal killed for Muslim consumption. Instead of evading this tax by buying their halal meat at Christian butcher shops (a workaround that was profitable to both parties), Muslims were required henceforth to have their own butchery for killing and selling meat and fish outside the walls of the town and the crown would collect its proper dues.[78]

The order that Muslim butchers in Elche and Crevillent relocate their business to outside the walls, or to some other area away from Christian butchers, was not uncommon by the fourteenth century. Sometimes Christian, Muslim, and Jewish meat stalls were all located in the same region of the city, as was normal with many medieval trades but especially relevant to butchers, who needed space for slaughtering, skinning, cutting, and selling meat, as well as pens for holding live animals.[79] But over time, with the development of established *morerías* and *juderías* in the fourteenth and fifteenth centuries, it became more common to move Muslim and Jewish butchers into these communally defined areas of a town. Thus, as in the case of bathhouses, *morerías* increasingly had their own communal facilities providing halal meat. This shift was presumably convenient for Muslim consumers and generally pleased both Christian and Muslim religious authorities, and it made it more straightforward for rulers and towns to collect revenue from butcher shops since these could now be leased as tax farms to the local *aljamas* for an annual fee.

Early in May 1321, Jaume II allowed the Muslims in Tortosa to build their own *carnicería* in return for an annual payment to the crown, but the location of this new butchery was not established in the original document and this omission would soon cause problems. For some period before the grant, the Muslim community had not had its own butcher and instead bought meat from Jewish butchers.[80] In consequence, Jewish butchers in the city complained to the king, after the grant, about competition from the new Muslim concession and won a ruling in late May to the effect that the Muslims were not to build their new butcher shop anywhere near the Jewish butchers. But apparently this amendment was not sufficient, since a month later, in June, the king further ordered that the just-constructed new Muslim butchery must be demolished and rebuilt within the walls of Tortosa's *morería*. The new Muslim butcher shop must have attracted a number of customers—including nonlocal Muslims and possibly also Christians and Jews—who might otherwise have patronized the Jewish butcheries. Relocated within the *morería*, its patrons would mainly be local Muslims.[81] Similar competition was evident in Huesca, where the Muslim butcher shop had once been located right by the city gate. A late thirteenth-century ordinance, forbidding Christians in Huesca to purchase meat from Christian and Jewish butchers, suggests that this conveniently situated butchery had attracted some Christian customers.[82] Although located in a prime spot for retail during peacetime, the butchery was burned down by official order in the 1360s when the space was needed for defense of the city during an attack. In 1369, King Pere IV allowed the butchery to be rebuilt, but only if it was in a different place and not larger than the city's Christian butcher shops. Disputes then continued for several years over the size and location of this new facility.[83] The relocation of Muslim butchers was intended to reduce commercial competition between different groups of butchers by encouraging consumers to favor shops run by coreligionists. At the same time, separation could make it easier for rulers and cities to collect the proper taxes.

On the other hand, complaints about competition indicate that medieval buyers were willing to cross religious boundaries in search of a better selection, quality, or price. There is also plenty of evidence (sometimes contradicting the kind of case noted above) that rulers and other legislators often supported consumers' freedom of choice over the claims of rival butchers. Before the dispute in Tortosa in 1321, Jaume II had ruled in 1298 that nobody in Tortosa could compel the local Muslims to use a particular butchery or meat shop (*carniceria seu macello*), and that they should be allowed to buy meat from any butcher in the city, including the Jewish butcher, without paying extra fees.[84] A few decades later, in 1359, the Synod of Tortosa explicitly allowed Christians to buy meat from Jewish and Muslim butchers.[85] In Valencia, Joan II responded in 1473 to a complaint from the city's butchering guild (the *carnicería mayor*) about Christians buying from Muslim butchers by citing the claims of continuity and tradition: "Today and for the past century, meat has been continually sold in that *morería*, as much to Christians as to Muslims and Jews, and they sell meat in the said *morería* to all people, of whatever law, status, or condition they may be" (axí a cristians com a moros e jueus, e axí, venent-se carns en la dita morería a totes persones, de qualsevol ley, stat o condició sien). In return, the butcher shops paid taxes that went to support Christian religious institutions in the city. The king went on to point out that if the butchers in the *morería* only sold meat to Muslims, the community would not bring in enough money to support itself (nor, presumably, would it be able to pay its annual dues to the crown and other entities).[86]

Even after the edicts of conversion, when all butchers were technically required to observe Christian slaughtering practices, the issue of consumer taste and preference became a new way of discussing a much older issue. In the early 1520s, when urban legislation in Granada banned sales of tongue, tripe, and other internal organs in the lower town (mainly populated by Old Christians), these meats could still be sold by butchers in the overwhelmingly Morisco neighborhood of the Albaicín. But in the Albaicín, butchers were required to offer these cuts to any Old or New Christian customers who wanted to buy them (that is, they could not be reserved for Moriscos only). Apparently there were buyers from other parts of the city who would make the trip up into the Albaicín to purchase certain types of meat that were unavailable elsewhere.[87]

Christian buyers seem to have been remarkably willing to buy meat from Muslim butchers and to seek out the butcher stalls that offered the best selection and prices, even if this entailed a shopping trip into the *morería*. During the thirteenth and fourteenth centuries, urban and royal legislation went back and forth on the issue of whether Christians should be allowed to purchase meat from Muslims, with no clear consensus emerging until the fifteenth century, when opinion increasingly rallied against cross-religious meat sales (as with other sales of food). Although there are a few earlier statutes prohibiting purchases of meat from Muslims and Jews, the 1412 edicts issued by Queen Catalina, forbidding Christians from buying meat, fish, or any other foodstuffs from Muslims or Jews, seems to have solidified legal opinion. After this, there was a wave of related legislation throughout the fifteenth century aimed at discouraging Christian purchases of meat from non-Christian butchers. Muslims were prohibited from selling meat to Christians in Murcia in 1434 and in Valencia in 1445.[88] Christians were likewise subject to fines if they were caught buying from a Muslim butcher.[89] Yet this increase in restrictions seems to have done little to cut down on cross-religious meat purchases, since much of the legislation bewailed continued Christian patronage of Muslim butchers despite the imposition of fines and other penalties.

Aside from its increasing stridency, the mood of fifteenth-century legislation also shifted. Rather than merely responding to commercial complaints from Christian butchers about competition, fifteenth-century mandates also claimed religious and cultural rationales that had not been cited in earlier legislation. For instance in Jérica, a mainly Christian town in the province of Castellón, a law issued in 1457 required that the Muslim butcher hire a Christian to work in his meat stall and sell to Christians, because—as the legislation explained—Christians did not want to buy meat that had been cut or touched by a Muslim.[90] In 1475, Christians in the same region refused to buy meat cut by a Muslim working in a Christian meat stall ("no és acostumat en aquesta vila que en les taules de xcristians tallen moros").[91] Twenty years later, in 1495, Christians who bought meat from Muslim meat stalls in Castellón were subject to a fine, on the grounds that, first, it was an affront to decency to buy meat in the proximity of a mosque and, second, that purchasing from a Muslim reduces the income of Christian butchers. Muslim butchers objected to this ruling, and disputes continued until at least 1503.[92]

Muslims were much less willing than Christians to buy meat across religious lines, and Muslim religious authorities also strongly discouraged purchases of non-halal meat.[93] But this sidestepped the question as to whether it was necessary to be Muslim in order to butcher and sell meat that Muslims could eat—a question that draws attention to the daily complexities and conundrums of Mudejar life. Not only were many of the butcher shops designated as "the butcher shop of the *morería*" run by Christians (though perhaps with Muslim employees), but there were also Christians who were cutting halal meat for sale to Muslim consumers. Meanwhile, there were Muslim butchers who were hired in "Christian" meat stalls to kill, cut, and sell to Muslim buyers. In some cases, a distinction was made between killing the animal (a ritual that needed to be performed by a Muslim) and cutting and selling the meat (actions that could be done by a Christian). Even the fact that Muslim communities sometimes objected to the circumstance in which a Christian butcher was handling their meat supports the existence of this scenario.

One of the earliest references to a meat stall in the *morería* of Valencia occurs when Jaume I leased this "tabulam ad taliandum et vendendum carnes" to a Christian, Dominico de Cavallo, in 1249. As Robert Burns has suggested, Dominico probably sublet the concession to a Muslim butcher who ran the meat stall on a day-to-day basis.[94] Two decades later however, in 1268, Jaume made new arrangements and granted an annual salary to Cahato Abinaia, *alcadi* of the Muslim community of Valencia, to run the "carnicerie sarracenorum Valentie." The salary was to be paid by the king out of profits from the butchery.[95] Whether this shift from Christian to Muslim oversight was owing to pressure from the Muslim community, or for some other reason, is not stated. Late in his reign, Jaume I strictly distinguished between Christian and non-Christian butchers. In 1274, all the Christian shops for selling meat and fish in Alcira were leased out as tax farms under the oversight of the bailiff of Valencia. Meat and fish stalls belonging to Jews and Muslims ("tabulis carnicerie et pischaterie iudeorum et sarracenorum") were excepted from this lease, although they also remained regalian monopolies.[96] Christians were not allowed to slaughter or sell meat and fish at the Jewish or Muslim stalls, nor were the latter allowed to do so at Christian stalls.

Later in the century, Muslim communities sometimes sought freedom to purchase meat wherever they wished, and at others they insisted on Muslim butchers. Several statutes issued by Jaume II explicitly allowed Muslims in Tarazona, Tortosa, Huesca, Zaragoza, and elsewhere in the kingdom of Aragon to buy meat from non-Muslim butchers, countermanding prohibitions issued by the local Muslim *aljamas*.[97] In 1291, Jaume II did side with the Muslims of Borja in opposing a move to appoint a Christian to supervise their butcher shop, but it is likely that he was protecting royal interests against urban attempts to garner profits rather than sympathizing with Muslim concerns.[98]

Despite evident Mudejar preferences to control their own butcher shops, it was common for these facilities to be under the oversight of Christian lease-holders and butchers. In 1354, the Muslims of Calatayud reminded King Pere IV that "in all cities and towns of the kingdom of Aragon, where Saracens live or where a Saracen aljama exists . . . the Saracens have their own legal, separate meat shop [*macellum*] and butcher who kills and cuts according to their rite or Sunna [*çunam*] the meats they need." In response to this request, Pere allowed them to build a butchery in either the Christian or Muslim section of the town, but the butcher (*carnifex*) was to be a Christian, though elected by the Muslims. To discourage competition with Christian butchers, and perhaps also to ensure that the Muslim community would be able to hire a suitable candidate, this butcher was to receive a higher amount per pound of meat than a normal Christian butcher, and any Christians buying from him also had to pay this higher price.[99] Late in the fifteenth century, the *morería's* butchery in Calatayud still received meat from a Christian supplier, and similar scenarios also played out elsewhere.[100] In 1436, Queen María (acting as regent for Alfonso V) issued ordinances for Lérida that included a meat stall ("una taula de carneceria") located within the *morería*, where a Christian butcher was to cut the meat ("en la qual un carnicer christià sia tengut de tallar carn") for the Muslim community. In order to ensure against any competition with Christian butcher shops, he was only allowed to sell his wares to Muslims.[101] Ten years later, concerns about competition were apparently less fervent in Teruel, where the meat stalls of the *morería* were leased for one year to a Christian butcher with the understanding that he would charge Christians the same prices that they paid for meat elsewhere in the city.[102]

Arrangements in Teruel also made explicit provision for a Muslim butcher to perform the tasks of killing and cutting under Christian oversight, a hybrid arrangement that was surely common even if not always specified in writing. In Teruel, the Christian lessee was only allowed to cut up the meat, not kill it, since that ritual was to be performed by a Muslim ("no cortarà carne sino travesada por moro").[103] Similarly, in Valencia, the qadi of the *aljama* farmed the rights to the meat stalls of the *morería* ("tabulas carniceria dicte moreria") to a Christian in 1479, but the contract stipulated that animals were to be properly killed and the blood drained, there was to be a special stall for goat meat, and a Muslim butcher would be hired to do the cutting of meat.[104]

Overall, the medieval data on Mudejar butcher shops in an era of coexistence demonstrate a complex web of religious expectations tempered by pragmatism, consumerism, and inconsistent legislation. Despite an apparently clear identification in the nomenclature of facilities designated as "for Muslims" (*de los moros*) or "for the Muslim community" (*de la morería*), in reality the religious and social identity of these meat sources was much more complicated. The most important distinction was in the nature of the meat itself that was universally indicated as conforming to halal requirements in its killing and preparation. Contracts and other sources were often careful to note that animals (cows, sheep, and goats—never pigs) will be brought alive to the butcher, who will cut the throat (*degollar*) and drain the blood before cutting up the meat. But aside from these indications, so-called "Muslim" butcheries were by no means run exclusively by or for Muslims, nor were they necessarily located in predominantly Muslim neighborhoods. Christians bought meat from butcheries in *morerías* until the end of the fifteenth century, despite increasing strident sanctions, while Muslims often bought meat from stalls owned by Christians, provided that they sold halal meat. Prices in Muslim butcheries were often competitive with other non-Muslim butcher shops in the same town, even though special taxes were charged on meat intended for Muslim consumption. These taxes signaled religious-based difference (despite the evidence of a variety of tax dodges), as did the fact that some Muslim holidays were recognized in tax arrangements. It was common to find tax exemptions granted for meat purchased on the Feast of the Greater 'Īd (often called "their Easter" [*pasqua de aquells*] in Christian Romance texts, or *paschua de las aldaheas*).[105]

After the edicts of conversion, the issues concerning butchers and sales of meat became, if anything, even more problematic in the sixteenth century

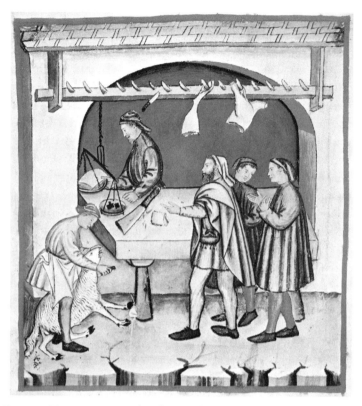

Figure 15. *Tacuinum sanitatis* (late fourteenth century). Biblioteca Casanatense
cod. 4182, fol. 138. Italian depiction of a butcher's shop.

than they had been previously. Although everybody was now officially Christian,
Moriscos continued to avoid pork products and to seek out butchers who
would kill and cut meat in an acceptable fashion, despite repeated ordinances
prohibiting all Islamic butchering practices, requiring that only Old Christians could be butchers, and forbidding New Christians from killing animals
except in the presence of Old Christians. Documents issued by Fernando and
Isabel at the time of conversion had ordered that New Christians must
butcher meat in a Christian manner, and these rules were reiterated by
their daughter, Queen Juana, in 1511, when it was brought to her attention that
Moriscos were still slaughtering in an Islamic fashion.[106] Two years later, she
revisited the issue (presumably in response to objections and appeals from
the New Christian community) and clarified certain issues. Among these, she

permitted New Christians to kill chickens and other birds in their houses, without the presence of an Old Christian, provided they did not perform any Muslim ceremonies. Likewise, an exception was made for hunters, allowing them to kill animals and birds without bringing them to an Old Christian butcher. And if Moriscos lived in a community in which there were no Old Christian butchers, then they were required to kill animals in the presence of a priest.[107]

It may be that Juana's clarifications were never fully enacted, because these same issues were addressed ten years later by Francisco Núñez Muley in his petition to Charles V. Although the emperor acknowledged reception of this document in 1523, it seems to have carried little weight, because Charles issued a comprehensive set of new ordinances restricting Morisco activities in 1526. Among these were reiterations of rules that New Christians must use Old Christian butchers, and if none were available, then a local priest could authorize a Morisco butcher to serve the community. The fact that priests were specifically forbidden from accepting any money for granting this approval suggests a small but potentially lucrative revenue stream that some priests had discovered.[108]

As well as stating restrictions on butchers, the 1526 decree also reveals a new twist in thinking about butchering that was directly tied to the context of the recently converted Morisco community. Whereas medieval discussions had simply referred to butchers as being either Muslim or Christian (including Christians who were authorized to kill and cut meat in the Muslim fashion), in the early sixteenth century it was suddenly necessary to distinguish butchers in a new way. Earlier religious titles were no longer useful in a society in which all people had been baptized, and no butchers were permitted to slaughter meat in an Islamic fashion. This makes it noteworthy that in 1526, the emperor stated that he had heard that New Christians in Granada refused "to eat meat unless it has been killed by somebody who has been circumcised" (no quieren comer carne si no es degollada por mano de alguno que esté circuncidado).[109] No medieval text mentioned circumcision as a marker of identity for butchers, but circumcision took on new meaning in the early sixteenth century, when it still stood as a potent physical marker of differentiation between Old Christians and recent converts. Symbolically, also, it made sense that butchers who still cut according to ritual (and clandestine) Islamic dictates had themselves been ritually cut.

The edicts of 1526 caused consternation and dismay in Granada, but they were almost immediately suspended, in return for a substantial payment from the New Christian community.[110] Nevertheless, tensions over butchering

continued, not only in Granada but also in Valencia and other regions
with New Christian populations. In Castelló de la Plana, a dispute in 1553
about a New Christian butcher who was accused of selling meat to Old
Christians (despite the fact that such sales had been prohibited since 1503)
grew so hot that one side even appealed to Charles V.[111] In the 1570s, Juan
de Ribera was still trying to enforce rules in Valencia that would prevent New
Christians from working as butchers, and at least twenty-three Moriscos
would be accused of working as butchers in Valencia during the decades leading up to the expulsions.[112]

As was noted at the start of this chapter, the wide-ranging restrictions on
New Christian life mandated by Felipe II in 1567 did not include references
to Morisco butchers or foodways, and neither were these topics mentioned in
the response penned by the elderly Francisco Núñez Muley. Nevertheless, just
because they were not mentioned in this context, we would be wrong to think
that the suppression of Muslim butchering practices was no longer important
to the New Christian community in the later sixteenth century. The edicts of
1567 inflamed Morisco passions and ignited a fierce and bloody rebellion in
the Alpujarras mountains in 1568–70, until the rebels were suppressed and
large segments of the Morisco population of the region was forcibly exiled,
partitioned, and resettled in distant areas of Castile. One of the issues at stake
in this rebellion (often called the "Wars of Granada") was surely the prohibition of Muslim foodways.

One of the best-known records of this Morisco revolt was the relatively
even-handed *Historia del rebelión y castigo de los moriscos del reyno de Granada*,
written by Luis del Mármol Carvajal, who lived through the events that he
described. His chronicle contains a reasonably accurate summary of Núñez
Muley's memorandum, and it is a reliable source for many other aspects of
the war. Nevertheless, there is surely more than straightforward narrative in
some stories that Mármol Carvajal tells about atrocities committed by Morisco
rebels in the Alpujarras. Among these, one story told of a pig butchered on
the altar of a church near Guadix, while another described the gruesome death
of a Christian child in the village of Canjáyar. Mármol Carvajal recounts how
they slit the throat (*degollaron*) of a nine-year-old boy named Hernandico, then
followed this by "cutting off his head and placing it in the local butcher shop
[*carnicería*], in the basket where the butcher normally kept the money from
meat that he sold to Christians, and leaving his flayed body on the butcher
block."[113] It is hard to accept this tale at face value; it contains too many traditional characteristics of the tales of the ritual murder of Christian children

by Jews that had been recounted in Europe since at least the twelfth century.[114] In Spain, there were examples of similar horror stories told against Muslims, including Moriscos.[115] And yet the particular details given here of the butcher shop, the basket for money, and the butcher block anchor this story in the real and ongoing conflict over butchering, religious identity, and the provision of halal meat in the later sixteenth century. Whether or not this barbarous act actually occurred, it fit into deeply established patterns of understanding and expectation for Castilian readers.

## Food Preparation and Consumption as Markers of Identity

The presence of Muslim butchers and the availability of halal meat were flash points in the encounter between Muslims and Christians in Spain throughout the Middle Ages and into the sixteenth century, but the particular foods that Muslims ate, and the ways in which they ate them, were more important markers of individual religious identity. Even though properly butchered meat and the avoidance of all pork products were required by the Qur'ān, many other foodstuffs and culinary techniques also came to be closely associated with Mudejar and Morisco identity. But unlike halal meat, which has blazed a clear trail through medieval and early modern documentation, most other foods have left only subtle and often ambiguous traces. Many edibles, especially sweets enriched with sugar, honey, and candied fruit, were widely enjoyed by anybody with a sweet tooth, whether Muslim or Christian. Even those items seen as most characteristic of Muslim and Morisco cuisine in Spain, such as couscous and fritters (buñuelos), were widely consumed by Christians. As we saw at the start of this chapter, couscous was even cooked in the royal kitchens of Felipe II. But perceptions of food were exceptionally complex, and, at the same time, couscous had become such a dangerous sign of Muslim identity that eating it could land one in front of the Inquisition.

Yet even as medieval and early modern Christians continued to enjoy foods that were often associated with Muslim culture, attitudes toward these foods changed dramatically over time. In the later Middle Ages, food items coming from the Islamic world such as sugar, pepper, cinnamon, and other Eastern spices, were perceived as expensive and highly sought-after luxuries. While medieval Christian clerics and crusaders struggled against Islamic doctrine and Arab armies, European cooks and consumers aspired to obtain the exotic delicacies provided by trade with Muslim markets. By the sixteenth century, however, the political and religious situation was completely different, and Europeans now had new channels of access to Eastern spices and other items. Direct trade with the Indian Ocean and the New World, and changing patterns of production for crops such as sugar (now grown in southern Spain and the Canary Islands), turned many luxuries into staples and disassociated these commodities from Islamic trade.[116] Whereas medieval Spanish Christians had once perceived Muslim cuisine as desirable and delicious, and Andalusi recipes and foodstuffs were widely adopted and assimilated, by the sixteenth century Morisco food was more often described as dirty and disgusting.

Late medieval cookbooks help to illuminate the assimilation of tastes and the integration of Andalusi-style food and cooking techniques into Spanish Christian kitchens and menus. They show that medieval Christians adopted and adapted a number of recipes and types of dish from Muslim cuisine. Recipe collections were a new and developing genre in fourteenth- and fifteenth-century Europe, and some early recipe books in Spain and Italy were translated from Arabic originals, since cooking manuals had existed in the Islamic world from at least the Abbasid period.[117] In other cases, European collections merely included recipes adapted from Eastern and Andalusi originals, or they required ingredients and culinary methods that were typical of the Islamic world.

At the same time that late medieval preachers and law codes were urging Christians to avoid Muslim meat and other foods, cookbook authors were writing down recipes with names that made open reference to Saracen or Moorish origins (giving them names like *carn al sarreÿnesca* or *cazuelas moriscas*). In a few cases, these recipes even acknowledged Muslim dietary requirements and may have been little changed from their original versions. A recipe for "eggplants in the Moorish style" (*albergínies a la morisca*) in the Catalan *Libre del coch*, which recorded recipes by the fifteenth-century master cook Roberto de Nola, instructed that eggplants be cooked in good salt pork, or else in oil because "the Moors do not eat salt pork" (que los moros no mengen carnsalada). Another recipe in the same collection, for squash in Moorish style (*carabasses a la morisca*) recommended simmering the squash in sheep, goat, or almond milk.[118] These ingredients would all have been perfectly familiar and acceptable to Muslim diners, as likewise in a Castilian recipe collection (dating to 1475–1525) that included instructions for making a Moorish stew (*olla morisca*), containing goat, garbanzos, onions, and spices.[119]

In other examples, a recipe's title might reference Moorish origins, but its ingredients had been changed to accommodate Christian culinary traditions. For example, a Catalan recipe for Saracen-style meat (*carn al sarreÿnesca*), from the early fourteenth-century cookbook the *Libre de Sent Soví*, also called for cooking the meat in salt pork lard (*lart de carnsalada*).[120] Similarly, a fifteenth-century Neapolitan cookbook, from the period of Aragonese rule in Naples, included a recipe for making a "Saracen Sauce" (*salza sarazinesca*), which began: "When you cook in the Saracen style . . ." and ended with the instruction to "prepare platters full of the sauce and serve it to Saracens." Yet despite this final instruction, and the stylistic claim, the directions called for the meat to be cooked with pork fat (*lardo*), so even if the recipe were based on a Muslim original, it had evidently been adapted for Christian tastes.[121]

More commonly, recipes repeated Arabic dishes and culinary techniques without any explicit link with Muslim cuisine. For example, the *Libre de Sent Soví* included a recipe for noodles, called *alatria*, derived from the Arabic word *al-itriyya*.[122] Likewise, a number of recipes for different varieties of *escabeche* (in Castilian) or *escabeig* (in Catalan), named for a technique of pickling and marinating derived from the Arabic term *sikbāj*, appear in both the *Libre de Sent Soví* and Roberto de Nola's *Libre del coch*.[123] Many other Arabic terms and techniques are also recorded in late medieval cookbooks. These have been extensively analyzed by modern scholars, who have shown, among other things, that European versions of Muslim recipes were usually significantly different from their Eastern originals.[124] Given the differences, there is no reason to believe that late medieval cooks and diners necessarily associated these dishes with their Arabic originals. Instead, it is more likely that most were simply seen as familiar local dishes.

In light of changing attitudes toward Muslim and Morisco foods in sixteenth-century Spain, one might expect to find significant differences between late medieval and early modern cookbooks. To some extent this is the case, since early modern recipe collections were more likely to cite classical authorities on food and cuisine, such as Marcus Gavius Apicius, than Muslim-style recipes.[125] The *Banquete de nobles caballeros*, a Castilian collection composed for Luis Lobera de Ávila in 1530, referenced both classical and Islamic sources (including Galen and Avicenna) but mentioned no explicitly Moorish dishes. Nevertheless, a number of medieval recipe collections emerged as printed editions in the early sixteenth century (for example, the *Libre del coch* by Roberto de Nola was published in Barcelona in 1520) without removing references to items cooked *a la morisca*. This reinforces the impression that there was little uniformity of opinion or practice regarding food and taste, and many Christians happily continued to eat dishes despite their association with Muslim foodways.

Aside from the plentiful references to Muslim and New Christian butchers, Mudejars and Moriscos also worked in other areas of the food industry in Christian cities, and at times they surely sold their wares to Christian buyers. The number of references to Muslim millers, oven keepers, and bakers is especially striking. This prevalence may be linked to the fact that mills and ovens were normally seigneurial properties, like butcheries, and this generated a degree of oversight, documentation, and fiscal accountability that we do not see for other areas of food production and sales.

Most ovens in medieval Iberian cities were shared public amenities, like bathhouses, butcher shops, and mills. Normally, they were not located in the home, for reasons of fuel economy and fire safety.[126] Instead, people brought their dough and other items for baking to a public oven and paid a fee for the service (much as they would when bringing grain to a mill). These revenues were collected by the community or the individual tax farmer, who in turn paid an annual rent to the king or local lord. Records of ovens indicate that, like butcher shops, some were designated for individual religious communities while others were shared by both Muslims and Christians. In 1258, Jaume I allowed a Christian to build, own, and operate an oven in Valencia's *morería* (thus presumably for the Muslim community) in return for an annual fee, while his son, Prince Alfonso, gave a grant to another Christian in Navarrés to build a public oven in which all Christians and Muslims in the town would henceforth cook their bread.[127] A year later, the master of the Hospitallers gave the farm of his oven (*furnum meum*) in Aldea (Tarragona) to the local Muslim community, with the promise that "no other Christian or Saracen would be able to build an oven or to cook bread except in this oven."[128] Ovens in Mudejar communities continued as seigneurial properties in later centuries, as when the *forno de los moros* was granted to the Muslim *aljama* in Zaragoza in 1459 in return for an annual fee.[129] Mills for flour operated under similar seigneurial assumptions, but unlike ovens, butchers, and baths, these facilities were not necessarily granted to Muslim communities for their exclusive use.[130]

Mudejars were employed as bakers, and in other areas of the grain trade as farmers, carters, and millers. Four Muslim *atahoneros* (millers) appear in notarial documents from Seville in the fourteenth century.[131] After the edicts of conversion, Moriscos continued to pursue similar trades in the food industry, working as bakers, millers, fritter makers (*buñoleros*), fruit vendors, and in other areas of food preparation and delivery in Granada, Valencia, Seville, and other cities.[132] They were likewise linked to these trades in Christian perceptions of Morisco labor. An image by the German artist Christophe Weiditz, who visited Granada in 1529, shows a Morisco man carrying a board on his head, bearing four round loaves of bread.[133] Likewise, a popular Castilian ballad told of Muslim women (Fátima and Xarifa) selling figs and raisins, while a man (Muça) made fritters (*buñuelos*).[134] Medieval Christians had even suspected that Muslims ate *buñuelos* in paradise, along with the more traditional afterlife fare of milk and honey, and the late fourteenth-century Catalan Franciscan Francesc Eiximenis praised devout Christians who eschewed the sin of gluttony—in this life—by avoiding honey, milk, butter, and fritters (*bunyols*).[135] In the sixteenth century, Moriscos were so closely associated with *buñuelos* that simply working as a *buñolero* could raise suspicions of improper belief and attract inquisitorial attention.[136] Eventually, a decade before expulsion, a measure brought to the Cortes in Madrid in 1593 barred Moriscos from working as bread makers or *buñoleros*, or in any other retail or wholesale food trades, restricting them to farming and selling produce.[137]

Fritters were not the only food that might provoke inquisitorial interest, since confessions about what was eaten, how it was eaten, what was not eaten, and in what kind of company, all provided fodder for trial evidence in Morisco cases. What entered one's mouth, in terms of food, should be as strictly observed as what came out of one's mouth in terms of words and language.[138] By far the majority of inquisitorial accusations about food and eating were concerned with specifically Islamic practices, either the observance of the Ramadan fast and rules for halal butchering or avoidance of pork products and—to a lesser extent—alcohol. Less common, but more indicative of cultural expectations, were accusations about making or eating other foods, such as fritters, couscous, figs, and raisins, sitting on the ground at a low table to eat, or eating with one's hands. In other words, as one Aragonese testimony from 1487 put it, "eating Moorish foods, in Moorish fashion, at a Moorish table" (comer las viandas de moros como moro a la mesa de los moros).[139]

The companions with whom one ate, as much as the food consumed and the manner of eating, also marked a bond of common identity. The dangers of backsliding posed by convivial and traditional gatherings such as weddings have already been noted above, but any shared meal could be suspect. This was clear in the case of Jerónima la Franca that opened this chapter, when she was not only accused of eating couscous with her hands, but doing so in the company of other Morisca women in Toledo. Another defendant, from Valencia in 1567 was asked why he had confessed to so many things, and he answered, simply, that "he would not hide the fact that he was a Morisco and that he had eaten and drunk among them" (no se recatan del por ser morisco y comer y bever entre ellos).[140] Isabel Ruiz and her daughter María, New Christians from Baza, were both accused in 1584 of having eaten a *capirotada* (a bread and fruit pudding) and a chicken killed according to Islamic rituals, "together with other people of their class and generation" (con otras personas de su casta y generacion).[141] The Inquisition heard another narrative, in 1586, recounted by Francisco Pablo, a Morisco who had retaken the Arabic name of Hamete and married a Muslim woman in Málaga, according to Muslim law. In the words of the report, Francisco/Hamete claimed that he had thought that this relationship was lawful, since "like a beast" (*como bestia*) he had not been properly taught "the law of Jesus Christ," nor what he ought to believe of it, and he had eaten couscous with the Muslim men and women in Málaga ("avia comido con los moros y moras de Malaga alcazcuz").[142]

Couscous has already appeared several times in the discussion above, but it deserves further comment, as the food most associated with this kind of testimony about communal meals. This dish was especially associated with the Islamic West, where it first appeared in the thirteenth century and became popular in Granada.[143] A Naṣrid poet, Ibn al-Azraq (who died in 1491), wrote a poem describing the cuisine of his homeland and mentioning couscous and other characteristic local dishes.[144] There is also material and documentary evidence of couscous in sixteenth-century Granada, since pots for cooking couscous survive, and they are mentioned in wills and inventories of Morisco possessions.[145] Traditionally, couscous was a shared dish that was served in a large common bowl from which diners scooped up small portions with their fingers. Hamete ate couscous together with other Moriscos, as did Jerónima la Franca, and a number of other women in Granada in the 1570s and 1580s who confessed to attending Morisco weddings, dancing, and eating couscous in the Moorish manner ("avia baylado y comido alcuzcucu como mora juntamente con otros moros").[146] In 1538, a Morisco man from Toledo was brought to trial for "playing music at night, dancing the *zambra*, and eating couscous."[147]

Late medieval Christians also ate couscous, and seem to have partaken of it in the same manner as Muslims. We have already seen Christians accepting the dish from Muslim hosts, as when Count Pero Niño was offered "great flat trays filled with couscous" in early fifteenth-century Gibraltar.[148] Later, the Catalan novel *Tirant lo Blanc* (published in 1490) described splendid fictional feasts, shared by Christians and Muslims, that included rice, couscous, and other "royal dishes" ("arròs, cuscusó e molts altres potatges . . . feren-lo molt ben server a la real").[149] In a more critical vein, a passage in Francesc Eiximenis's discussion of Christian table manners listed couscous (*cuçcuçó*) among messy foods that "are eaten greedily from a common bowl."[150]

These comments by Eiximenis reflect a pattern in which late medieval Christian table manners were beginning to shift away from eating with one's fingers out of common dishes (a habit that had been common even in elite Iberian Christian society through the fourteenth century) and toward the use of forks and individual plates.[151] Muslim manners, in contrast, continued to favor eating from shared dishes without utensils (see Figure 16). In the early sixteenth century, Leo Africanus drew attention to these now striking differences in foodways, together with associated value judgments, when he described table manners in Fez for a Christian audience.[152] In his 1526 *Cosmografia*, he wrote that "in comparison to men in Europe, the life of those in Africa seems lowly and mean, not for a lack of material things, but because of the lack of orderliness in their habits and because they eat on the ground at low tables without any cloth or napkins for their hands. When they eat couscous or any other food, they eat it all together in one dish, and they eat with their hands without using a spoon. . . . Although educated men and nobles live more politely, an Italian gentleman lives more politely than anybody in Africa."[153]

These emerging distinctions in foodways gave rise to a new early modern discourse that emphasized what Christian observers saw as the brutish, disgusting, and uncivilized nature of Muslim table manners. The perception that Muslims and Moriscos ate with their hands from a common bowl, that they sat on the floor around a raised tray or low table, and that they used neither napkins nor tablecloths was increasingly exploited to depict them as both uncouth and unclean. In fact, many Christians in Spain—and especially in Castile—may also have sat on the floor for meals and used their fingers to eat, even into the fifteenth century, but ideas about these practices were changing.[154] The association between eating with one's hands, lack of hygiene, and bad manners went back at least to the thirteenth century, when the *Siete Partidas* recommended that diners should wipe their fingers "on towels and nothing else; for they should not wipe them on their clothes, like some people do who do not know anything about cleanliness or politeness."[155] By 1500,

Figure 16. Al-Harīrī, *Maqāmāt* (thirteenth century). British Library Or. 1200, fol. 146v. Arabic depiction of men eating from shared bowls, seated on floor. © The British Library Board

Figure 17. Mestre de Soriguerola, *Taula de Sant Miquel* (late thirteenth century). Museu Nacional d'Art de Catalunya. Aragonese portrayal of Last Supper, showing expectation of eating seated at table with individual plates.

Iberian Christians made a point of the fact that they ate in a civilized manner, at tables using implements and napkins (see Figure 17). Hernando de Talavera taught Christian manners (*costumbres Christianas*) to new converts and made sure that they had dining tables and chairs in their houses, while the Synod of Guadix emphasized the fact that New Christians "must not eat *en ataifor*."[156]

Many of the early modern discussions of Muslim foodways by Spanish authors cited manners in North Africa and Egypt rather than Spain. Although the habits that they described were similar to those noted by Leo Africanus, their disdainful comments and critique reflected Christian Iberian sentiments of superiority. When Pedro Mártir de Anglería visited Egypt in 1501, as an ambassador from Fernando and Isabel, he reported that "it is the custom among all the Muslim people to . . . eat on the ground, with their heads bent low, like brutish animals [*veluti animalia bruta*]."[157] In his *Descripción general de Africa*, Luis del Mármol Carvajal (also the chronicler of the Alpujarras war), wrote that people in Morocco commonly ate couscous "while seated on the ground, both men and women," and their law forbids spoons and only allows them to eat with their right hand, after which they lick their fingers or wipe them on their sleeves "because they have neither tablecloths or napkins."[158] Another sixteenth-century observer, Diego de Torres, remarked that Muslims "eat all kinds of food with their hands, even things that need a spoon, and in place of a table and cloth, the floor is covered with a mat or piece of leather that they call a *taifor*. Instead of napkins, they use their tongues to lick their fingers, which is the dirtiest thing in the world."[159] Later, at the start of the eighteenth century, a Franciscan author went even further, describing how meals in Morocco invariably began with a plate of couscous (*alcuzcuz*), which diners ate with their hands, keeping their arms bare so that they could dip up to the elbow in the deep serving dishes. After the meal, they did not wash their hands, but licked their arms instead. The king of Morocco, rather than using a napkin, wiped his hands in the hair of two black serving boys, saying: "these napkins are better, because they are more valuable and more durable than those used by Christian kings."[160]

Contemporary with these negative descriptions of Muslim manners in foreign lands, Inquisition records in Spain were accusing Moriscos of similar habits, and thus branding their foods and foodways as fundamentally incompatible with a civilized and orthodox Christian lifestyle. In Toledo, again, Jerónima la Franca, was charged with "squatting around a tray on which they served couscous, and eating the couscous with [her] hands . . . as the Moors used to do according to the tradition and custom of the sect of Muhammad." In that same town, Juan de Flores was condemned on the evidence that "he ordinarily did not sit in a chair, nor did he eat at a table, according to the custom and ceremony of the said sect of Muhammad."[161] And in 1576, a group of Moriscos in Arcos confessed to eating at the house of Beatriz de Padilla, "reclining on the floor, without tables, as is the custom of the Moors."[162] What, how, and with whom you ate had potentially become a matter of life and death for those suspected of retaining vestiges of Muslim identity in early modern Iberia.


## Conclusion


By the later sixteenth century, Inquisition evidence and other reports about Morisco foodways combined to support arguments that it was impossible to assimilate the New Christian population and that they would have to be expelled. Just as Moriscos continued to distinguish themselves from Old Christians in their dress and bathing habits, they would never be fully civilized or Christianized in their eating habits so long as maintained their affinity for the manners of their coreligionists in the Islamic world. A report sent to King Felipe III in 1588 recommended that all Moriscos should be considered as openly declared enemies ("hemos de tener por enemigos declarados todos los moriscos") because they refused to adapt themselves to Christian ways, including the fact that "in their manner of eating and drinking they follow the same law as those who live in Africa."[163] Any Morisco ties with the Maghrib were considered dangerous in an age of rebellion within the Peninsula and external hostilities between Spain and states in North Africa.

Apologists picked up on these arguments and deployed the perception of uncivilized foodways as a rationale for expulsions even of fully baptized and faithful Christian Moriscos in the early seventeenth century. Both Pedro Aznar Cardona and Jaime Bleda (often echoing Aznar Cardona's words) wrote lengthy treatises shortly after the expulsions (in 1612 and 1618 respectively), justifying this action on the grounds that, among other things, Moriscos "were brutish at their meals [*eran brutos en sus comidas*], always eating on the ground (as was suited to their station) without a table or any other furniture."[164] A year later, in 1619, Pedro de León reflected on the primitive tastes of Moriscos, describing them as idlers with bad habits (*malas costumbres*), a "miserable and impoverished people, who sustained themselves on a bit of dried bread, or acorns and chestnuts," or "the worst kind of bread [*pan malísimo*] crumbled or cooked into a mush, with meat or fish only very occasionally when they could find it."[165] Others, including Juan de Ribera, added that the extreme frugality of Moriscos as regards eating and drinking undercut economic opportunities for Old Christians.[166] Whereas Hernando de Talavera had tried to domesticate (*domesticarles*) the eating habits of the Morisco population in Granada in the early sixteenth century, a century later this project was abandoned as unattainable. By the early seventeenth century, apologists for the expulsion used the desperation of Morisco poverty and their continued attachment to their traditional diet to emphasize the almost subhuman aspects of Morisco life and the fact that they would never truly be able to find a place at the Old Christian table.

There can be no definitive conclusion to this book. The author's primary enthusiasm was for data gathering and her research was ongoing at the time of her death. Notes and conversations suggest that she kept an open mind throughout, ever questioning, and willing to follow up with whatever conclusions the evidence might eventually point to. This was perhaps her greatest strength as a historian—she followed her clues wherever they led, rather than seeking to prematurely impose order on them or to press them into support for a predetermined hypothesis. And since the goal here has been to retain her original authorial voice as much as possible, there seems no need to attempt a reconstruction of what she "might have said." Instead, I will offer a few brief observations of my own by way of reflection on the significance of her findings.

Clearly, there was a marked evolution in Spanish Christian perceptions of and reactions to Islamic identity over the centuries. One *could* characterize this as movement from a more or less "tolerant" period of medieval Christian rule—in which religious differences could freely be expressed in habits of dress, hygiene, and diet as well as language and ritual behavior—to a more "intolerant" early modern Christian regime, characterized by almost obsessive demands for conformity in nearly all aspects of daily life. But of course these apparently simple words mask complex realities and beg more questions than they resolve. Medieval toleration for markers of difference should by no means be equated with modern ideals of intercultural acceptance that imply "respect," "appreciation," or "understanding." On the contrary it was a matter of enforced differentiation, generally for the sake of segregation and all too often for persecutory discrimination. Similarly, the imposition of homogeneity by sixteenth-century legislators was ostensibly intended to foster communal inclusivity, rather than to exacerbate factional discontent in the style of more recent xenophobic demagoguery. It was also highly contingent, coming as it did as the end result of other long-standing processes that had already brought about the conquest and subsequent wholesale coercive conversion of Muslim (and Jewish) populations. It did not emerge merely for the sake of indulging some newfound distaste for pluralism.

It is therefore impossible to reduce the findings of this book to a simple narrative of decline from "better" to "worse" models of intercultural relations, or vice versa. Rather, what has been traced is a set of modalities by which Muslim-identified subject "otherness" was defined and perceived in gradually shifting terms from one generation to the next across centuries of Spanish Christian domination. Sometimes these terms were derived from scriptural mandates and points of religious law. Sometimes they were driven more by sociological observations and political anxieties that identified proscribed behaviors as somehow having (or threatening to have) a negative impact on community well-being. The overall achievement of this book has simply been to describe, as fully and objectively as possible, just how such changes came about over a long stretch of time.

Of course, what is also plainly evident is the fact that markers of differentiation rarely reflected static, objective realities of division that inherently set one group apart from the next. Instead such markers tended to be *invented* and infused with significance only as and when necessary, to serve the discriminatory needs of a given regime or population. Differences of religion, for example, may indeed place communities in opposition to one another— but only if the terms of their respective religious beliefs were understood to demand such opposition. And such an understanding cannot really explain the shifts in policy that have been documented here. Being "Muslim" is, at its essential core, a matter of religious belief: in one God, in the prophethood of Muhammad, and so on. It may also involve certain practices, perhaps including modes of dress, ablution, and dietary regulation, but it is hard to see how any of these could be legitimately proscribed in and of themselves by normative Christianity. Even inquisitorial prosecutions against those who avoided pork, or otherwise maintained non-Christian lifeways, depended on intentionality, the belief behind the act, rather than on the act itself. The crime, in other words, was not having eaten eggplant or couscous, but of having acted on a lack of faith in the church's exclusive promise of salvation, which should have made resort to such alternatives to pork unnecessary. Yet inquisitors knew all too well that belief is invisible, changeable, and easily dissimulated. Visible traits and behaviors, on the other hand, provide a convenient shorthand for discerning who is or is not a member of a given group. Hence the tendency to emphasize external indicators of cultural affiliation, rather than internal character and belief—in spite of all the potential for unfairness and misunderstanding this necessarily entails—as a means of cleanly separating human communities into "insiders" and "outsiders."

The artificial nature of such moves, the fact that they tend to displace one putative locus of difference with another, is nowhere more clear than in the exaggerated emphasis placed on distinctively "female" practice at key phases in this evolution. What women wore, how they washed and decorated their bodies, how they prepared and served food—all these might well be tangential at best to the practice of Islam per se. And yet by the end of the period under study, they were all matters of serious inquisitorial inquiry. The significance of gender as a factor in medieval and early modern perceptions of Islam emerges repeatedly in the findings of this book, and though its exploration did not necessarily emerge as one of the author's initial research objectives, it is a topic that deserves further consideration.[1]

The relevance of medieval and early modern Spanish perceptions of Islam to other histories, unfolding in other places and times, is also worthy of mention here. Dr. Constable, in her typically understated and down-to-earth fashion, asserts in Chapter 1 that there is little to be gained by directly comparing medieval or early modern anti-Islamic attitudes and legislation to modern Islamophobia. And while her point about the very real and important differences between the two is certainly valid, recent experience suggests that there may also be more instructive similarities than she first suspected. The vehemence with which so-called "old stock" populations were mobilized to support anti-veiling legislation in recent Canadian elections—as if eliminating an allegedly "foreign" item of women's clothing would somehow decrease the presence of Islam in society, and thereby assist in wider struggles against Islamist "terrorism"—is certainly reminiscent of some sixteenth-century Spanish attitudes.[2] And food has also played an inordinate role in modern Islamophobia, as evidenced by the Front National's demand that pork be made a mandatory ingredient in French school cafeterias, or British popular revulsion over the prospect of halal meats being served in fast-food restaurants.[3] There may not be direct connections between such modern emphases and their medieval or early modern antecedents, but the enduring propensity for human beings to judge and condemn one another based on corporeal (as opposed to ideological) differences does invite further discussion. This was indeed the subject of one of my last conversations with Dr. Constable, and she was in agreement that current events had brought an undeniable new urgency to her research.

My appreciation of that research, and my gratitude at having been able to help bring it to light, has been enhanced by its potential significance not only to the immediate fields of medieval and early modern Christian-Muslim relations but to wider questions of colonial history and its ongoing effects on the modern world. Returning again to the Canadian context I know best, there are few political topics so important today as how the perceived differences of suspect immigrant minority groups—whether Muslim in terms of religion, or just culturally "Middle Eastern"—should be accommodated by a non-Islamic host society. And if there *is* a topic of greater importance, it is probably the related realization of just how destructively alien standards of dress, hygiene, diet (and, yes, language) were imposed on North American indigenous peoples over a century of coercive attendance at residential schools. Similar colonial legacies exist in different forms around the world, and their study is greatly facilitated when it can be placed in solid historical perspective.

Nevertheless, it is important above all to comprehend medieval and early modern Spanish perceptions of Muslim identity on their own terms. By advancing historians' understanding of how and why Muslim-Christian relations developed as they did in the specific circumstances of the Iberian Peninsula, as it shifted from situations of long-standing religious pluralism to the emergence of more unified Christian polities, this book stands as its author's final contribution to a field of study that she very much helped to define. It is to be hoped that it will inspire or otherwise assist others to further their own scholarship, as this vital field continues to develop, and that our understanding of intergroup dynamics will continue to grow in the challenging decades to come.

# NOTES

## FOREWORD

1. Antonio Gallego Burín and Alfonso Gámir Sandoval, *Los moriscos del Reino de Granada según el sínodo de Guadix de 1554* (facsimile; Granada: Universidad de Granada, 1996), 162–63; cited in Chapter 4.

2. "Muslim Spain and Mediterranean Slavery: The Medieval Slave Trade as an Aspect of Muslim-Christian Relations," in *Christendom and Its Discontents: Exclusion, Persecution, and Rebellion, 1000–1500*, ed. Scott L. Waugh and Peter D. Diehl (Cambridge: Cambridge University Press, 1996), 264–84; "Chess and Courtly Culture in Medieval Castile: The *Libro de ajedrez* of Alfonso X, el Sabio," *Speculum* 82, no. 2 (April 2007): 301–47; *Medieval Iberia: Readings from Christian, Muslim, and Jewish Sources* (Philadelphia: University of Pennsylvania Press, 1997; 2nd ed., with the assistance of Damian Zurro, 2012).

## EDITOR'S PREFACE

1. For related studies using different methodological approaches and different types of sources, see, for example, John Tolan, *Saracens: Islam in the Medieval European Imagination* (New York: Columbia University Press, 2002); and Barbara Fuchs, *Exotic Nation: Maurophilia and the Construction of Early Modern Spain* (Philadelphia: University of Pennsylvania Press, 2009).

2. Olivia Remie Constable, *Housing the Stranger in the Mediterranean World: Lodging, Trade, and Travel in Late Antiquity and the Middle Ages* (Cambridge: Cambridge University Press, 2003) xi; Constable, *Trade and Traders in Muslim Spain: The Commercial Realignment of the Iberian Peninsula, 900–1500* (Cambridge: Cambridge University Press, 1994), xix.

## CHAPTER 1

1. As explained in the preface, a planned fifth chapter on the significance of Muslim music, naming, and language practices must await future publication.

2. Martín Pérez de Ayala, *Sínodo de la Diócesis de Guadix y de Baza*, facsimile of original edition (Alcalá, 1556) with preliminary study by Carlos Asenjo Sedano (Granada: University of Granada, 1994) fols. 90v–91v.

3. "Pues los moriscos tenian baptismo y nombre de cristianos, y lo habian de ser y parecer, dejasen el hábito y la lengua y las costumbres de que usaban como moros." Luis del Mármol Carvajal, *Historia del rebelión y castigo de los moriscos del Reyno de Granada* (Málaga, 1600); ed. Cayetano Rosell et al., as *Historia del rebelión y castigo de los moriscos del Reino de Granada*, Biblioteca de autores españoles 21 (Madrid: Ediciones Atlas, 1852); repr. with new pagination as *Rebelión y castigo de los moriscos* (Málaga: Editorial Arguval, 1991), 2.5, p. 67. A slightly different English translation of this passage by Vincent Barletta can be found in his appendix to Francisco Núñez Muley, *A Memorandum for the President of the Royal Audiencia and Chancery Court of the City and Kingdom of Granada* (Chicago: University of Chicago Press, 2007) 104; emphasis mine.—Ed.

4. Francisco Bermúdez de Pedraza, *Historia eclesiástica de Granada*, facsimile of original edition (Granada, 1639) with preliminary study by Ignacio Henares Cuéllar (Granada: Editorial don Quijote, 1989), 4.82, fol. 238r.

5. Núñez Muley, *Memorandum*, Barletta trans., 70 (here given with slight variation). The original text is in Ana Isabel Carrasco Manchado, *De la convivencia a la exclusión: Imágenes legislativas de mudéjares y moriscos, siglos XIII–XVII* (Madrid: Sílex, 2012), 379.

6. Núñez Muley, *Memorandum*, Barletta trans., 87; Carrasco Manchado, *De la convivencia a la exclusión*, 391.

7. "La cristianidad no va en el ávito ni en el calçado, que agora se calçan, ni la seta de los moros tanbién. . . . Desto verá vuestra señoría reberendísima, tendrá por cierto, y esto es verdad, que no toca en cosa alguna del ávito y traxe y calçado en cosa alguna en favor de la seta ni contra ella, por todas causas arriba declaradas." Núñez Muley, *Memorandum*, Barletta trans., 70, 72; Carrasco Manchado, *De la convivencia a la exclusión*, 379, 381.

8. See Barletta's introduction to Núñez Muley, *Memorandum*, 11–13.

9. Núñez Muley, *Memorandum*, Barletta trans. 79; Carrasco Manchado, *De la convivencia a la exclusión*, 386. See also Bermúdez de Pedraza, *Historia eclesiástica*, 4.10, fol. 187r.

10. The complexities of these varied struggles are laid out in Bernard F. Reilly, *The Medieval Spains* (Cambridge: Cambridge University Press, 1993). Though it appeared too late to be fully consulted for this book, Brian A. Catlos, *Muslims of Medieval Latin Christendom, c. 1050–1614* (Cambridge: Cambridge University Press, 2014), esp. 20–41 and 51–75, further outlines the political conflicts that unfolded among and between Christian and Muslim forces in this period.

11. L. P. Harvey, *Muslims in Spain, 1500–1614* (Chicago: University of Chicago Press, 2005), 2–6.

12. Núñez Muley, *Memorandum*, Barletta trans., 56; Carrasco Manchado, *De la convivencia a la exclusión*, 369.

13. Núñez Muley, *Memorandum*, Barletta trans., 76; such sentiments are echoed again at the end of the *Memorandum*, Barletta trans., 97; Carrasco Manchado, *De la convivencia a la exclusión*, 383 and 399.

14. Mármol Carvajal, *Historia del rebelión y castigo de los moriscos*, 2.5, p. 67.

15. Henry Charles Lea, *The Moriscos of Spain: Their Conversion and Expulsion* (New York and London, 1901; reprint, New York: Haskell House Publishers, 1968), 215–17; Harvey, *Muslims in Spain*, 105–6. The precise content of the edict of December 7, 1526, is difficult to reconstruct. A copy from Granada's cathedral archive is transcribed in Antonio Gallego Burín and Alfonso Gámir Sandoval, *Los moriscos del Reino de Granada según el sínodo de Guadix de 1554* (Granada, 1968; facsimile ed., Granada: Universidad de Granada, 1996), 198, doc. 31. Later legal compilations such as the *Ordenanzas de la Real Audiencia y Chancillería de Granada* (Granada: Sebastian de Mena, 1601) 4.3.7, fols. 368v–371v, and the *Segunda parte de las leyes del Reyno*, also known as the *Nueva Recopilación de las leyes del Reyno* (first published Alcalá de Henares: Andrés de Angulo, 1567), 8.2.13, also given in Carrasco Manchado, *De la convivencia a la exclusión*, 248–53, contain many but not all of the same clauses. Later summaries, perhaps colored by the events of 1567, tend to add more details regarding types of clothing (such as *almalafas*) that were to be banned; the original texts of the edict apparently mentioned only charm necklaces "con ciertas letras moriscas" for specific prohibition. See, for example, Bermúdez de Pedraza's abbreviated version in the *Historia eclesiástica*, 4.46, fols. 212v–214r; and Núñez Muley, *Memorandum*, Barletta trans., 63–96; Carrasco Manchado, *De la convivencia a la exclusión*, 375–98. The latter gives his rambling account from memory, and claims that the total bribe paid was at least ninety thousand ducats—including ten thousand to secure the agreement of various nobles and officials, with further payments in the years to follow.

16. José Luis Corral Lafuente, "El proceso de represión contra los mudéjares aragoneses," *Aragón en la Edad Media* 14–15 (1999): 350; Catlos, *Muslims of Medieval Latin Christendom*, 223–25.

17. We know of the Audiencia's decree mainly through Mármol Carvajal's description and Núñez Muley's response as noted above, but it also seems to have closely mirrored royal legislation introduced several weeks earlier at Madrid: *Segunda parte de las leyes del Reyno*, 8.2.14–17.

18. Kathryn Miller, *Guardians of Islam* (New York: Columbia University Press, 2008), 20–24; cf. Catlos, *Muslims of Medieval Latin Christendom*, 314–19.

19. "Cuanto al hábito, se mandó que no se hiciesen de nuevo marlotas, almalafas, calzas, ni otra suerte de vestido de los que se usaban en tiempo de moros; y que todo lo que se cortase y hiciese fuese a uso de cristianos." Mármol Carvajal, *Historia del rebelión y castigo de los moriscos*, 2.6, p. 67; trans. Barletta, in appendix to Núñez Muley, *Memorandum*, 105, here slightly altered.

20. Fatima Mernissi, *The Veil and the Male Elite*, trans. Mary Jo Lakeland (New York: Addison-Wesley, 1991), remains a classic statement of Muslim feminist analysis on the subject. For more recent discussion of women's autonomy and choice with regard to veiling in the modern world, see Leila Ahmed, *A Quiet Revolution: The Veil's Resurgence, from the Middle East to America* (New Haven, CT: Yale University Press, 2011).

21. Leila Ahmed, *Women and Gender in Islam* (New Haven, CT: Yale University Press, 1992), 55.

22. "The Islamic Veil Across Europe," *BBC News*, September 22, 2011. See also Anastasia Vakulenko, *Islamic Veiling in Legal Discourse* (New York: Routledge, 2012).

23. Louise Leduc, "L'appui à la charte est maintenant majoritaire," *La Presse*, March 3, 2014, http://www.lapresse.ca/actualites/dossiers/charte-de-la-laicite/201403/03/01-4744020-lappui-a-la-charte-est-maintenant-majoritaire.php. This initiative, also known as the "Charte des valeurs québécoises," was withdrawn after an electoral defeat in April 2014.

24. Núñez Muley, *Memorandum*, Barletta trans., 98–99; Carrasco Manchado, *De la convivencia a la exclusión*, 399–400.

25. Núñez Muley, *Memorandum*, Barletta trans., 99; Carrasco Manchado, *De la convivencia a la exclusión*, 399–401.

## CHAPTER 2

1. José Damián González Arce, *Apariencia y poder: La legislación suntuaria castellana en los siglos XIII y XV* (Jaén: Universidad de Jaén, 1998), 171–73; José Damián González Arce, "Cuadernos de ordenanzas y otros documentos sevillanos del reinado de Alfonso X," *Historia, Instituciones, Documentos* 16 (1989): 122. In all of this legislation, the words *moro* in Castilian and *sarrayn* in Catalan were terms signifying religious identity, meaning "Muslim" as opposed to "Christian," although they may also have had ethnic significance.

2. Miguel Ángel Ladero Quesada, *Los mudéjares de Castilla en el tiempo de Isabel I* (Valladolid: Instituto "Isabel la Católica" de Historia Eclesiástica, 1969), 295, doc. 127.

3. "Porque las personas y las cosas se conosçen por las señales que tienen y se juzgan ser de aquél cuyas señales traen." Joaquín Gil Sanjuán, "El parecer de Galíndez de Carvajal sobre los moriscos andaluces (año 1526)," *Baetica* 11 (1988): 394.

4. *Segunda parte de las leyes del Reyno*, 8.2.16.

5. "No era honesto, y se compadecia mal, que las Christianas se anduviesen vestidas como Moras." Mármol Carvajal, *Historia del rebelión y castigo de los moriscos*, 2.7, p. 68; slightly different trans. Barletta, in appendix to Núñez Muley, *Memorandum*, 108–9.

6. Núñez Muley, *Memorandum*, Barletta trans., 70.

7. Mármol Carvajal contrasts the situation in Granada with that in Aragon, where he claims that New Christians had acquiesced to prohibitions and given up earlier styles of dress and face veiling (*Historia del rebelión y castigo de los moriscos*, 2.6, p. 67; trans. Barletta, in appendix to Núñez Muley, *Memorandum*, 105. This source may overstate the case, and some Morisco communities, especially in Valencia, clung to earlier vestimentary traditions. For more on Morisco clothing in Aragon and northern Castile (and its similarity to Old Christian dress), see Mercedes García-Arenal, *Los moriscos* (Granada: Universidad de Granada, 1996) 165, 169; Israel Lasmarías Ponz, "Vestir al morisco, vestir a la morisca: El traje de los moriscos en Aragón en la edad moderna," in *Actas: X Simposio Internacional de Mudejarismo, Teruel, 14–15–16 septiembre 2005* (Teruel: Centro de Estudios

Mudéjares, 2007), 629–39. A 1507 apprenticeship contract between two Muslims in Calatayud includes mention of various articles of clothing, none of which are notably Muslim (Francisco Fernández y González, *Estado social y político de los mudéjares de Castilla* [Madrid: Imprenta a cargo de Joaquin Muñoz, 1866], 437–38, doc. 92).

8. Circumcision was an overtly religious sign of Muslim and Jewish identity in medieval Spain, and New Christians were strictly prohibited from circumcising their children (although many continued to do so). As a religious requirement, circumcision falls into a different category from clothing and will not be discussed here. On this topic, see Bernard Vincent, "The *Moriscos* and Circumcision," in *Culture and Control in Counter-Reformation Spain*, ed. Anne J. Cruz and Mary Elizabeth Perry (Minneapolis: University of Minnesota Press, 1992), 78–92; María Desamparados Martínez San Pedro, "La práctica de la circuncisión, un 'pecado' morisco," in *VII Simposio Internacional de Mudejarismo, Teruel, 19–21 de septiembre de 1996* (Teruel: Centro de Estudios Mudéjares, 1999), 467–74; Ridha Mami, "Algunos ritos de los mudejares del siglo XV: Bodas, divorcios y circuncisión," in *Famille morisque: Femmes et enfants*, ed. Abdeljelil Temimi (Zaghouan: Fondation Temimi pour la Recherche Scientifique et l'Information, 1997), 218–23.

9. For a summary of scholarship on perceptions of Muslim identity and race in medieval Europe, see Jeffrey J. Cohen, *Medieval Identity Machines* (Minneapolis: University of Minnesota Press, 2003), 188–206. On Morisco physical appearance, see Bernard Vincent, "¿Qué aspecto físico tenían los moriscos?" *Andalucía moderna: Actas II Coloquios Historia de Andalucía, Córdoba, noviembre 1980* (Córdoba: Monte de Piedad y Caja de Ahorros de Córdoba, 1983), 2:335–40; Bernard Vincent, "Morisques et mobilité: L'exemple de Pastrana," in *Exils, passages et transitions: Chemins d'une recherche sur les marges; Hommage à Rose Duroux*, ed. Anne Dubet and Stéphanie Urdician (Clermont-Ferrand: Presses Universitaires Blaise Pascal, 2008), 17–24; José Manuel Prieto Bernabé, "Aproximación a las características antropológicas de la minoria morisca asentada en Pastrana en el último tercio del siglo XVI," *Wad-al-Hayara: Revista de estudios de Guadalajara* 14 (1987): 355–62.

10. Mark Cohen, "What Was the Pact of 'Umar? A Literary-Historical Study," *Jerusalem Studies in Arabic and Islam* 23 (1999): 100–157; see also Milka Levy-Rubin, *Non-Muslims in the Early Islamic Empire: From Surrender to Coexistence* (Cambridge: Cambridge University Press, 2011).

11. As an example of the Pact of 'Umar in al-Andalus, see the version reproduced by the jurist al-Ṭurṭūshī (d. 1126) in Bernard Lewis, *Islam from the Prophet Muhammed to the Fall of Constantinople* (New York: Oxford University Press, 1974), 2:217–19.

12. For evidence of such continuity see the examples of Ibn 'Abdūn and Ibn Rushd, given below.

13. *Decrees of the Ecumenical Councils*, ed. Norman Tanner (London: Sheed and Ward, 1990), 1:266–67; translated in *English Historical Documents*, vol. 3, *1189–1327*, ed. Harry Rothwell (London: Methuen, 1975), 672–73.

14. Olivia Remie Constable, "Clothing, Iron, and Timber: The Growth of Christian Anxiety about Islam in the Long Twelfth Century," in *European Transformations. The*

*Long Twelfth Century*, eds. Thomas F. X. Noble and John Van Engen (Notre Dame, IN: University of Notre Dame Press, 2012), 279–313.

15. Alonso de Santa Cruz, *Crónica de los reyes católicos*, ed. Juan de Mata Carriazo (Seville: Escuela de Estudios Hispano-Americanos de Sevilla, 1951), 190. The Castilian *almalafa* is from Arabic *al-milḥafa*.

16. Hernando de Talavera, *Breve e muy provechosa doctrina christiana* (Granada: Meinardus Ungut and Johann Pegnitzer, 1496); Teresa de Castro, "El tratado sobre el vestir, calzar y comer del arzobispo Hernando de Talavera," *Espacio, Tiempo y Forma* 14 (2001): 11–92.

17. Although this account was written a century later, by the chronicler Francisco Bermúdez de Pedraza, his wording probably still reflects Talavera's sentiments. The same (cognate) verb appears in a French document issued by Fernando and Isabel in 1492 that outlines their plans to oversee the "domestication" of the habits and conditions of the Muslims of Granada ("apaise et domestique les meurs et condicions des maures habitans et residans en la cite"); see Miguel Garrido Atienza, *Las capitulaciones para la entrega de Granada* (Granada, 1910; facsimile edition, Granada: Universidad de Granada, 1992), 320.

18. Bermúdez de Pedraza, *Historia eclesiástica*, 4.10, fol. 187r. On *sayas*, see María del Carmen Martínez Meléndez, *Los nombres de los tejidos en castellano medieval* (Granada: Universidad de Granada, 1989), 217–19.

19. Lea, *Moriscos of Spain*, 25–56.

20. On Baza and Huéscar, see Gallego Burín and Gámir Sandoval, *Los moriscos del Reino de Granada*, 165, 168; on Vélez Rubio, see Juan Grima Cervantes, *Almería y el Reino de Granada en los inicios de la modernidad (s. XV–XVI)* (Almería: Arráez Editores, 1993), 222. See also Harvey, *Muslims in Spain*, 47.

21. Pascual Boronat y Barrachina, *Los moriscos españoles y su expulsión* (Valencia: Imprenta de Francisco Vives y Mora, 1901), 1:123; Carrasco Manchado, *De la convivencia a la exclusión*, 255. See also Benjamin Ehlers, *Between Christians and Moriscos: Juan de Ribera and Religious Reform in Valencia, 1568–1614* (Baltimore: Johns Hopkins University Press, 2006), 16.

22. Gallego Burín and Gámir Sandoval, *Los moriscos del Reino de Granada*, 174.

23. Gallego Burín and Gámir Sandoval, *Los moriscos del Reino de Granada*, 177.

24. Gallego Burín and Gámir Sandoval, *Los moriscos del Reino de Granada*, 178–80; Harvey, *Muslims in Spain*, 72–73.

25. Gallego Burín and Gámir Sandoval, *Los moriscos del Reino de Granada*, 202–3. The ornament surely refers to what is now often called the "hand of Fatima" design. On this document and its variants, see Chapter 1, note 15, above.

26. Prudencio de Sandoval, *Primera parte de la vida y hechos del emperador Carlos Quinto* (Valladolid: Sebastian de Cañas, 1604), fol. 443r; republished in *Historia de la vida y hechos del emperador Carlos V*, ed. Carlos Seco Serrano, in Biblioteca de autores españoles 81 (Madrid: Ediciones Atlas, 1951), 173. On the *marlota*, see Robert Ricard, "Espagnol et Portugais 'marlota': Recherches sur le vocabulaire du vêtement hispano-mauresque," *Bulletin Hispanique* 53 (1951): 131–56.

27. Harvey, *Muslims in Spain*, 105–6; David Coleman, *Creating Christian Granada: Society and Religious Culture in an Old-World Frontier City, 1492–1600* (Ithaca, NY: Cornell University Press, 2003), 120.

28. Gallego Burín and Gámir Sandoval, *Los moriscos del Reino de Granada*, 215–17.

29. Gallego Burín and Gámir Sandoval, *Los moriscos del Reino de Granada*, 220.

30. Pérez de Ayala, *Sínodo de la Diócesis de Guadix y de Baza*, fol. 63v.

31. *Segunda parte de las leyes del Reyno*, 8.2.16. Cf. Mármol Carvajal, *Historia del rebelión y castigo de los moriscos*, 2.6, p. 67; trans. Barletta, in appendix to Núñez Muley, *Memorandum*, 105–6.

32. Núñez Muley, *Memorandum*, Barletta trans., 57 and 60.

33. Núñez Muley, *Memorandum*, Barletta trans., 66.

34. Núñez Muley, *Memorandum*, Barletta trans., 66–67.

35. Núñez Muley, *Memorandum*, Barletta trans., 69–70.

36. Núñez Muley, *Memorandum*, Barletta trans., 70.

37. Sixty years later, Francisco Bermúdez de Pedraza would claim that it was a particular problem that Morisca brides would be married in church in Christian clothes, then return home and change into Moorish clothing ("se vestian de Moras") for further wedding festivities (*Historia eclesiástica*, 4.82, fol. 238r).

38. Núñez Muley, *Memorandum*, Barletta trans., 72–73.

39. Núñez Muley, *Memorandum*, Barletta trans., 77 and 86–87.

40. Mármol Carvajal, *Historia del rebelión y castigo de los moriscos*, 2.9–11.

41. Diego Hurtado de Mendoza, *Guerra de Granada hecho por el Rei de España don Philippe II nuestro señor contra los moriscos de aquel reino, sus rebeldes* (Lisbon: Giraldo de la Viña, 1627), 1.7, fol. 12r; trans. Martin Shuttleworth, *The War in Granada* (London: Folio Society, 1982), 1.9, pp. 48–49.

42. See Robin Vose, *Dominicans, Muslims, and Jews in the Medieval Crown of Aragon* (Cambridge: Cambridge University Press, 2009).

43. Enforcement of Lateran IV's canon 68, which was vague to begin with in terms of differentiating "signs" to be imposed, varied tremendously from one region to the next throughout the later Middle Ages and beyond. In Iberia, despite early recognition of its demands, the wearing of Jewish badges was only sporadically imposed before the mid-fourteenth century (Pamela Anne Patton, *Art of Estrangement: Redefining Jews in Reconquest Spain* [University Park: Pennsylvania State University Press, 2012], 31–32). Studies of enforcement in other jurisdictions include Nora Berend, "Medieval Patterns of Social Exclusion and Integration: The Regulation of Non-Christian Clothing in Thirteenth-Century Hungary," *Revue Mabillon*, n.s., 8 (1997): 155–76; and Ariel Toaff, "The Jewish Badge in Italy During the 15th Century," in *Die Juden in ihrer Mittelalterlichen Umwelt*, ed. Alfred Ebenbauer and Klaus Zatloukal (Vienna: Böhlau, 1991), 275–80.

44. Carrasco Manchado, *De la convivencia a la exclusión*, 176–78, doc. 52. The blue half-moon patch would also be imposed on Aragonese Mudejars by 1526 (Corral Lafuente, "El Proceso," 350).

45. Dwayne E. Carpenter, *Alfonso X and the Jews: An Edition of and Commentary on "Siete Partidas" 7.24 "De los judíos"* (Berkeley: University of California Press, 1986), 36–37; *Siete Partidas*, 7.24.11; trans. Samuel Parsons Scott and ed. Robert I. Burns (Philadelphia: University of Pennsylvania Press, 2001), 5:1437.

46. *Documents arabes inédits sur la vie sociale et économique en occident musulmane au moyen âge,* ed. Évariste Lévi-Provençal (Cairo: Institut français d'archéologie orientale, 1955), 50–51. In the same collection, see also later rulings by al-Jarsīfī (late thirteenth century), 122.

47. Ibn Rushd, *Fatāwā Ibn Rushd,* ed. Al-Mukhtar ibn al-Tāhir al-Talīlī (Beirut: Dār al-Gharb al-Islāmī, 1987), 3:1618, no. 634.

48. *Colección de cánones y de todos los concilios de la iglesia española,* ed. and trans. Juan Tejada y Ramiro (Madrid: Imprenta de J. M. Alonso, 1849–62), 3:368.

49. These rules were originally promulgated in 1252 and repeated in other royal documents in 1253 and 1256. Carrasco Manchado, *De la convivencia a la exclusión,* 105–6; González Arce, *Apariencia y poder,* 171–72. On *çendal,* a type of very light silk or linen cloth, see Martínez Meléndez, *Los nombres de los tejidos en castellano medieval,* 386–98.

50. *Cortes de los antiguos reinos de León y de Castilla* (Madrid: Real Academia de la Historia, 1861–1903), 1:59; Carrasco Manchado, *De la convivencia a la exclusión,* 108–9.

51. *Cortes de los antiguos reinos de León y de Castilla,* 1:69. See discussion in González Arce, *Apariencia y poder,* 173.

52. Miguel Ángel Ladero Quesada, "Los mudéjares de Castilla en la baja edad media," *Historia, Instituciones, Documentos* 5 (1978): 285.

53. Juan Sempere y Guarinos, *Historia del luxo y de las leyes suntuarias de España* (Madrid: Imprenta Real, 1788), 1:87–97; Carmen Bernis, *Trajes y modas en la España de los Reyes Católicos* (Madrid: Consejo Superior de Investigaciones Científicas, 1978–79), 1:57–63.

54. Manuel Gómez Moreno, *El Panteón Real de Las Huelgas de Burgos* (Madrid: Consejo Superior de Investigaciones Científicas, 1946); Concha Herrero Carretero, *Museo de telas medievales: Monasterio de Santa María la Real de Huelgas* (Madrid: Patrimonio Nacional, 1988); María Judith Feliciano, "Muslim Shrouds for Christian Kings? A Reassessment of Andalusi Textiles in Thirteenth-Century Castilian Life and Ritual," in *Under the Influence: Questioning the Comparative in Medieval Castile,* ed. Cynthia Robinson and Leyla Rouhi (Leiden: Brill, 2005), 101–31.

55. González Arce, "Cuadernos de ordenanzas y otros documentos sevillanos," 122.

56. Mercedes García-Arenal, "Los moros en las Cantigas de Alfonso X el Sabio," *Al-Qantara* 6 (1985): 133–51; Rafael Ocasio, "Ethnic Underclass Representation in the *Cantigas*: The Black Moro as a Hated Character," in *Estudios alfonsinos y otros escritos en homenaje a John Esten Keller y a Aníbal A. Biglieri,* ed. Nicolás Toscano Liria (New York: National Endowment for the Humanities, 1991), 183–88; Rachel Arié, "Le costume des musulmans de Castille au XIIIᵉ siècle d'après les miniatures du *Libro de Ajedrez,*" *Mélanges de la Casa de Velázquez* 2 (1966): 59–69; Constable, "Chess and Courtly Culture in Medieval Castile."

57. On Christian and Muslim clothing styles depicted in Alfonsine texts, see Gonzalo Menéndez Pidal, *La España del siglo XIII leída en imágenes* (Madrid: Real Academia de la Historia, 1986), 51–104.

58. Elena Lourie, "Anatomy of Ambivalence: Muslims Under the Crown of Aragon in the Late Thirteenth Century," in *Crusade and Colonization: Muslims, Christians, and Jews in Medieval Aragon* (Aldershot: Variorum, 1990) essay 7, p. 55.

59. *Diplomatarium of the Crusader Kingdom of Valencia*, ed. Robert I. Burns (Princeton, NJ: Princeton University Press, 1985–2007), 2:229–30.

60. María Teresa Ferrer i Mallol, *Els sarraïns de la corona catalano-aragonesa en el segle XIV: Segregació i discriminació* (Barcelona: Consell Superior d'Investigacions Científiques, 1987), 45–55. Ferrer i Mallol cites an ordinance from Lérida in 1436 that described the *garceta* as wearing "los cabells en dret de les orelles, pus lonchs, en manera que sien tan larchs, que basten a miges orelles."

61. Menéndez Pidal, *La España del siglo XIII leída en imágenes*, 82.

62. Bukhārī, *Ṣaḥīḥ al-Bukhārī*, trans. Muhammad Muhsin Khan (Riyadh: Darussalam, 1997), 7.77, 421, no. 5892; Muslim, *Ṣaḥīḥ Muslim*, trans. 'Abdul Ḥamīd Ṣiddīqī (Lahore: Sh. Muhammad Ashraf, 1971), 1.103, 159–60, nos. 498–501.

63. On the Cid's beard, and its cross-cultural message of power and virility that would have been understood by both his Muslim and Christian contemporaries, see Constable, "Clothing, Iron, and Timber," 300–301.

64. Laws on Jewish appearance were enacted much earlier in the thirteenth-century Crown of Aragon; see Lourie, "Anatomy of Ambivalence," 55.

65. *Costums de Tortosa*, ed. Jesús Massip i Fonollosa (Barcelona: Fundació Noguera, 1996); 71; José Hinojosa Montalvo, *Los mudéjares: La voz del Islam en la España cristiana* (Teruel: Centro de Estudios Mudéjares, 2002), 1:294.

66. Hinojosa Montalvo, *Los mudéjares*, 2:290–91; Ferrer i Mallol, *Els sarraïns de la corona catalano-aragonesa*, 213, doc. 1.

67. Jaime Villanueva, *Viage literario a las iglesias de España* (Madrid: Real Academia de la Historia, 1803–52), 16:231; John Boswell, *The Royal Treasure: Muslim Communities Under the Crown of Aragon in the Fourteenth Century* (New Haven, CT: Yale University Press, 1977), 332. The Cortes of Lérida (with the statute requiring short hair) is dated to July 17, 1301, in the *Cortes de los antiguos reinos de Aragon y de Valencia y Principado de Cataluña* (Madrid: Real Academia de la Historia, 1896), 190, by Lourie, "Anatomy of Ambivalence," 55; and by Ferrer i Mallol, *Els sarraïns de la corona catalano-aragonesa*, 43. Elsewhere, it is dated to 1300; see Francisco A. Roca Traver, "Un siglo de vida mudéjar en la Valencia medieval (1238–1338)," *Estudios de Edad Media de la Corona de Aragón* 5 (1952): 160; Fernández y González, *Estado social y político de los mudéjares de Castilla*, 369, doc. 56.

68. Elena Lourie has argued that this case was the direct cause of Jaume's decree in Lérida in July 1301 ( "Anatomy of Ambivalence," 55). Despite this clear and early attention to hair in Valencia, there is no recorded mention of the *garceta* in Valencian law until 1341, when Pere IV ordered that Muslims must not dress like Christians and must not

wear the *garceta*. Originally, violators were to be enslaved, but in 1345 the penalty was reduced to a monetary fine (Hinojosa Montalvo, *Los mudéjares*, 1:294–95, 2:292–93, docs. 221 and 222; Ferrer i Mallol, *Els sarraïns de la corona catalano-aragonesa*, 44 and 258, doc. 49).

69. Fernández y González, *Estado social y político de los mudéjares de Castilla*, 369, doc. 57; Carrasco Manchado, *De la convivencia a la exclusión*, 140–41, doc. 26; Ferrer i Mallol, *Els sarraïns de la corona catalano-aragonesa*, 43.

70. For Albalate de Cinca, see Ferrer i Mallol, *Els sarraïns de la corona catalano-aragonesa*, 44; María Blanca Basáñez Villaluenga, *Las morerías aragonesas durante el reinado de Jaime II: Catálogo de la documentación de la Cancelleria Real* (Teruel: Centro de Estudios Mudéjares, 1999), 264. For Calatayud, see Basáñez Villaluenga, *Las morerías aragonesas*, 368. In 1312, in Tarazona, Jaume reissued his order for Muslims to wear short hair (Ferrer i Mallol, *Els sarraïns de la corona catalano-aragonesa*, 44).

71. Ferrer i Mallol, *Els sarraïns de la corona catalano-aragonesa*, 48.

72. Ferrer i Mallol, *Els sarraïns de la corona catalano-aragonesa*, 48.

73. Ferrer i Mallol, *Els sarraïns de la corona catalano-aragonesa*, 47 and 270–71, doc. 60. In 1358, Pere reminded the bailiff of Valencia to impose this law (Ferrer i Mallol, *Els sarraïns de la corona catalano-aragonesa*, 284, doc. 73).

74. For this and other cases, see Ferrer i Mallol, *Els sarraïns de la corona catalano-aragonesa*, 49–51.

75. Ferrer i Mallol, *Els sarraïns de la corona catalano-aragonesa*, 51–52 and 318–19, doc. 103. Laws requiring the *garceta* in the kingdom of Valencia were repeated in 1390 and 1394 (Ferrer i Mallol, *Els sarraïns de la corona catalano-aragonesa*, 52–53).

76. Ferrer i Mallol, *Els sarraïns de la corona catalano-aragonesa*, 331, doc. 117.

77. Regulations in Zaragoza reiterated that hair should be cut short all around the head and in front, and without the *garceta* ("thonsis capillis in rotundo supra fronte et absque garceta"). Boswell, *The Royal Treasure*, 331; Ferrer i Mallol, *Els sarraïns de la corona catalano-aragonesa*, 44.

78. Ferrer i Mallol, *Els sarraïns de la corona catalano-aragonesa*, 48, 54–55.

79. Hinojosa Montalvo, *Los mudéjares*, 1:295.

80. María Blanca Basáñez Villaluenga, *La aljama sarracena de Huesca en el siglo XIV* (Barcelona: Consejo Superior de Investigaciones Científicas, 1989), 65 and 212–13, doc. 75.

81. Ferrer i Mallol, *Els sarraïns de la corona catalano-aragonesa*, 328, doc. 114.

82. Statements to this effect appeared at the Cortes of Palencia (1312), Synod of Zamora (1313), Cortes of Burgos (1315), Ordinances of Seville (1327), and Cortes of Burgos (1338). See Hinojosa Montalvo, *Los mudéjares*, I, 297; Carrasco Manchado, *De la convivencia a la exclusión*, p. 146, doc. 31, and p. 156, doc. 37; González Arce, *Apariencia y poder*, 174; *Cortes de los antiguos reinos de León y de Castilla*, 1:227. Similar laws continued to be repeated in the fifteenth century in Castile.

83. *Cortes de los antiguos reinos de León y de Castilla*, 1:19; Carrasco Manchado, *De la convivencia a la exclusión*, 161–63, doc. 42; González Arce, *Apariencia y poder*, 174–75.

84. Carrasco Manchado, *De la convivencia a la exclusión*, 166–67, doc. 46.

85. Hinojosa Montalvo, *Los mudéjares*, 1:295; Ferrer i Mallol, *Els sarraïns de la corona catalano-aragonesa*, 54.

86. Maria Filomena Lopes de Barros, "Body, Baths and Cloth: Muslim and Christian Perceptions in Medieval Portugal," *Portuguese Studies* 21 (2005): 9.

87. "Cum certo tallio seu signo crinium, habitu, vestitu." Ferrer i Mallol, *Els sarraïns de la corona catalano-aragonesa*, 52.

88. Josefa Mutgé Vives, *L'aljama sarraïna de Lleida a l'edat mitjana: Aproximació a la seva història* (Barcelona: Consell Superior d'Investigacions Científiques, 1992), 372, doc. 191; Hinojosa Montalvo, *Los mudéjares*, 2:293, doc. 223.

89. Ferrer i Mallol, *Els sarraïns de la corona catalano-aragonesa*, 56 and 333–34, doc. 120.

90. Ferrer i Mallol, *Els sarraïns de la corona catalano-aragonesa*, 56 and 335–36, doc. 122.

91. Hinojosa Montalvo, *Los mudéjares*, 1:296–97; Basáñez Villaluenga, *La aljama sarracena de Huesca*, 66; Ferrer i Mallol, *Els sarraïns de la corona catalano-aragonesa*, 57–59 and 336–37, doc. 123.

92. Ferrer i Mallol, *Els sarraïns de la corona catalano-aragonesa*, 58–59 and 343–44, doc. 129.

93. Ferrer i Mallol, *Els sarraïns de la corona catalano-aragonesa*, 354–55, doc. 137.

94. Ferrer i Mallol, *Els sarraïns de la corona catalano-aragonesa*, 57 and 359–60, doc. 140.

95. Ferrer i Mallol, *Els sarraïns de la corona catalano-aragonesa*, 59–60.

96. "Los varones traian sobre todas las vestiduras un capuz de paño, color amarillo vestido, é un señal tamaña de luna, de paño, color torquesado, tan grande como esta, toda llena manifiestamente de yuso de el hombro derecho en tal manera, que pareçca toda. É las mujeres que traian eso mesmo, cada una la dicha señal á manera de luna del paño color de torquesado, tan grande como esta toda llena, que traian manifiestamente sobre todas las vestiduras de yuso de el hombro derecho en tal manera, que pareçca toda." Fernández y González, *Estado social y político de los mudéjares de Castilla*, 397–99, doc. 76; Carrasco Manchado, *De la convivencia a la exclusión*, 176–78, doc. 52. Although not stated in the text, it is possible that Catalina was reiterating legislation initiated during the reign of her late husband Enrique III (1390–1406), since an ordinance from Murcia in 1418 affirmed the laws requiring *capuzes* and moon symbols "according to the said ordinances of our said lord, don Enrique" (Hinojosa Montalvo, *Los mudéjares*, 1:297). More likely, the Murcian law may have confused the reign in which the law was given or its contents. Enrique III had cited an almost identical law for Castilian Jews (mandating yellow circles) at the Cortes of Valladolid in 1405 (*Cortes de los antiguos reinos de León y de Castilla*, 2:553).

97. Hinojosa Montalvo, *Los mudéjares*, 1:298; González Arce, *Apariencia y poder*, 176. The Synod of Ávila in 1481 ruled that "todos los judios y moros trayan sus señales acostumbradas para que puedan ser conoscidos entre los fieles christianos . . . y los moros capuzes amarillos con lunas azules, y las moras lunas de paño azul en los mantos,

publicamente, por que sean conoscidos entre los otros y se eviten los pecados y yerros suso dichos." Antonio García y García, "Jews and Muslims in the Canon Law of the Iberian Peninsula in the Late Medieval and Early Modern Period," *Jewish History* 3 (1988): 47.

98. Fernández y González, *Estado social y político de los mudéjares de Castilla*, 400–405, doc. 77; Carrasco Manchado, *De la convivencia a la exclusión*, 176–78, doc. 53; Ana Echevarría Arsuaga, "Política y religión frente al Islam: La evolución de la legislación real castellana sobre musulmanes en el siglo XV," *Qurtuba* 4 (1999): 66–67.

99. Carrasco Manchado, *De la convivencia a la exclusión*, 187–92, doc. 56 (Juan II, 1443); 209, doc. 58 (Enrique IV, 1465); 212–13, doc. 59 (Fernando and Isabel, 1476). See also Hinojosa Montalvo, *Los mudéjares*, 1:297.

100. Carrasco Manchado, *De la convivencia a la exclusión*, 212–13, doc. 59.

101. Lopes de Barros, "Body, Baths and Cloth," 9–10.

102. Luis Rubio García, *La procesión de Corpus en el siglo XV en Murcia y religiosidad medieval* (Murcia: Academia Alfonso X el Sabio, 1983), 67–68.

103. There is no mention of Christian clothing in either the early fourteenth-century Castilian so-called *Leyes de moros* or the early fifteenth-century Valencian *Llibre de la çuna e xara*. See respectively "Leyes de Moros," in *Tratados de legislación musulmana*, ed. Pascual de Gayangos (Madrid: Real Academia de la Historia, 1853), 11–235; and *Un tratado catalán medieval de derecho islámico: El llibre de la çuna e xara dels moros*, ed. Carme Barceló Torres (Córdoba: Universidad de Córdoba, 1989).

104. Yça Gidelli, "Suma de los principales mandamientos y devademientos de la ley y çunna," in *Tratados de legislación musulmana*, 282.

105. Ibn Saʿīd, quoted by al-Maqqarī in his *Analectes sur l'histoire et la littérature des arabes d'Espagne*, ed. R. Dozy et al. (Leiden: Brill, 1855), 1:137; Emilio García Gómez, *Cinco poetas musulmanas: Biografías y estudios* (Madrid: Espasa-Calpe, 1959), 176; Ibn al-Khaṭīb, *Historia de los reyes de la Alhambra: El resplandor de la luna llena acerca de la dinastía nazarí (Al-Lamha al-badriyya fī l-dawlat al-nasriyya)*, trans. José María Casciaro Ramírez and Emilio Molina López (Granada: Universidad de Granada, 2010), 127–28.

106. Ibn Khaldūn, *Muqaddimat ibn Khaldūn. Prolégomènes d'ebn-Khaldoun*, ed. M. Quatremère (Paris: Benjamin Duprat, 1858), 1:267; *The Muqaddimah*, trans. Franz Rosenthal (New York: Pantheon Books, 1958), 1:300.

107. The most comprehensive study of clothing in Naṣrid Granada is Rachel Arié's "Quelques remarques sur le costume des musulmans d'Espagne au temps des Naṣrides," *Arabica* 12 (1965): 244–61. On earlier clothing in al-Andalus, see Évariste Lévi-Provençal, *Histoire de l'Espagne musulmane* (Paris: Maisonneuve, 1950–53), 3:422–29; Reinhart Dozy, *Dictionnaire détaillé des noms des vêtements chez les Arabes* (Amsterdam: J. Muller, 1845); Manuela Marín, *Mujeres en al-Andalus* (Madrid: Consejo Superior de Investigaciones Científicas, 2000), 198–217.

108. Roser Salicrú i Lluch, "La diplomacia y las embajadas como expresión de los contactos interculturales entre cristianos y musulmanes en el Mediterráneo occidental durante la baja edad media," *Estudios de Historia de España* 9 (2007): 89.

109. David Nirenberg, *Communities of Violence: Persecution of Minorities in the Middle Ages* (Princeton, NJ: Princeton University Press, 1996), 143–48; David Nirenberg, "Conversion, Sex, and Segregation: Jews and Christians in Medieval Spain," *American Historical Review* 107 (2002): 1075–76.

110. Ferrer i Mallol, *Els sarraïns de la corona catalano-aragonesa*, 285, doc. 74.

111. Arié, "Quelques remarques sur le costume des musulmans d'Espagne," 255–56.

112. Carmen Bernis, "Modas moriscas en la sociedad cristiana española del siglo XV y principios del XVI," *Boletín de la Real Academia de la Historia* 144 (1959): 199–236; Carmen Bernis, *Indumentaria medieval española* (Madrid: Consejo Superior de Investigaciones Científicas, 1956), 35; Bernis, *Trajes y modas en la España de los Reyes Católicos*, 1:49–56, 2:19–24; Fuchs, *Exotic Nation*, 60–72; Ruth M. Anderson, *Hispanic Costume, 1480–1530* (New York: Hispanic Society of America, 1979), 92–97, 202–3, 215–17.

113. A number of late medieval Castilian and Aragonese kings and queens wore "Moorish garments" on occasion (Bernis, "Modas moriscas," 200–201). Even Queen Isabel wore such garments (Andrés Bernáldez, *Memorias del reinado de los Reyes Católicos*, ed. Manuel Gómez-Moreno and Juan de M. Carriazo [Madrid: Real Academia de la Historia, 1962], 170). Miguel Lucas de Iranzo was famous for his delight in *ábito morisco* (*Relación de los hechos del muy magnífico e más virtuoso señor, el señor don Miguel Lucas, muy digno condestable de Castilla*, ed. Juan Cuevas Mata, Juan del Arco Moya, and José del Arco Moya [Jaén: Universidad de Jaén, 2001], 46, 85, 116, 143, 161, 212). A German traveler to Burgos in the 1460s visited the household of a local noble and reported seeing everybody dressed in Muslim styles ("Viaje del noble bohemio Léon de Rosmithal de Blatna por España y Portugal, hecho del año 1465 a 1467: Fragmentos de la Relación del Viaje por Tetzel," in J. García Mercadal, ed., *Viajes de extranjeros por España y Portugal desde los tiempos mas remotos, hasta fines del siglo XVI* (Madrid: Aguilar, 1952), 296. See also Ana Echevarría Arsuaga, *Knights on the Frontier: The Moorish Guard of the Kings of Castile (1410–1467)*, trans. Martin Beagles (Leiden: Brill, 2009), 104–5; Manuel Jódar Mena, "El gusto por lo morisco como símbolo de identidad del poder: El caso del Condestable Iranzo en el reino de Jaén," *Revista de Antropología Experimental* 12 (2012): 341–42.

114. Menéndez Pidal, *La España del siglo XIII leída en imagenes*, 56–57, 65, 88–89. The letter written by Jaume II of Aragon in 1300, reminding Christians in Lérida not to wear Muslim or Jewish clothes, stands almost alone in this regard (Villanueva, *Viage literario*, 16:231).

115. *Escribir y gobernar: El último registro de correspondencia del Conde de Tendilla (1513–1515)*, ed. María Amparo Moreno Trujillo, María José Osorio Pérez, and Juan María de la Obra Sierra (Granada: Universidad de Granada, 2007), 195–96; Helen Nader, *The Mendoza Family in the Spanish Renaissance, 1350–1550* (New Brunswick, NJ: Rutgers University Press, 1979), 187.

116. Ramon Llull, *Libre de Meravelles*, ed. M. Salvador Galmés (Barcelona: Editorial Barcino, 1931–34), 3:44–45; Jocelyn Hillgarth, *The Spanish Kingdoms, 1250–1516* (Oxford: Clarendon Press, 1976), 1:168–69.

117. *El Fuero de Teruel*, ed. Max Gorosch (Stockholm: Almqvist & Wiksells Boktryckeri, 1950), 328; Basáñez Villaluenga, *Las morerías aragonesas*, 67.

118. Ferrer i Mallol, *Els sarraïns de la corona catalano-aragonesa*, 215–16, doc. 4; Hinojosa Montalvo, *Los mudéjares*, 2:291, doc. 220; González Arce, *Apariencia y poder*, 171–73; González Arce, "Cuadernos de ordenanzas y otros documentos sevillanos," 122.

119. Lea, *Moriscos of Spain*, 27–28.

120. Joaquín Gil Sanjuán, "La inquisición de Granada: Visita a Málaga y su comarca en 1568," *Baetica* 1 (1978): 325.

121. William Monter, *Frontiers of Heresy: The Spanish Inquisition from the Basque Lands to Sicily* (Cambridge: Cambridge University Press, 1990), 189 and 206.

122. On Morisco dress, see Rachel Arié, "Acerca del traje musulmán en España desde la caída de Granada hasta la expulsión de los moriscos," *Revista de Instituto Egipcio de Estudios Islámicos* 13 (1965–66): 103–17; Julio Caro Baroja, *Los moriscos del Reino de Granada (ensayo de historia social)* (Madrid: Instituto de Estudios Políticos, 1957), 124–30; Manuel Barrios Aguilera, *Granada morisca, la convivencia negada: Historia y textos* (Granada: Editorial Comares, 2002), 256–61.

123. Christoph Weiditz, *Authentic Everyday Dress of the Renaissance: All 154 Plates from the "Trachtenbuch"* (New York: Dover, 1994), plates 79–91. On images of Morisco dress, see Manuel Barrios Aguilera, "Religiosidad y vida cotidiana de los moriscos," in *Historia del Reino de Granada*, ed. Manuel Barrios Aguilera (Granada: Universidad de Granada, 2000), 2:406–10.

124. Manuela García Pardo, "Las moriscas granadinas: Notas para su estudio," in *Famille morisque: Femmes et enfants*, ed. Abdeljelil Temimi (Zaghouan: Fondation Temimi pour la Recherche Scientifique et l'Information, 1997), 121–22.

125. *Correspondencia del Conde de Tendilla*, ed. Emilio Meneses García (Madrid: Real Academia de la Historia, 1973–74), 2:533–34.

126. See above, note 20.

127. Ladero Quesada, *Los mudéjares de Castilla en tiempos de Isabel I*, 284–92, doc. 125.

128. Bermúdez de Pedraza, *Historia eclesiástica*, 4.10, fol. 187r.

129. Legislation on Morisco dress said nothing about male head coverings or turbans. According to Ibn al-Khaṭīb (d. 1374), turbans were rarely worn in Naṣrid Granada, except by men in certain religious and administrative offices (*Historia de los reyes de la Alhambra*, 127). In consequence, perhaps Morisco men did not wear this style, although the *toca* (a turban-like hat) was popular among late medieval Christian men. Moriscos must have been aware of the turban, since a late sixteenth-century *aljamiado* manuscript (known from 1591), translated from a medieval Arabic collection of *'aḥādīth*, quoted the well-known saying that "turbans are the crowns of the Arabs" (Abdeljalil Temimi, "Attachement des morisques à leur religion et à leur identité à travers les hadiths dans deux manuscrits morisques," in *Actes du II Symposium Internacional du C.I.E.M. sur Religion, Identité et Sources Documentaires sur les Morisques Andalous*, ed. Abdeljelil Temimi [Tunis: Publications de l'Institut Supérieur de Documentation, 1984], 2:159). Distinctive haircuts would of course have become less relevant if Muslim men regularly covered their heads.

130. Arié, "Quelques remarques sur le costume des musulmans d'Espagne," 248. In the 1520s, Leo Africanus described women in Fez wearing long mantles that covered their whole bodies and face veils that revealed only their eyes. This was presumably similar to styles worn in Granada, Leo's birthplace, although he actually compared it to "the manner of women in Syria." This analogy may be because Leo was writing for an Italian readership that may have been more familiar with accounts of costume in the Near East than in Spain (Jean-Léon l'Africain, *Description de l'Afrique*, trans. A. Épaulard [Paris: Adrien-Maisonneuve, 1956], 1:208).

131. Lasmarías Ponz, "Vestir al morisco, vestir a la morisca," 639.

132. James T. Monroe, *Hispano-Arabic Poetry. A Student Anthology* (Berkeley: University of California Press, 1974), 376.

133. The *milḥafa* and other coverings are recorded in medieval Andalusi sources; see Marín, *Mujeres en al-Andalus*, 200; Lévi-Provençal, *Histoire de l'Espagne musulmane*, 3:424. Women depicted in the thirteenth-century Andalusi manuscript *Ḥadīth Bayāḍ wa Riyāḍ* show some women with head coverings and others without, but only one woman holds a veil across her lower face as she delivers a letter in public; see Cynthia Robinson, ed., *Medieval Andalusian Courtly Culture in the Mediterranean* (New York: Routledge, 2007), fol. 17r.

134. Lourie, "Anatomy of Ambivalence," 3.

135. Ferrer i Mallol, *Els sarraïns de la corona catalano-aragonesa*, 54; Hinojosa Montalvo, *Los mudéjares*, 1:295.

136. Hillgarth, *The Spanish Kingdoms*, 1:168.

137. See above, note 15.

138. Antoine de Lalaing, "Relation du premier voyage de Philippe le Beau en Espagne en 1501," in *Collection des voyages des souverains des Pays-Bas*, ed. M. Gachard (Brussels: F. Hayez, 1876), 1:208.

139. Luigi Monga, ed., *Un mercante di Milano in Europa: Diario di viaggio del primo Cinquecento* (Milan: Jaca Book, 1985), 131.

140. Andrea Navagero, *Opera omnia* (Venice: Typographia Remondiniana, 1754), 289, 340.

141. Antonio Gallego Morell, "La corte de Carlos V en la Alhambra en 1526," in *Miscelánea de estudios dedicados al profesor Antonio Marín Ocete* (Granada: Universidad de Granada, 1974), 1:274.

142. Weiditz, *Authentic Everyday Dress of the Renaissance*, plates 84–86.

143. Gallego Burín and Gámir Sandoval, *Los moriscos del Reino de Granada*, 178–79. L. P. Harvey translates this edict in *Muslims in Spain*, 72–73.

144. Gallego Burín and Gámir Sandoval, *Los moriscos del Reino de Granada*, 184.

145. *Correspondencia del Conde de Tendilla*, 2:534. This letter is also reproduced by Rafael Gerardo Peinado Santaella, *"Como disfrutan los vencedores cuando se reparten el botín": El reino de Granada tras la conquista castellana (1483–1526)* (Granada: Comares, 2011), 233–34.

146. *Escribir y gobernar*, 574–75, doc. 970.

147. *Escribir y gobernar*, 657, doc. 1092.

148. *Escribir y gobernar*, 905, doc. 1498 (August 1515); the matter of *almalafas* also comes up in docs. 194 (February 1514), 1034 (March 1515), 1194 (May 1515).

149. Gallego Burín and Gámir Sandoval, *Los moriscos del Reino de Granada*, 194–95.

150. Gallego Burín and Gámir Sandoval, *Los moriscos del Reino de Granada*, 202–3.

151. Gallego Burín and Gámir Sandoval, *Los moriscos del Reino de Granada*, 214, 218–19.

152. Gallego Burín and Gámir Sandoval, *Los moriscos del Reino de Granada*, 27; Gloria López de la Plaza suggested a connection between Guevara's threat and the queen's intervention; see her article "Las mujeres moriscas granadinas en el discurso político y religioso de la Castilla del siglo XVI (1492–1567)," *En la España Medieval* 16 (1993): 310.

153. Pérez de Ayala, *Sínodo de la Diócesis de Guadix y de Baza*, fol. 23r.

154. López de la Plaza, "Las mujeres moriscas granadinas," 310; *Colección de cánones y de todos los concilios*, 5:389.

155. *Segunda parte de las leyes del Reyno*, 8.2.16.

156. Hurtado de Mendoza, *Guerra de Granada*, 1.5, fol. 8v; trans. Shuttleworth, *War in Granada*, 1.5, p. 41.

157. Núñez Muley, *Memorandum*, Barletta trans., 86.

158. Núñez Muley, *Memorandum*, Barletta trans., 77.

159. Núñez Muley, *Memorandum*, Barletta trans., 87.

160. Teresa de Castro, "El tratado sobre el vestir, calzar y comer," 32.

161. Camilo Borghese, "Diario de la relación de viaje de monseñor Camilo Borghese, enviado a la Corte como nuncio extraordinario del Papa Clemente VIII el año 1594 al rey Felipe II," in García Mercadal, *Viajes de extranjeros por España*, 1472.

162. Antonio de León Pinelo, "Velos antiguos y modernos en los rostros de las mujeres: Sus conveniencias y daños," ed. Enrique Suárez Figaredo, *Lemir* 13 (2009): 311. The translation is from Fuchs, *Exotic Nation*, 71. Half-veiling was a style in which only the eyes (sometimes only one eye) were revealed. Overall, León Pinelo's treatise was a defense and explication of traditions of veiling, and he opened his text with the observation that "women have used veils and covered their faces for almost as long as there have been women in the world" ("Velos antiguos y modernos," 273).

163. León Pinelo, "Velos antiguos y modernos," 314. León Pinelo's treatise is filled with diligent erudition and quotations from sources, some verifiable and others not. Strikingly, he includes a passage (316) claimed as being from Núñez Muley's memorandum, but he must have consulted a very different text from the ones we know today (see Vincent Barletta's discussion of manuscripts and editions, *Memorandum*, 13–20). Although there are recognizable phrases in common, León Pinelo's quotation of Núñez Muley includes rather unlikely mention of the work of both Vincent Ferrer and Jean Gerson. This suggests that there may have been a number of versions of the memorandum circulating in the early seventeenth century.

164. Monga, *Un mercante di Milano in Europa*, 131–32.

165. Navagero, *Opera omnia*, 290; "Viaje en España," in García Mercadal, *Viajes de extranjeros por España*, 891.

166. Gallego Morell, "La corte de Carlos V," 276.

167. Luc Renaut, "Recherches sur le henné antique," *Journal of Near Eastern Studies* 68, no. 3 (2009): 193–212.

168. Abū Dā'ūd Sulaymān ibn al-Ash'ath al Sijistānī, *Sunan Abu Dawud: The third correct Tradition of the Prophetic Sunna*, trans. Muḥammad Mahdī Sharīf (Beirut: Dar al-Kotob al-Ilmiyah, 2008), 4:222, nos. 4164 and 4166.

169. *Tratados de legislación musulmana*, CIII, 77–78.

170. *Crónicas de los reyes de Castilla desde Alfonso el Sabio, hasta los Católicos Don Fernando y Doña Isabel*, ed. Cayetano Rosell, in Biblioteca de autores españoles 68 (Madrid: M. Rivadeneyra, 1877), 2:319.

171. Alfonso Martínez de Toledo, *Archipreste de Talavera o Corbacho*, ed. J. González Muela (Madrid: Clásicos Castalia, 1982), 137; Alfonso Martínez de Toledo, *Little Sermons on Sin: The Archpriest of Talavera*, trans. Lesley Byrd Simpson (Berkeley: University of California Press, 1959), 118.

172. Bartolomé Miranda Díaz and Francisco de Córdoba Soriano, *Los moriscos de Magacela* (Magacela: Ayuntamiento de Magacela, 2010), 222; Harvey, *Muslims in Spain*, 52; Gallego Burín and Gámir Sandoval, *Los moriscos del Reino de Granada*, 183. Henna was just one aspect of traditional wedding practice affected by the Ordenanzas, which explicitly demanded that henceforth all marriages were to be performed "en la manera que los cristianos viejos hacen las suyas."

173. Harvey, *Muslims in Spain*, 107–8; Gallego Burín and Alfonso Gámir Sandoval, *Los moriscos del Reino de Granada*, 203.

174. Gallego Burín and Alfonso Gámir Sandoval, *Los moriscos del Reino de Granada*, 207.

175. Pérez de Ayala, *Sínodo de la Diócesis de Guadix y de Baza*, fols. 23r and 91r; the synod's importance in defining Morisco custom as "superstitiones y ritos" is emphasized in López de la Plaza, "Mujeres moriscas granadinas," 311–12.

176. Mármol Carvajal, *Historia del rebelión y castigo de los moriscos*, 2.6; trans. Barletta, in appendix to Núñez Muley, *Memorandum*, 106.

177. Henry Charles Lea, *A History of the Inquisition of Spain* (New York: Macmillan, 1906–7), 3:329; also Lea, *Moriscos of Spain*, 130.

178. Jean-Pierre Dedieu, "Morisques et vieux-chrétiens à Daimiel au XVIᵉ siècle," in *Actes du II Symposium International du C.I.E.M. sur Religion, Identité et Sources Documentaires sur les Morisques Andalous*, ed. Abdeljelil Temimi (Tunis: Institut Supérieur de Documentation, 1984), 1:214. Of course Gonzalo was quite wrong about his ancestral religion, as the virgin birth of Jesus is in fact a central tenet of orthodox Islam; see Qur'ān 19:17–21.

179. In 1560, Isabel Garçía was penanced for a "baño y pinturas en el rostro" (images on the face); María la Paxaruca was similarly treated "por baño para su boda y pinturas" (bathing for her wedding, and images—presumably drawn on with henna). See María

Isabel Pérez de Colosía Rodríguez and Joaquín Gil Sanjuán, "Los moriscos del Algarbe malagueño: Orígenes y presión inquisitorial," *Jábega* 56 (1987): 21–23; and Isabel Pérez de Colosía Rodríguez, "La religiosidad en los moriscos malagueños," in *Actes du II Symposium Internacional du C.I.E.M. sur Religion, Identité et Sources Documentaires sur les Morisques Andalous*, ed. Abdeljelil Temimi (Tunis: Publications de l'Institut Supérieur de Documentation, 1984), 1:188. Inquisitor Martín de Coscojales was one of those who considered it to be a *poca cosa* and dismissed many prisoners with little or no punishment.

180. Seven paintings were commissioned in all, and executed over the period of 1612 to 1613. See José María Calleja Maestre, "La expulsión de los moriscos en las artes plásticas," extracts from a conference of the Asociación Amigos del Legado Andalusí, ed. Guillermo Muñoz Vera (2010), http://www.arauco.org/SAPEREAUDE/terraaustralisincognita /historiasdealandalus/laexpulsionenlapintura.html; and Christina H. Lee, *The Anxiety of Sameness in Early Modern Spain* (Manchester: Manchester University Press, 2015), 153–56. The Morisco men stand apart from the women in this striking image, some stripped-down and engaged in formal wrestling matches to pass the time.

181. See, for example, the list of grievances recited to the Ottoman sultan Bayezid II, in a *qaṣīda* dating to the early 1500s, as cited in Maqqarī's *Azhar al-Riyāḍ* (trans. García-Arenal, *Los moriscos*, 34, esp. verse 13).

CHAPTER 3

1. *Segunda parte de las leyes del Reyno*, fol. 153. These prohibitions were also reported by Luis del Mármol Carvajal in his *Historia del rebelión y castigo de los moriscos*, 2.6, p. 67.

2. On Islamic rules for ritual washing, see A. J. Wensinck, "The Origin of the Muslim Laws of Ritual Purity," in *The Development of Islamic Ritual*, ed. Gerald Hawting (Aldershot: Ashgate, 2006), 75–93.

3. Washing is one of the very few rituals (along with circumcision) the Aragonese inquisitor Nicholas Eymeric saw fit to draw attention to in his description of Islam (first written ca. 1376), which was printed and widely circulated in the early modern period. Nicholas Eymeric, *Directorium inquisitorum*, ed. Francisco Pegnae (Venice: Apud Marcum Antonium Zalterium, 1607), 306 (part 2, q. 21, "De erroribus Sarracenorum"): "Per lotionem manum, pedum, et partium exteriorum corporis, etiam pudendorum, credunt mundari a peccatorum maculis."

4. Gallego Burín and Gámir Sandoval, *Los moriscos del Reino de Granada*, 161; Ladero Quesada, *Los mudéjares de Castilla en tiempos de Isabel I*, 293.

5. Gallego Burín and Gámir Sandoval, *Los moriscos del Reino de Granada*, 235–37. This ordinance was repeated in the Synod of Guadix (Pérez de Ayala, *Sínodo de la Diócesis de Guadix*, fol. 61r).

6. Pérez de Ayala, *Sínodo de la Diócesis de Guadix y de Baza*, fols. 60v, 91r.

7. Manuel Danvila y Collado, *La expulsión de los moriscos españoles* (Madrid: Librería de Fernando Fé, 1889), 171; Boronat y Barrachina, *Los moriscos españoles y su expulsión,* 1:538; Lea, *Moriscos of Spain,* 162.

8. Pérez de Ayala, *Sínodo de la Diócesis de Guadix,* fol. 60r.

9. Gallego Burín and Gámir Sandoval, *Los moriscos del Reino de Granada,* 183.

10. *El Fuero de Teruel,* 225–26.

11. Pérez de Ayala, *Sínodo de la Diócesis de Guadix,* fol. 60v.

12. Gallego Burín and Gámir Sandoval, *Los moriscos del Reino de Granada,* 202.

13. Pérez de Ayala, *Sínodo de la Diócesis de Guadix,* fol. 61r.

14. Núñez Muley, *Memorandum,* Barletta trans., 82, 84; Carrasco Manchado, *De la convivencia a la exclusión,* 388–89.

15. Núñez Muley, *Memorandum,* Barletta trans., 82.

16. Núñez Muley, *Memorandum,* Barletta trans., 82–83.

17. Caroline Fournier, "Bains publics et mosquées dans les villes d'al-Andalus," in *I Congreso internacional: Escenarios urbanos de al-Andalus y el Occidente musulmán; Vélez-Málaga, 16–18 de junio de 2010,* ed. Virgilio Martínez Enamorado (Málaga: Iniciativa Urbana de "Toda la Villa," 2011), 337–54.

18. Núñez Muley, *Memorandum,* Barletta trans., 83.

19. Núñez Muley, *Memorandum,* Barletta trans., 84.

20. For example, in 1501 it was reported that men were entering the bathhouses in Granada while women were bathing (Gallego Burín and Gámir Sandoval, *Los moriscos del Reino de Granada,* 170).

21. Núñez Muley, *Memorandum,* Barletta trans., 84.

22. Núñez Muley, *Memorandum,* Barletta trans., 87.

23. Núñez Muley, *Memorandum,* Barletta trans., 84.

24. Núñez Muley, *Memorandum,* Barletta trans., 85.

25. Núñez Muley, *Memorandum,* Barletta trans., 85.

26. Núñez Muley, *Memorandum,* Barletta trans., 84.

27. Núñez Muley, *Memorandum,* Barletta trans., 85.

28. Núñez Muley, *Memorandum,* Barletta trans., 85.

29. *Primera crónica general de España,* ed. Ramón Menéndez Pidal (Madrid: Editorial Gredos, 1955), 2:555.

30. Lucas of Tuy, *Lucae Tudensis Chronicon Mundi,* ed. Emma Falque, Corpus Christianorum. Continuatio Mediaevalis, 74 (Turnhout: Brepols, 2003), 306–7.

31. Rodrigo Sánchez de Arévalo, *Compendiosa historia hispánica* (Rome: Udalricus Gallus, 1470), part 3, chap. 29, fol. 47v (image 148 of the unpaginated Biblioteca Nacional de España exemplar, http://bibliotecadigitalhispanica.bne.es:80/webclient/DeliveryManager ?pid=1604755&custom_att_2=simple_viewer); Alonso López de Corella, *Secretos de philosophia y astrologia y medicina y delas quatro mathematicas sciencias* (Zaragoza: En la casas de George Coci a costas de Pedro Bernuz, 1547), fols. 58v–59r; Luis de Escobar, *Las quatrocientas respuestas a otras tantas preguntas* (Valladolid: Por Francisco de Cordoua y a

costa de Francisco de Alfaro, 1552), part 2, fol. 101v; Reem F. Iversen, "El discurso de la higiene: Miguel de Luna y la medicina del siglo XVI," in *Morada de la palabra: Homenaje a Luce y Mercedes López-Baralt*, ed. William Mejías López (San Juan: Universidad de Puerto Rico, 2002), 1:907; Sebastián de Covarrubias Orozco, *Tesoro de la lengua castellana o española, según la impresión de 1611, con las adiciones de Benito Remigio Noydens publicadas en 1674*, ed. Martín de Riquer (Barcelona: Horta, 1943), 190–91. See also María José Ruiz Somavilla, "Los valores sociales, religiosos y morales en las respuestas higiénicas de los siglos XVI y XVII: El problema de los baños," *Dynamis: Acta Hispanica ad Medicinae Scientiarumque Historiam Illustrandum* 12 (1992): 161–62.

32. Luis Lobera de Ávila, *Vergel de Sanidad que por otro nombre se llamava Banquete de nobles cavalleros, y orden de bivir* (Alcalá de Henares: Joan de Brocar, 1542); repr. as *Banquete de nobles caballeros* (Madrid: Reimpresiones Bibliográficas, 1952), 35; Alonso Díez Daza, *Libro de los provechos y dannos que provienen con la sola bevida del agua* (Seville: Alonso de la Barrera, 1576), fol. 89v.

33. Nothing on bathhouses is noted in Alfonso's surviving documents from after the Battle of Uclés; see Andrés Gambra, *Alfonso VI: Cancillería, curia, e imperio* (León: Centro de Estudios e Investigación "San Isidro," 1997), 98–100.

34. Bathing in early medieval Spain probably had origins in Roman and late antique practice. This is not documented, but there were likely parallels with the situation described for Italy and southern France by Paolo Squatriti, *Water and Society in Early Medieval Italy, AD 400–1000* (Cambridge: Cambridge University Press, 1998), 44–65.

35. Aníbal Ruiz Moreno, "Los baños públicos en los fueros municipales españoles," *Cuadernos de Historia de España* 3 (1945): 152.

36. Alfonso Andrés, "Monasterio de San Juan de Burgos," *Boletín de la Real Academia de la Historia* 71 (1917): 119–20; Leopoldo Torres Balbás, *Algunos aspectos del mudejarismo urbano medieval* (Madrid: Imprenta y Editorial Maestre, 1954), 46.

37. Julio González, *Repoblación de Castilla la Nueva* (Madrid: Universidad Complutense, 1975), 2:264.

38. On stylistic changes, see Ana María Echaniz Quintana et al., "Aguas mudéjares: Aguas para la salud," in *Actas del XI simposio internacional de mudejarismo, Teruel, 18–20 de septiembre de 2008* (Teruel: Centro de Estudios Mudéjares, 2009), 329–30.

39. Patrice Cressier, "Prendre les eaux en al-Andalus: Pratique et fréquentation de la Hamma," *Médiévales* 43 (2002): 41–54; Samuela Pagani, "Un paradiso in terra: Il Ḥammām e l'economia della salvezza," in *Hammam: Le terme nell'Islam; Convegno internazionale di studi, Santa Cesarea Terme, 1516 maggio 2008*, ed. Rosita D'Amora and Samuela Pagani (Florence: Leo S. Olschki, 2011), 133–58.

40. There are many studies of Andalusi bathhouse architecture. These include Mikel de Epalza, *Baños árabes en el pais Valenciano* (Valencia: Generalitat Valenciana, Conselleria de Cultura, Educació i Ciència, 1989); Leopoldo Torres Balbás, "La judería de Zaragoza y su baño," *Al-Andalus* 21 (1956): 172–90; Leopoldo Torres Balbás, "El baño musulmán de Murcia y su conservación," *Al-Andalus* 17 (1952): 433–38; Catherine B.

Asher, "The Public Baths of Medieval Spain: An Architectural Study," in *The Medieval Mediterranean: Cross-Cultural Contacts*, ed. Marilyn J. Chiat and Kathryn L. Reyerson (St. Cloud, MN: North Star Press, 1988), 25–34; André Bazzana, *Maisons d'al-Andalus: Habitat médiéval et structures du peuplement dans l'Espagne orientale* (Madrid: Casa de Velázquez, 1992), 257–59. See other notes elsewhere in this chapter for more architectural and archaeological references.

41. Henri Pérès, *La poésie andalouse en arabe classique au XI siècle* (Paris: Adrien-Maisonneuve, 1953), 339; María Jesús Rubiera, *La arquitectura en la literatura árabe* (Madrid: Hiperión, 1988), 102–3.

42. On bathhouses in the region of Granada, see Carlos Vílchez Vílchez, *Baños árabes* (Granada: Disputación de Granada, 2001); María Elena Díez Jorge, "Purificación y placer: El agua y las mil y una noches en los Baños de Comares," *Cuadernos de la Alhambra* 40 (2004): 123–50; Cecilio Gómez González and Carlos Vílchez Vílchez, "Baños árabes inéditos de la época almohade (siglos XII–XIII) de la judería de Granada," *Actas del I Congreso de arqueologia medieval española* 3 (1986): 545–67; Mariano Martín García, "Baños árabes de la provincia de Granada: El Baño de la Zubia," *Andalucía Islámica* 4–5 (1986): 307–15; Rafael Manzano Martos, "El baño termal de Alhama de Granada," *Al-Andalus* 32 (1958): 408–17.

43. Al-Idrīsī, *Description de l'Afrique et de l'Espagne par Edrîsî*, ed. and trans. R. Dozy and M. J. de Goeje (Leiden: Brill, 1866); on Córdoba, see p. 208 (Arabic), p. 257 (French); Almería, 197/240; Málaga, 204/250; Tarifa, 176/212; Adra, 198/242; Quesada, 203/249. Seville is listed as having "a great many baths" (178/215), as did Elche (193/234), while both Lisbon (184/223) and Pechina (200/245) had hot springs. Also on bathhouses in Málaga, see María Dolores Aguilar García, "Mezquitas y baños de Málaga musulmana," in *Simposio internacional sobre la ciudad islámica* (Zaragoza: Institución Fernando el Católico, 1991), 396–98.

44. Al-Shaqundī, *Elogio del Islam español (Risāla fī faḍl al-Andalus)*, trans. Emilio García Gómez (Madrid: Estanislao Maestre, 1934), 108.

45. Al-Himyarī, *La péninsule ibérique au moyen-age d'après le Kitāb ar-rawd al-miʿtār*, ed. and trans. Évariste Lévi-Provençal (Leiden: Brill, 1938), 19 (Arabic), 25 (French).

46. Ibn ʿIdhārī al-Marrākushī, *Kitāb al-bayān al-mughrib*, ed. G. S. Colin and E. Lévi-Provençal (Leiden: Brill, 1951), 2:232; al-Maqqarī, *Analectes sur l'histoire et la littérature des Arabes d'Espagne*, 1:355. See also Lévi-Provençal, *Histoire de l'Espagne musulmane*, 3:430.

47. Vílchez Vílchez, *Baños árabes*, 26–74.

48. Al-Himyarī, *La péninsule ibérique*, 70–71 (Arabic), 88 (French). One of the state-run establishments was called the "Bath of the Bull" (Ḥammām al-Thawr), because it contained the marble image of a bull, a feature that suggests the continued use of a former Roman bathhouse.

49. *Documents arabes inédits*, 31.

50. Federico Corriente Córdoba, *Relatos píos y profanos del manuscrito aljamiado de Urrea de Jalón* (Zaragoza: Institución Fernando el Católico, 1990), 213–20; Z. David Zuwiyya, "Arab Culture and Morisco Heritage in an Aljamiado Legend: Al-hadit del baño de Zaryeb," *Romance Quarterly* 48 (2001): 32–46; Miguel Asín Palacios, "El original árabe de la novela aljamiada 'El baño de Zarieb,'" in *Homenaje ofrecido a Menéndez Pidal* (Madrid: Librería y Casa Editorial Hernando, 1925), 1:377–88.

51. Cressier, "Prendre les eaux en al-Andalus," 49; Lévi-Provençal, *Histoire de l'Espagne musulmane*, 3:430.

52. Giorgio Levi Della Vida, "Il regno di Granata nel 1465–66 nei ricordi di un viaggiatore egiziano," *Al-Andalus* 1 (1933): 320.

53. Ibn 'Abdūn, in *Documents arabes inédits*, 49. Al-Wansharīsī, *Al-Mi'yar al-mu'rib wa al-jami' al-mughrib* (Rabat: Wizarat al-Awqaf, 1981), 9:20–21. See also Vincent Lagardère, *Histoire et société en Occident musulman au Moyen Âge: Analyse du "Mi'yār" d'al-Wanšarīsī* (Madrid: Consejo Superior de Investigaciones Científicas, 1995), 362, no. 316.

54. Images of medieval Muslims bathing are rare, and there are none from al-Andalus. Frescoes on the walls of the early eighth-century bathhouse at Qusayr 'Amra in Jordan show nude female bathers, presumably continuing Byzantine traditions of either decoration or actual bathing. See Helen C. Evans and Brandie Ratliff, eds. *Byzantium and Islam, Age of Transition, 7th–9th Century* (New York: Metropolitan Museum of Art, 2012), 202. Later medieval Persian manuscript illustrations also depict scenes set in bathhouses, but men are always shown with towels wrapped around their waists or wearing loose breeches. See, for example, fifteenth and sixteenth century images of Hārūn al-Rashīd in the bathhouse (see Harvard Art Museums/Arthur M. Sackler Museum, 2002.50.43; St. Johns College Cambridge, MS Browne 1434; see also the British Library image reproduced in Figure 8).

55. Ibn 'Abdūn, in *Documents arabes inédits*, 48.

56. Al-Saqatī, *Un manuel hispanique de hisba*, ed. G. S. Colin and Évariste Lévi-Provençal (Paris: Ernest Leroux, 1931), 26.

57. Rubiera, *La arquitectura en la literatura árabe*, 103.

58. Pérès, *La poésie andalouse*, 340–43.

59. This inscription was cited in the eighteenth century by Juan Velázquez de Echeverría, *Paseos por Granada y sus contornos* (Granada: N. Moreno, 1764), 372. See also Rafael Contreras, *Estudio descriptivo de los monumentos árabes de Granada, Sevilla y Córdoba, ó sea, la Alhambra, el Alcázar y la Gran mezquita de occidente* (Madrid: Ricardo Fé, 1885), 347–48; Manuel Espinar Moreno, "Apuntes de arqueología y cultura material Granadina: El baño del Albaicín (siglos XIII–XVI)," *Cuadernos de arte de la Universidad de Granada* 21 (1990): 75–76.

60. Ibn al-Khatīb, *Libro del cuidado de la salud durante las estaciones del año, o, "Libro de higiene,"* ed. and trans. María Concepción Vázquez de Benito (Salamanca: Universidad de Salamanca, 1984), 146–49.

61. Ibn 'Abdūn mentioned barbers and masseurs in bathhouses, adding that a Muslim should never be required to massage a Jewish or a Christian client (*Documents arabes inédits*,

48). The *aljamiado* story of the Baño de Zaryeb describes washing hair and using henna in the bathhouse (Corriente Córdoba, *Relatos píos y profanos*, 217). See also Marín, *Mujeres en al-Andalus*, 233–35; and Caroline Fournier, "Les bains publics d'al-Andalus, espaces de 'convivialité'? (IXᵉ–XVᵉ siècles)," in *La convivencia en las ciudades medievales*, ed. Beatriz Arízaga Bolumburu and Jesús Ángel Solórzano Telechea (Logroño: Instituto de Estudios Riojanos, 2008), 328–30. These bathhouse services were not unique to al-Andalus. Usama ibn Munqidh famously described shaving and hair washing in bathhouses in twelfth-century Syria (*The Book of Contemplation: Islam and the Crusades*, trans. Paul M. Cobb [London: Penguin, 2008], 148–50).

62. Al-Saqaṭī, *Un manuel hispanique de hisba*, 57, 67.

63. On bathhouses in Toledo, see Jean Passini, Juan Manuel Rojas Rodríguez-Malo, and J. Ramón Villa, "Los baños extramuros de San Sebastián," *Al-Qanṭara* 18 (1997): 187–219; Jean Passini, "El baño de Bāb al-Mardūm (o de la Cruz): Localización e identificación," *Al-Qanṭara* 31 (2010): 211–23.

64. The best study of bathhouses in medieval Spanish legal texts is James F. Powers, "Municipal Baths and Social Interaction in Thirteenth-Century Spain," *American Historical Review* 84 (1979): 659–60.

65. *Colección diplomática de Alfonso I de Aragón y Pamplona, 1104–1134*, ed. José Ángel Lema Pueyo (San Sebastián: Editorial Eusko Ikaskuntza, 1990), 125. The date on this document (September 1117) is problematic, since this is two years before Alfonso's conquest of Tudela in 1119. Lema Pueyo notes the date as "muy manipulado." For Pamplona, see *Fueros de Navarra*, ed. José María Lacarra and Ángel J. Martín Duque (Pamplona: Institución Príncipe de Viana, 1975), 2:402–3.

66. Robert I. Burns, "Baths and Caravanserais in Crusader Valencia," *Speculum* 46 (1971): 456. After the conquest of Játiva, Jaume gave a gift of bathhouse buildings to be used as houses or cellars; see Burns, *Diplomatarium*, 2:81, no. 93a.

67. We may infer that Jaume I of Aragon was familiar with steam baths from his analogy of tossing and turning in bed while sweating "as if we were in a bath" in *The Book of Deeds of James I of Aragon: A Translation of the Medieval Catalan "Llibre dels Fets,"* trans. Damian J. Smith and Helena Buffery (Aldershot: Ashgate, 2003), 206.

68. Jesús Ernesto Martínez Ferrando, *Jaime II de Aragón: Su vida familiar* (Barcelona: Consejo Superior de Investigaciones Científicas, 1948), 2:139–40.

69. *Ordinaciones de la Casa Real de Aragón* (Zaragoza: Impr. y Lit. De M. Peiro, 1853), 288. The text notes that Pere bathed secretly (*bañese secretamente*), suggesting a very private event.

70. Leopoldo Torres Balbás, "El baño de doña Leonor de Guzmán en el palacio de Tordesillas," *Al-Andalus* 24 (1959): 409–25; Torres Balbás, *Algunos aspectos del mudejarismo urbano medieval*, 59, 62.

71. Martínez Ferrando, *Jaime II de Aragón*, 2:178.

72. Antònia Carré and Lluís Cifuentes, "Práctica social, saber médico y reflejo literario de la cultura del baño en el contexto catalan medieval," *Anuario de Estudios Medievales* 39 (2009): 206–9.

73. The recommendations about bathing in Ibn al-Khaṭīb's fourteenth-century treatise *Kitāb al-wuṣūl li ḥifẓ al-ṣiḥḥa fī al-fuṣūl* (*Libro del cuidado de la salud durante las estaciones del año, o, "Libro de higiene"*) have already been noted above (n. 60). Ibn al-Khaṭīb (d. 1374) served as physician at the Naṣrid court in Granada. On his medical writings, see María Concepción Vázquez de Benito, "La materia médica de Ibn al-Jaṭīb," *Boletín de la Asociación Española de Orientalistas* 15 (1979): 139–50.

74. Arnau de Vilanova, *Regimen sanitatis ad regem aragonum*, ed. Luis García-Ballester and Michael R. McVaugh, vol. 10.1 of *Arnaldi de Villanova Opera medica omnia* (Barcelona: Seminarium Historiae Scientiae Barchinone [C.S.I.C.], 1996), 428.

75. Juan de Aviñón, *Sevillana medicina que trata el modo conservativo y curativo de los que habitan en la muy insigne ciudad de Sevilla* (Seville: Imprenta de Enrique Rasco, 1885), 236–42.

76. Manuscripts of this text, produced at the court of Naples, are held in the Biblioteca Universitaria de Valencia (MS 860), in the Biblioteca Ambrosiana in Milan (MS J.6 inf., SP II bis), and in the Bibliothèque Nationale in Paris (MS Lat. 8161). On the latter two, see Raymond J. Clark, "Peter of Eboli, 'De Balneis Puteolanis': Manuscripts from the Aragonese Scriptorium in Naples," *Traditio* 45 (1989–90): 380–89. C. M. Kauffmann, *The Baths of Pozzuoli* (Oxford: Bruno Cassirer, 1959), provides an overview of the poem and its illuminations in a wide variety of manuscripts.

77. Josep Puig i Cadafalch, "Els banys de Girone i la influencia moresca a Catalunya," *Anuari* 5 (1913): 687–728; Josep Puig i Cadafalch, *Les bains de Girone, guide descriptive* (Barcelona: Imprenta de la Casa de Caritat, 1936); Lluís Bayona i Prats, "La rehabilitació en els monuments: El cas dels Banys Àrabs," *Revista de Girona* 139 (1990): 181–85; César Martinell, "Los baños medievales en el Levante español," *Cuadernos de arquitectura* 2 (1944): 4–19.

78. Mónica Ann Walker Vadillo, *Bathsheba in Late Medieval French Manuscript Illumination: Innocent Object of Desire or Agent of Sin?* (Lewiston, NY: Edwin Mellen Press, 2008).

79. Mónica Ann Walker Vadillo, "Emotional Responses to David Watching Bathsheba Bathing in Late Medieval French Manuscript Illumination," *Annual of Medieval Studies at the Central European University* 13 (2007): 97–109.

80. *The Pamplona Bibles: A Facsimile Compiled from Two Picture Bibles with Martyrologies Commissioned by King Sancho el Fuerte of Navarra (1194–1234); Amiens Manuscript Latin 108 and Harburg MS. 1, 2, Lat. 4°, 15*, ed. François Bucher (New Haven, CT: Yale University Press, 1971); the images under discussion here are in vol. 2, plates 225 and 226.

81. David Alegría Suescun, "Baños urbanos del patrimonio real en Navarra (siglos XII–XIV)," in *Usos sociales del agua en las ciudades hispánicas a fines de la edad media*, ed. María Isabel del Val Valdivieso (Valladolid: Universidad de Valladolid, 2002), 315–65; David Alegría Suescun, *Agua y ciudad: Aprovachamientos hidráulicos urbanos en Navarra (siglos XII–XIV)* (Pamplona: Gobierno de Navarra, 2004).

82. This differs from French images, which sometimes depicted a naked Bathsheba in the thirteenth century (for example, in the St. Louis Psalter, Bibliothèque Nationale de France, MS Lat. 10525, fol. 85v) and normally displayed her fully unclothed in later manuscripts, especially in Books of Hours (for example, Morgan Library MSS M. 12, fol. 41r; M. 52, fol. 329r; M. 61, fol. 70r; M. 85, fol. 72v; and M. 261, fol. 61v). See Figure 14 in this volume.

83. *Lapidario,* Biblioteca de El Escorial, MS H.l.15, fol. 69r.

84. Magdalena Santo Tomás Pérez, *Los baños públicos en Valladolid: Agua, higiene y salud en el Valladolid medieval* (Valladolid: Ayuntamiento de Valladolid, 2002), 87.

85. *Lapidario,* fol. 69r; also Alfonso el Sabio, *Lapidario and Libro de las formas & ymagenes,* ed. Roderic C. Diman and Lynn W. Winget (Madison, WI: Hispanic Seminary of Medieval Studies, 1980), 88–89. As noted earlier, pumice was used in Muslim bathhouses.

86. *Lapidario,* fol. 49v; Alfonso el Sabio, *Lapidario and Libro de las formas,* 64.

87. Juan Manuel, "El Conde Lucanor," in *Obras completas,* ed. José Manuel Blecua (Madrid: editorial Gredos, 1982–83), 2:343–47 ex. 43, "De lo que le contescio al Bien y al Mal, et al cuerdo con el loco."

88. *Ordenanzas para el buen régimen y gobierno de . . . la ciudad de Toledo* (Toledo: Imprenta de José de Cea, 1858), title 14, chap. 18, p. 20; *Ordenanças de Sevilla* (Seville: Juan Varela, 1527), chap. 18, fols. 143v–144r, and chap. 34, fol. 145v (cited in Torres Balbás, *Algunos aspectos del mudejarismo urbano medieval,* 62).

89. Juan Manuel, "Conde Lucanor," in *Obras completas,* 2:495–503, ex. 51, "Lo que contesçio a un rey christiano que era muy poderoso et muy soberbioso." This section does not appear in all manuscripts; see the introductory notes in *Obras completas,* 2:9–18.

90. Martínez de Toledo, *Archipreste de Talavera,* 136–37; Martínez de Toledo, *Little Sermons on Sin,* 117; *"The Mirror" of Jaume Roig: An Edition and an English Translation of MS. Vat. Lat. 4806,* ed. and trans. María Celeste Delgado-Librero (Tempe: Arizona Center for Medieval and Renaissance Studies, 2010), 296–97; "Refundición de la Crónica de 1344," ed. Ramón Menéndez Pidal in *Rodrigo, el ultimo godo* (Madrid: Espasa-Calpe, 1942–56), 1:148–49.

91. Alfonso el Sabio, *Cantigas de Santa María,* no. 212; trans. in *Songs of Holy Mary of Alfonso X, the Wise: A Translation of the "Cantigas de Santa Maria,"* by Kathleen Kulp-Hill (Tempe: Arizona Center for Medieval and Renaissance Studies, 2000), 254.

92. *Forum Conche, Fuero of Cuenca: The Latin Text of the Municipal Charter and Laws of the City of Cuenca, Spain,* ed. George H. Allen (Cincinnati: University Studies published by the University of Cincinnati, 1909–10), 28; *The Code of Cuenca: Municipal Law on the Twelfth-Century Castilian Frontier,* trans. James F. Powers (Philadelphia: University of Pennsylvania Press, 2000), chap. 2.32, pp. 40–41. On concerns about bathhouse theft, see also Powers, "Municipal Baths and Social Interaction," 659–60.

93. Twelfth and thirteenth-century *fueros* and urban codes from northern Spanish cities often contain clauses relating to bathhouses, including those from Albarracín,

Brihuega, Cáceres, Calatayud, Coria, Cuenca, Iznatoraf, Pamplona, Plasencia, Sepúlveda, Soria, Teruel, Tortosa, Tudela, Usagre, Valencia, and Zorita. Many of these have already been discussed by James Powers, Aníbal Ruiz Moreno, Leopoldo Torres Balbás, Magdalena Santo Tomás Pérez, and others, and do not need further discussion here.

94. These concerns crop up in canon law as well as secular codes; see James A. Brundage, *Law, Sex, and Christian Society in Medieval Europe* (Chicago: University of Chicago Press, 1990), 392.

95. Josefina Mutgé Vives, "La aljama sarracena en la Lleida cristiana: Noticias y conclusiones," *VII Simposio Internacional de Mudejarismo, Teruel 19–21 de septiembre de 1996* (Teruel: Centro de Estudios Mudéjares, 1999), 106; *Las Siete Partidas* 7.24.7, ed. Burns, 5:1436.

96. Statutes enacted under Juan II in 1443 ordered that Christians should not bathe with either Jews or Muslims (Carrasco Manchado, *De la convivencia a la exclusión*, 189).

97. James Powers has identified different patterns in *fueros* from Leonese Extremadura, Aragon, Valencia, Tortosa, and the family of Cuenca-influenced charters; see James F. Powers "Baths," in *Medieval Iberia: An Encyclopedia*, ed. Michael Gerli (New York: Routledge, 2003), 152–53; also Powers, "Municipal Baths and Social Interaction," 661, 664.

98. *The Code of Cuenca*, 2.32, pp. 40–41.

99. *El Fuero de Teruel*, 225–26.

100. *Fuero de Usagre (siglo XIII) anotado con las variantes del de Cáceres*, ed. Rafael de Ureña y Smenjaud and Adolfo Bonilla y San Martín (Madrid: Hijos de Reus, 1907), 48, no. 127; *Fuero de Plasencia*, ed. Jesús Majada Neila (Salamanca: Librería Cervantes, 1986), 105, no. 438.

101. Heath Dillard, *Daughters of the Reconquest: Women in Castilian Town Society, 1100–1300* (Cambridge: Cambridge University Press, 1984), 152; H. Salvador Martínez, *La Convivencia en la España del siglo XIII: Perspectivas alfonsíes* (Madrid: Ediciones Polifemo, 2006), 326.

102. In Marseille, a statute from 1253 had already clarified this point, ruling that both Jewish men and women (*judeum vel judeam*) could only use the bathhouse on Fridays. The same was likely to have been true in the Crown of Aragon. See Régine Pernoud, ed., *Les statuts municipaux de Marseille* (Paris: Librairie Auguste Picard, 1949), 171.

103. David Romano, "Los judíos en los baños de Tortosa (siglos XIII–XIV)," *Sefarad* 40 (1980): 60–61, 63–64.

104. Jean Régné, *History of the Jews in Aragon: Regesta and Documents, 1213–1327* (Jerusalem: Magnes Press, 1978), 569, no. 3034.

105. *Costums de Tortosa*, 1.1.15; Romano, "Los judíos en los baños de Tortosa," 62; see also Ruiz Moreno, "Los baños públicos," 153.

106. *Código de las costumbres escritas de Tortosa a doble texto*, ed. Ramon Foguet et al. (Tortosa: Impr. Querol, 1912), book 1, rubric 1, para. 15, p. 34, and book 9, rubric 13, para. 5, p. 430; also Ruiz-Moreno, "Los baños públicos," 156.

107. *Repartimiento de Sevilla*, ed. Julio González (Madrid: Consejo Superior de Investigaciones Científicas, 1951), 1:524. This is a later law, from the sixteenth century, but claiming to reflect earlier practice.

108. On royal bathhouses in Lisbon, see Lopes de Barros, "Body, Baths and Cloth," 4.

109. Fernández y González, *Estado social y político de los mudéjares de Castilla*, 346–47; Manuel González Jiménez, ed., *Diplomatario Andaluz de Alfonso X* (Seville: El Monte, Caja de Huelva y Sevilla, 1991), 158–60; Manuel González Jiménez, "Los mudéjares andaluces (ss. XIII–XV)," in *Actas del V coloquio internacional de historia medieval de Andalucia: Andalucia entre Oriente y Occidente (1236–1492)*, ed. Emilio Cabrera (Córdoba: Excma. Diputación Provincial de Córdoba, 1988), 541.

110. In 1266, revenues from the Jewish bathhouses in Zaragoza went toward construction of a new bridge over the Ebro (Régné, *History of the Jews in Aragon*, 62, no. 348). Bathhouse revenues in Tortosa were to be used to maintain the walls of the city (*Costums de Tortosa*, 1.1.15).

111. Grant issued by Ramiro II in 1135–36, in *El Libro de la Cadena del Concejo de Jaca*, ed. Dámaso Sangorrín y Diest-Garcés (Zaragoza: Imprenta de F. Martínez, 1920), 138; cited in Torres Balbás, *Algunos aspectos del mudejarismo urbano medieval*, 46–47. Grant issued by Alfonso VII in 1144 and reconfirmed by Fernando II, in Julio González, "Repoblación de la 'Extremadura' leonesa," *Hispania* 3, no. 11 (1943): 222.

112. Burns, "Baths and Caravanserais," 443–58; Robert I. Burns, *Medieval Colonialism: Postcrusade Exploitation of Islamic Valencia* (Princeton, NJ: Princeton University Press, 1975), 57–63.

113. Danvila y Collado, *La expulsión de los moriscos españoles*, 347–51; Fernández y González, *Estado social y político de los mudéjares de Castilla*, 324–27. There may have been other bathhouses in the city, but no longer in use, because seven years later, in 1258, Jaume gave a bathhouse (*balnea*) in Játiva "in perpetuity, for use as housing" to Sanç Pere de Ribabellosa; see Burns, *Diplomatarium*, 2:81.

114. *Ordenanzas para el buen régimen y gobierno de . . . la ciudad de Toledo*, title 14, chap. 18, p. 20; *Ordenanças de Sevilla*, chap. 18, fol. 143v. See also Leopoldo Torres Balbás, "Crónica Arqueológica de la España Musulmana: Los baños públicos en los fueros municipales españoles," *Al-Andalus* 11:2 (1946): 443; and *El registro del Merino de Zaragoza el Caballero Don Gil Tarín, 1291–1312* (Zaragoza: Imprenta del Hospicio Provincial, 1889), 5. *Trehuderas* (Aragonese *treudo/treudero*), from Latin *tributum*, denotes revenue-producing property.

115. Burns, *Diplomatarium*, 2:41, 48, 60.

116. Burns, "Baths and Caravanserais," 455, errs in thinking this bathhouse was also in Alcira; cf. Régné, who, in *History of the Jews in Aragon*, 95, no. 556, correctly cites ACA reg. 19, fol. 19.

117. *Documentos del Archivo general de la villa de Madrid*, ed. Ángel Pérez Chozas, Agustín Millares Carlo, and Eulogio Varela Hervías (Madrid: Artes gráficas municipales,

1932), 325–33. This bathhouse was located in the parish of San Pedro, thus not in a *morería*.

118. Danvila y Collado, *La expulsión de los moriscos españoles*, 347–51. Other baths in the city had been earlier given to Christians; the *repartimiento* of Valencia noted a *balnea* in Játiva given to a Christian cleric in 1242 (Leopoldo Torres Balbás, "El baño de Torres Torres y otros levantinos," *Al-Andalus* 17 [1952]: 185).

119. *Catálogo de la documentación relativa al antiguo reino de Valencia*, ed. Jesús Ernesto Martínez Ferrando (Madrid: Cuerpo Facultativo de Archiveros, Bibliotecarios y Arqueólogos, 1934), 2:46–47, no. 173; Burns, "Baths and Caravanserais," 455–56.

120. Manuel Vicente Febrer Romaguera, ed., *Cartas pueblas de las morerías valencianas y documentación complementaria* (Zaragoza: Anubar, 1991), 1:108.

121. *Catálogo de la documentación relativa al antiguo reino de Valencia*, 2:392, no. 1835; Burns, *Medieval Colonialism*, 62–63.

122. Roca Traver, "Un siglo de vida mudéjar," 206–8; and Burns, *Medieval Colonialism*, 63.

123. *Fuero de Plasencia*, 24; *Fori antiqui Valentiae*, ed. Manuel Dualde Serrano (Madrid: Consejo Superior de Investigaciones Científicas, 1950–67), 80.

124. Villanueva, *Viage literario*, 18:294–97. Torres Balbás reports that this bathhouse remained almost intact until its destruction in 1834 (*Algunos aspectos del mudejarismo urbano medieval*, 53).

125. Burns, *Diplomatarium*, 3:489 gives a slightly different translation; see also Robert I. Burns, "Women in Crusader Valencia: A Five-Year Core Sample, 1265–1270," *Medieval Encounters* 12 (2006): 37–47.

126. Francisco de Bofarull y Sans, "Jaime y los Judíos," in *Congrés d'historia de la corona d'Aragó dedicat al rey en Jaume I y a la seua época* (Barcelona: Stampa d'en Francisco Altés, 1913), 907–8.

127. Régné, *History of the Jews in Aragon*, 106, no. 623.

128. Passini, "El baño de Bāb al-Mardūm (o de la Cruz)," 211.

129. Julio González, *Reinado y diplomas de Fernando III* (Córdoba: Publicaciones del monte de Piedad y Caja de Ahorros de Córdoba, 1986), 214–15, no. 671.

130. *Repartimiento de Sevilla*, 1:522–24; 2:17.

131. Juan Torres Fontes, "Los baños de la reina," *Murgetana* 40 (1975): 64.

132. Burns, *Medieval Colonialism*, 62; *Catálogo de la documentación relativa al antiguo reino de Valencia*, 2:136, no. 602.

133. In 1268, Guillem de Plana and his wife Francesca owned baths in Valencia City (Burns, *Diplomatarium*, 3:311); in 1296, the wife of Pedro Fernández de Valdenebro owned a bathhouse in Seville (*Repartimiento de Sevilla*, 1:523); in 1338, Teresa, the widow of the lord of Rebollet, received a pension of four hundred solidi from baths in the Muslim quarter of Valencia City, and this grant was reconfirmed in 1346 (Roca Traver, "Un siglo de vida mudéjar," 206–7; Burns, *Medieval Colonialism*, 63); in 1391, Gonzalo Martínez and his wife Olalla held a bathhouse in Murcia (Torres Fontes, "Los baños de la reina," 67–73).

134. María Barceló Crespí and Guillem Rosselló Bordoy, *La ciudad de Mallorca: La vida cotidiana en una ciudad mediterránea medieval* (Palma: Lleonard Muntaner, 2006), 428; *Documentos del Archivo general de la villa de Madrid*, 325–33.

135. Torres Balbás, *Algunos aspectos del mudejarismo urbano medieval*, 48.

136. Luciano Serrano, *El obispado de Burgos y Castilla primitiva desde el siglo V al XIII* (Madrid: Instituto de Valencia de San Juan, 1936), 147–48; Laura Burguete Ors and Josemi Lorenzo Arribas, "Limpieza y contaminación en la villa de Madrid durante la edad media: Casas de baño y tenerías," in *Agua y sistemas hidráulicos en la edad media hispana*, ed. Cristina Segura (Madrid: Asociación Cultural al-Mudayna, 2003), 99; González, *Repoblación de Castilla la Nueva*, 2:263; Gonzalo Viñuales Ferreiro, "Aproximación al estudio de la comunidad mudéjar de Guadalajara en la Edad Media," in *Actas: X simposio internacional de mudejarismo, Teruel 14–15–16 septiembre 2005* (Teruel: Centro de Estudios Mudéjares, 2007), 507; Martinell, "Los baños medievales en el Levante español," 10; González, "Repoblación de la 'Extremadura' leonesa," 222; Enrique Claudio Girbal, *Estudio histórico-artístico de los llamados baños árabes de Gerona* (Girona: Paciano Torres, 1888), 12.

137. *Repartimiento de Sevilla*, 1:522.

138. Magdalena Santo Tomás Pérez, "El agua en la documentación eclesiástica," in *El agua en las ciudades castellanas durante la edad media*, ed. María Isabel del Val Valdivieso (Valladolid: Universidad de Valladolid, 1998), 28; Francisco de Bofarull y Sans, "Documentos para escribir una monografía de la Villa de Montblanch, leidos en la Real Academia de Buenas Letras de Barcelona," *Memorias de la Real Academia de Buenas Letras de Barcelona* 6 (1898): 437; Ricardo del Arco, "El monasterio de Santa Cristina de 'Summo Portu,'" *Linajes de Aragón* 5 (1914): 106.

139. González, *Repoblación de Castilla la Nueva*, 2:263; Robert I. Burns, *The Crusader Kingdom of Valencia: Reconstruction on a Thirteenth-Century Frontier* (Cambridge, MA: Harvard University Press, 1967), 1:188.

140. Bernard F. Reilly, *The Kingdom of León-Castilla Under King Alfonso VII, 1126–1157* (Philadelphia: University of Pennsylvania Press, 1998), 74; Serrano, *El obispado de Burgos*, 161–62.

141. The 1188 rules for the Hospitaller convent of Sixena, in Aragon, included regulations on bathing; see *Cartulaire général de l'ordre des Hospitaliers de S. Jean de Jérusalem (1100–1310)*, ed. Joseph Delaville Le Roulx (Paris: E. Leroux, 1906), 1:535, no. 859.

142. Santo Tomás Pérez, "El agua en la documentación eclesiástica," 28.

143. Manuel Vallecillo Ávila, "Los judíos de Castilla en la alta edad media," *Cuadernos de historia de España* 14 (1950): 57–58.

144. Ramón Menéndez Pidal, *Documentos lingüísticos de España* (Madrid: Consejo Superior de Investigaciones Científicas, 1919), 432–33. Torres Balbás indicates that this bathhouse had to be rebuilt a year after Alfonso's grant, and the contract documenting this work, written in Arabic, provides minute details about the structure (*Algunos aspectos del mudejarismo urbano medieval*, 52). In 1256, another grant (again written in Arabic) gave the convent rights to use a spring on a neighboring property to supply this

bathhouse with water. See Ángel González Palencia, *Los mozárabes de Toledo en los siglos XII y XIII* (Madrid: Instituto de Valencia de San Juan, 1928), 3:49, no. 780.

145. Alegría Suescun, "Baños urbanos del patrimonio real en Navarra," 342–44, 350–59; Alegría Suescun, *Agua y ciudad*, 367. The bathhouses in Tudela appear to have been more consistently profitable than those in Estella, which were turned over to the convent of Santo Domingo de Estella by Jeanne II of Navarre (and her French husband Philip IV) some time before her death in 1305; see Torres Balbás, *Algunos aspectos del mudejarismo urbano medieval*, 52.

146. Burns, "Baths and Caravanserais," 457–58; Burns, *Medieval Colonialism*, 63.

147. Cristina Sanz Gándara, "El arrendamiento de los baños de una villa bajomedieval en el sudeste peninsular: Elche," in *El món urbà a la Corona d'Aragó del 1137 als decrets de nova planta: XVII Congrés d'Història de la Corona d'Aragó* (Barcelona: Universitat de Barcelona, 2003), 2:375–76.

148. Sanz Gándara, "El arrendamiento de los baños," 376.

149. Alegría Suescun, "Baños urbanos del patrimonio real en Navarra," 361–62.

150. According to Torres Balbás, Christians in Tarazona used the bathhouse in the *morería* until as late as 1375 (*Algunos aspectos del mudejarismo urbano medieval*, 55).

151. Fernández y González, *Estado social y político de los mudéjares de Castilla*, 402.

152. Fernández y González, *Estado social y político de los mudéjares de Castilla*, 391.

153. Manuel Vicente Febrer Romaguera, ed., *Les aljames mudèjars valencianes en el segle XV* (Valencia: Universitat de València, 2006), 73–74, 99–100, 134–36, 254, 319.

154. Febrer Romaguera, ed., *Les aljames mudèjars valencianes*, 240–43.

155. Alegría Suescun, "Baños urbanos del patrimonio real en Navarra," 363–64.

156. Vílchez Vílchez, *Baños arabes*, 37–65.

157. Garrido Atienza, *Las capitulaciones para la entrega de Granada*, 242; Ladero Quesada, *Los mudéjares de Castilla en tiempos de Isabel I*, 168.

158. Levi Della Vida, "Il regno di Granata nel 1465–66," 320. This thermal bath continued to be popular into the later sixteenth century, when it was depicted (in 1564) by the Flemish engraver and traveler Joris Hoefenagel. See also Manzano Martos, "El baño termal de Alhama," 408–17.

159. *Los repartimientos de Vélez-Málaga: Primer repartimiento*, ed. María Teresa Martín Palma (Granada: Editorial Universidad de Granada, 2005), 94, 98, 112, 113, 116, 146, 174 (mention of the bathhouse of Fernando de Çafra), 169 (mention of the bathhouse of Françisco Enrríques).

160. The thermal sulfur baths in Baza remained free of charge at least into the early sixteenth century (Javier Castillo Fernández, "Nuevos datos en torno a la ubicación de la judería de Baza y de sus baños árabes," *Miscelánea de estudios árabes y hebraicos: Sección de hebreo* 47 [1998]: 61).

161. Manuel Espinar Moreno, "Rentas y tributos de los baños de las tierras de Guadix: El baño de La Peza (1494–1514)," in *Actas del VI coloquio internacional de historia medieval de Andalucía* (Málaga: Universidad de Málaga, 1991), 177–87.

162. Pedro María Rubio, *Tratado completo de las fuentes minerales de España* (Madrid: D. R. R. de Rivera, 1853), xlii–xliii.

163. Gallego Burín and Gámir Sandoval, *Los moriscos del Reino de Granada*, 170.

164. Ladero Quesada, *Los mudéjares de Castilla en tiempos de Isabel I*, 293, 276; Gallego Burín and Gámir Sandoval, *Los moriscos del Reino de Granada*, 161, 168; Grima Cervantes, *Almería y el reino de Granada*, 223; Harvey, *Muslims in Spain*, 47.

165. Data on rents, oversight, and water provision for a bathhouse in the Albaicín, especially in the years 1517–19, have been studied in detail in Espinar Moreno, "Apuntes de arqueología y cultura material Granadina," 71–85.

166. Inquisitorial interest in bathing extended to both Moriscos and conversos, with trials of converted Jews beginning earlier than those of converted Muslims. As an example of accusations of converso bathing, see Haim Beinart's *Records of the Trials of the Spanish Inquisition in Ciudad Real* (Jerusalem: Israel Academy of Sciences and Humanities, 1977), 2:151, 214, 224, 254, 263–64, 274–75, 278, 280, 284, 294, 307, 380, 383, 388–89, 392, 394, 427, 435–36, 473, 481, 485, 489, 506, 531.

167. Pérez de Colosía Rodríguez and Gil Sanjuán, "Los moriscos del Algarbe malagueño," 13–28. See also Pérez de Colosía Rodríguez, "La religiosidad en los moriscos malaguenos," 188, 192–94.

168. María Isabel Pérez de Colosía Rodriguez and Joaquín Gil Sanjuán, *Málaga y la Inquisición* (Málaga: Diputación Provincial de Málaga, 1982), 58. Christian writers often confused partial ablution (*al-wuḍū'*) with full body washing (*al-ghusl*); see Norman Daniel, *Islam and the West: The Making of an Image* (Oxford: Oneworld, 1993), 235–36.

169. Pérez de Colosía Rodriguez and Gil Sanjuán, *Málaga y la Inquisición*, 58. In 1568, a Morisco man from Málaga was also accused of bathing; see Gil Sanjuán, "La inquisición de Granada," 327, 334.

170. Mercedes García-Arenal, *Inquisición y moriscos: Los procesos del Tribunal de Cuenca* (Madrid: Siglo Veintiuno, 1978), 50–51.

171. Pérez de Ayala, *Sínodo de la Diócesis de Guadix*, fols. 60v and 91r; Danvila y Collado, *La expulsión de los moriscos españoles*, 171; Boronat y Barrachina, *Los moriscos españoles y su expulsión*, 1:538.

172. On illuminated images of Bathsheba, see above note 78ff. Graphic images from several manuscripts of the *De balneis Puteolanis* can be found in Kauffmann, *Baths of Pozzuoli*.

173. On the legend of La Cava, see Elizabeth Drayson, *The King and the Whore: King Roderick and La Cava* (New York: Palgrave Macmillan, 2007); and Patricia Grieve, *The Eve of Spain: Myths of Origins in the History of Christian, Muslim, and Jewish Conflict* (Baltimore: Johns Hopkins University Press, 2009).

174. "Refundición de la Crónica de 1344," in Menéndez Pidal, *Rodrigo, el ultimo godo*, 1:148–49.

175. Roig, *The Mirror of Jaume Roig*, 98–99, 335.

176. Roig, *The Mirror of Jaume Roig*, 296–97. Chickens, partridges, eggs, and sweet wine were all seen as sexual stimulants (Carré and Cifuentes, "Práctica social, saber médico y reflejo literario de la cultura del baño," 218).

177. Joanot Martorell and Martí Joan de Galba, *Tirant lo Blanc*, ed. Martí de Riquer (Barcelona: Editorial Seix Barral, 1970), 2:98 (chap. 231); *Tirant lo Blanc*, trans. David H. Rosenthal (New York: Schocken Books, 1983), 370–72.

178. Martínez de Toledo, *Archipreste de Talavera*, 136–37; Martínez de Toledo, *Little Sermons on Sin*, 116–18. The Catalan author Bernat Metge also directly translated a passage from Boccaccio's *Corbaccio*, on bathing and sexual pleasure, in *Lo somni* (1389–99), ed. Lola Badia (Barcelona: Quaderns Crema, 1999), 131; *The Dream of Bernat Metge*, trans. Richard Vernier (Aldershot: Ashgate, 2002), 49; cited in Carré and Cifuentes, "Práctica social, saber médico y reflejo literario de la cultura del baño," 216–17.

179. Corriente Córdoba, *Relatos píos y profanos*, 215–16. Significantly, the second half of the tale about the Baño de Zaryeb treats bathhouse dangers, moving on from describing the construction of this marvelous bathhouse, to telling of how a young woman who was seeking to visit it was accosted and raped when she arrived at the wrong building.

180. Francisco Delicado, *Retrato de la Lozana Andaluza*, ed. Jacques Joset and Folke Gernert (Barcelona: Círculo de Lectores, 2007), 35, 50, 55, 58, 308. Delicado uses the word *estufa* or *stufa* (steam bath), not *baño*, to clarify the public nature of these facilities. Later Golden Age writing also drew on the theme of bathhouse culture and female vanity, for instance in Augustín de Rojas Villandrando's *Viaje entretenido*, composed in 1602 (*El viaje entretenido de Agustín de Rojas*, ed. Manuel Cañete [Madrid: Rodriguez Serra, 1901], 1:75).

181. Cristóbal de Castillejo, *Obras*, ed. J. Domínguez Bordona (Madrid: Espasa-Calpe, 1957–60), 2:276–79; Álvaro Alonso, "Un poema erótico de Cristóbal de Castillejo: "Estando en los baños," in *Venus venerada: Tradiciones eróticas en la literatura española*, ed. José Ignacio Díez and Adrienne L. Martín (Madrid: Editorial Complutense, 2006), 39–56.

182. Christian fantasies about Muslim women in general, often involving exoticism and sexual domination, have become the subject of a growing literature; see for example Janet Levarie Smarr, "Non-Christian People and Spaces in the *Decameron*," in *Approaches to Teaching Boccaccio's "Decameron,"* ed. James H. McGregor (New York: Modern Language Association of America, 2000), 33–34; Louis Mirrer, *Women, Jews, and Muslims in the Texts of Reconquest Castile* (Ann Arbor: University of Michigan Press, 1996), 17–30; and articles by Olivia Remie Constable ("Muslim Women in Christian Spain") and Sahar Amer ("Muslim Women: Western Literature") in *Women and Gender in Medieval Europe: An Encyclopedia*, ed. Margaret Schaus (New York: Routledge, 2006), 593–95, along with the sources cited therein.

183. Alfonso Fernández de Palencia, *Guerra de Granada*, trans. D. A. Paz y Meliá (Madrid: Revista de Archivos, 1909; facsimile ed., Granada: Universidad de Granada, 1998), 30.

184. The Baño de Comares was repaired a number of times in the course of the sixteenth century and must have been considered something of a showpiece for visitors (Díez Jorge, "Purificación y placer," 135–36).

185. Navagero, *Opera omnia*, 290, 330, 340; "Viaje en España," in García Mercadal, *Viajes de extranjeros por España*, 854, 860.

186. Jerónimo Münzer, *Viaje por España y Portugal (1494–1495)* (Madrid: Ediciones Polifemo, 1991), 95; Adolf Hasenclever, "Die tagebuchartigen Aufzeichnungen des pfälzischen Hofarztes Dr. Johannes Lange über seine Reise nach Granada im Jahre 1526," *Archiv für Kulturgeschichte* 5 (1907): 422; see also Gallego Morell, "La corte de Carlos V," 275.

187. Monga, *Un mercante di Milano in Europa*, 130.

188. Pedro Guerra de Lorca, *Catecheses mystagogicae pro advenis ex secta Mahometana* (Madrid: Apud Petrum Madrigal, 1586), fols. 60v–61r.

189. Hurtado de Mendoza, *Guerra de Granada*, 1.7, fols. 12v–13r; trans. Shuttleworth, *War in Granada*, 1.9, 50.

190. Conrad Schellig, *In pustulas malas morbum quem malum de Francia vulgus appellat consilium* (Heidelberg: Friedrich Misch, ca. 1495–96, unpaginated); facsimile ed. in Karl Sudhoff and Charles Singer, *The Earliest Printed Literature on Syphilis: Being Ten Tractates from the Years 1495–1498* (Florence: R. Lier, 1925), 13.

191. Ruiz Somavilla, "Los valores sociales, religiosas y morales," 155–87, examines negative Spanish attitudes toward bathing in this period. On medical approaches to syphilis and its treatments, see Jon Arrizabalaga, John Henderson, and Roger French, *The Great Pox* (New Haven, CT: Yale University Press, 1997); also Roger French and Jon Arrizabalaga, "Coping with the French Disease: University Practitioners' Strategies and Tactics in the Transition from the Fifteenth to the Sixteenth Century," in *Medicine from the Black Death to the French Disease*, ed. Roger French et al. (Aldershot: Ashgate, 1998), 248–87.

192. Nicolò Massa, *Liber de morbo gallico* (Venice: In aedibus Francisci Bindoni, ac Maphei Pasini, 1527?), tract. 4, chap. 5 (unpaginated). The colophon to Massa's treatise claims publication in 1507, but it has been persuasively redated to 1527 by Peter Krivatsy, "Nicola Massa's *Liber de morbo gallico*—Dated 1507 but Printed in 1527," *Journal of the History of Medicine and Allied Sciences* 29 (1974): 230–33.

193. Lobera de Ávila, *Vergel de Sanidad*, chap. 10, "Del baño y de los provechos y daños que de usarle se siguen"; *Banquete de Nobles Caballeros* (1952 ed.), 35–36. He did acknowledge that "this matter of bathing is good for those who are used to it and in lands where it is the custom" (esto del baño es bueno a los que lo tienen en uso y en la tierra que está en costumbre); but while presumably this would apply to many contemporary inhabitants of Granada and other parts of Spain, they were not the people he had in mind when thinking of *senores de España*.

194. Francisco López de Villalobos, *El sumario de la medicina* (Salamanca: Antonio de Barreda, 1498); López de Villalobos, *El sumario de la medicina con un tratado de las pestiferas bubas*, ed. María Teresa Herrera (Salamanca: Ediciones del Instituto de Historia de

la Medicina Española, 1973), 174; López de Villalobos, *The Medical Works of Francisco Lopez de Villalobos, the Celebrated Court Physician of Spain*, trans. George Gaskoin (London: John Churchill and Sons, 1870), 126. Erasmus famously observed that steam baths were falling out of fashion in Brabant as a result of the "new pox" (syphilis), but public fear should not be exaggerated and its impact on bath closures was sporadic; see Arrizabalaga, Henderson, and French, *The Great Pox*, 36; and Guy Poirier, "A Contagion at the Source of Discourse on Sexualities: Syphilis During the French Renaissance," in *Imagining Contagion in Early Modern Europe*, ed. Claire L. Carlin (Basingstoke: Palgrave Macmillan, 2005), 158–61.

195. Serena Stefanizzi, "Sulla trasmissione di testi arabi nel 'De Balneis' (1553)," in D'Amora and Pagani, *Hammam: Le terme nell'Islam*, 223–36. There is no evidence to suggest, however, that therapeutic bathing comprised an important element in practical Morisco folk medicine of the later sixteenth or early seventeenth centuries—perhaps because facilities for such treatment were simply no longer available. It is not mentioned in an anonymous nonelite Arabic medical treatise of this period, MS Biblioteca Nacional de España, caja xviiii, 585, xxi; this newly discovered work is currently being edited by Ron Barkai, and a preliminary sense of its contents may be found in Alexander Borg, "The Language of Folk Medicine—a Philological Note on the Pathology of Syphilis and Leprosy in a Morisco Arabic MS," *Korot* 21 (2011–12): 293–313 [the editor thanks Dr. Barkai for providing a further description of this manuscript].

196. Mercedes García-Arenal and Fernando Rodríguez Mediano, *Un oriente español: Los moriscos y el Sacromonte en tiempos de Contrarreforma* (Madrid: Marcial Pons Historia, 2010), 177; rev. and trans. as *The Orient in Spain: Converted Muslims, the Forged Lead Books of Granada, and the Rise of Orientalism*, ed. and trans. Consuelo López-Morillas (Leiden: Brill, 2013), 170–71. Full text of the letter is in Mercedes García-Arenal and Fernando Rodríguez Mediano, "Médico, traductor, inventor: Miguel de Luna, cristiano arábigo de Granada," *Chronica Nova* 32 (2006): 226–30, appendix 1, "Escrito de Miguel de Luna sobre la conveniencia de restaurar los baños y estufas."

197. García-Arenal and Rodríguez Mediano, "Médico, traductor, inventor," 228.

198. Pedro de Torres, *Libro que trata de la enfermedad de las bubas* (Madrid: Luis Sanchez, 1600), chap. 30, pp. 90–92.

199. Bathing and induced perspiration are mentioned throughout Andrés de León, *Practico de morbo gallico* (Valladolid: Luis Sanchez, 1605), but only as preparatory stages for herbal and drug treatments; for example, fol. 22r. On Andrés de León and his contemporaries, see Luis Sánchez Granjel, "El tema de la sifilis en la literatura médica española del siglo XVII," in *Capitúlos de la medicina española* (Salamanca: Instituto de Historia de la Medicina Española, 1971), 77–86. Treatment by *unciones y sudores* remained common practice for syphilitics well into the eighteenth century, but administered in special beds rather than bathing facilities; see Agustín Muñoz Sanz, *Los hospitales docentes de Guadalupe: La respuesta hospitalaria a la epidemia de bubas del Renacimiento (siglos XV y XVI)* (Badajoz: Junta de Extremadura, 2008), 55–57.

200. María José Ruiz Somavilla points out, however, that new types of river bathing would ultimately be seen as healthy and desexualized popular activities in the seventeenth century ("Los valores sociales, religiosas y morales," 176–77).

## CHAPTER 4

1. "Jerónima la Franca y sus familiares con otras personas moriscas se pusieron en cuclillas y echaron alcuzcuz en un batena [*batea*], y todas con ésta a la redonda, comían del alcuzcuz con la mano haziendo unas pellicas [*pellizcas*] como los Moros lo hazían por guarda y ceremonia de la secta de Mahoma." Madrid, Archivo Histórico Nacional, Inquisición, leg. 192, no. 23; cited by Louis Cardaillac, *Morisques et chrétiens: Un affrontement polémique (1492–1640)* (Paris: Klincksieck, 1977), 19. Corrections in square brackets are from Mercedes García-Arenal, *Moriscos y cristianos: Un enfrentamiento polémico (1492–1640)* (Madrid: Fondo de cultura económica, 1979), 27. My thanks to Robin Vose for providing the place and date for this case.

2. Núñez Muley, *Memorandum*, Barletta trans., 81; Carrasco Manchado, *De la convivencia a la exclusión*, 387.

3. This is the version of current laws stated by Francisco Núñez Muley in his petition. In fact, the legal situation was more complex, as will be discussed later in this chapter.

4. Gallego Burín and Gámir Sandoval, *Los moriscos del Reino de Granada*, 68, 192–94.

5. For further discussion, see Olivia Remie Constable, "Food and Meaning: Christian Understandings of Muslim Food and Food Ways in Spain, 1250–1550," *Viator* 44 (2013): 199–235; Teresa de Castro, "L'émergence d'une identité alimentaire: Musulmans et chrétiens dans le royaume de Grenade," in *Histoire et identités alimentaires en Europe*, ed. Martin Bruegel and Bruno Laurioux (Paris: Hachette littératures, 2002), 199–215.

6. Gallego Burín and Gámir Sandoval, *Los moriscos del Reino de Granada*, 162–63.

7. Bermúdez de Pedraza, *Historia eclesiástica de Granada*, fol. 187r.

8. Pérez de Ayala, *Sínodo de la Diócesis de Guadix y de Baza*, fol. 90v.

9. Gil Sanjuán, "El parecer de Galíndez de Carvajal," 396.

10. See Paul Freedman, *Out of the East: Spices and the Medieval Imagination* (New Haven, CT: Yale University Press, 2008).

11. Daniel, *Islam and the West*, 172–76; John Tolan, *Sons of Ishmael: Muslims Through European Eyes in the Middle Ages* (Gainesville: University Press of Florida, 2008), 35–45; Suzanne Conklin Akbari, *Idols in the East: European Representations of Islam and the Orient, 1100–1450* (Ithaca, NY: Cornell University Press, 2009), 257–58; Ana Echevarría Arsuaga, *The Fortress of Faith: The Attitude Towards Muslims in Fifteenth Century Spain* (Brill: Leiden, 1999), 93–94. The tenacity of this image of a Muslim paradise in the Christian imagination was surely bolstered by the fact that Christians were already conditioned to

such associations by biblical passages linking milk and honey with the land of Canaan (Exodus 3:8, 13:5).

12. Coleman, *Creating Christian Granada*, 67. Church officials had to be warned once more not to refer to converted Moriscos as *moros perros* at a provincial council held at Granada in 1565; *Colección de cánones y de todos los consilios*, 5:390.

13. Matthew 15:26–27; Mark 7:27–28.

14. *Castigos e documentos para bien vivir ordenados por el rey don Sancho IV*, ed. Agapito Rey (Bloomington: Indiana University Press, 1952), 130, 132.

15. García-Arenal, *Inquisición y moriscos*, 68–76.

16. Pedro de Valencia, *Tratado acerca de los moriscos de España: manuscrito del siglo VII*, ed. Joaquín Gil Sanjuán (Málaga: Algazara, 1997), 76.

17. Muslim restrictions on wine were never as strictly observed as those on pork products in medieval and early modern Spain. In Islamic law, alcohol is considered *makrūh* (to be avoided), while pork is forbidden (*ḥarām*). In consequence, abstinence from wine was less commonly noted by Christians as a marker of Islamic identity. See Peter Heine, *Food Culture in the Near East, Middle East, and North Africa* (Westport, CT: Greenwood Press, 2004), 7–8.

18. Pedro Aznar Cardona, *Expulsion iustificada de los moriscos* (Huesca: Pedro Cabarte, 1612), fol. 33r–v. Aznar Cardona also comments on avoiding salt pork (*tocino*) (34r). This passage is also translated by Harvey, *Muslims in Spain*, 413–16. On Aznar Cardona's views of Moriscos, see Julio Caro Baroja, "Los moriscos aragoneses segun un autor de comienzos del siglo XVII," in *Razas, Pueblos, y Linajes* (Madrid: Revista de Occidente, 1957), 81–98. Jaime Bleda, writing in support of the expulsion six years later in 1618, and copying some materials directly from Aznar Cardona's treatise, added that in Valencia Moriscos ate rice every day and that they also enjoyed eggplants, goat meat, mutton, and various types of fish (*Coronica de los moros de España* [Valencia: En la Impresion de Felipe Mey, 1618], 1024).

19. For example, information brought to the Inquisition in Benquerencia in 1510 contained a long discussion of cooking habits and salt pork (Miranda Díaz and Córdoba Soriano, *Los moriscos de Magacela*, 223). See also Américo Castro, "Sentido histórico-literario del jamón y del tocino," in *Cervantes y los casticismos españoles* (Madrid: Alianza Editorial, 1974), 25–32; Mohammed Hocine Benkheïra, "Tabou du porc et identité en Islam," in *Histoire et identités alimentaires en Europe*, ed. Martin Bruegel and Bruno Laurioux (Paris: Hachette littératures, 2002), 37–51.

20. Gallego Burín and Gámir Sandoval, *Los moriscos del Reino de Granada*, 72.

21. Harvey, *Muslims in Spain*, 62; Pedro Longás Bartibás, *Vida religiosa de los moriscos* (Madrid: E. Maestre, 1915), 306.

22. García-Arenal, *Inquisición y moriscos*, 71; Teresa de Castro, "L'émergence d'une identité alimentaire," 209.

23. Constable, *Trade and Traders in Muslim Spain*, 183–85, 220–22; Karl W. Butzer, Elizabeth K. Butzer, and Juan F. Mateu, "Medieval Muslim Communities of the Sierra de Espadán, Kingdom of Valencia," *Viator* 17 (1986): 346–47.

24. Lope de Vega, *Los Porceles de Murcia*, in *Obras completas de Lope de Vega*, ed. Jesús Gómez and Paloma Cuenca (Madrid: Biblioteca Castro, 1993–98), 15:663. Lope de Vega's contemporary Miguel de Cervantes also makes a point in book 1, chap. 9, of *Don Quixote* that he paid fifty pounds of raisins and two bushels of wheat to a Morisco for translating the original Arabic tale; trans. Charles Jarvis (Oxford: Oxford University Press, 1992), 76. On Cervantes's use of eggplants to hint at Morisco identity (as explicitly in book 2, chap. 2 of *Don Quixote*, trans. Jarvis, 537), see also Anita Savo, "'Toledano, ajo, berenjena': The Eggplant in *Don Quixote*," *La Corónica* 43, no. 1 (2014): 231–52.

25. *Romancero general (1600, 1604, 1605)*, ed. Ángel González Palencia (Madrid: Consejo Superior de Investigaciones Científicas, 1947), 1:220.

26. Francisco Martínez Montiño, *Arte de cocina, pasteleria, vizcocheria, y conserveria* (Barcelona: En la imprenta de Maria Angela Martí, 1763), 360–64. There is also a recipe for Moorish chicken ("Gallina Morisca"), 63–64. The first edition of the book was published in 1611.

27. David M. Freidenreich, *Foreigners and Their Food: Constructing Otherness in Jewish, Christian, and Islamic Law* (Berkeley: University of California Press, 2011).

28. King Pere IV of Aragon had Muslims serving at his table, a fact that earned him papal reproof in 1337 (*Regesta de letras pontificias del Archivo de la Corona de Aragón*, ed. Francisco J. Miquel Rosell (Madrid: Cuerpo de Archiveros, Bibliotecarios, y Arqueólogos, 1948), 289, no. 578). Lords also relied on Muslim tenants to provide food for their households, as when the lord of Gaibel ordered the local *aljama* to provide chickens, eggs, and goats "por nuestra provisión" in 1379 (Febrer Romaguera, *Les aljames mudèjars valencianes*, 59).

29. Bermúdez de Pedraza, *Historia eclesiástica*, fol. 238r.

30. José María García Fuentes, ed., *La Inquisición en Granada en el siglo XVI: Fuentes para su estudio* (Granada: Universidad de Granada, 1981), 142–43, 166.

31. González Arce, "Cuadernos de ordenanzas y otros documentos sevillanos," 122; Echevarría Arsuaga, "Política y religión frente al Islam," 50.

32. I have found very little documentation of sharing food before this period, but it surely happened on a regular basis, both among the elite (during diplomatic visits, friendly exchanges, or exiles, as when the future Alfonso VI spent time at the Taifa court of Toledo) and among more ordinary people (merchants, travelers, neighbors).

33. Jaume [James] I of Aragon, *Llibre dels fets del rei en Jaume*, ed. Jordi Bruguera (Barcelona: Barcino, 1991), 2:321 (chap. 438); trans., *The Book of Deeds of James I*, 316.

34. Bernat Desclot, *Crònica*, ed. M. Coll i Alentorn (Barcelona: Barcino, 1949–51), 2:129–30 (chap. 45).

35. Desclot, *Crònica*, 3:67 (chap. 79).

36. Ramon Muntaner, *Crònica*, ed. Enric Bagué (Barcelona: Barcino, 1951), 2:57 (chap. 85).

37. Basáñez Villaluenga, *Las morerías aragonesas*, 224.

38. Gutierre Díaz de Gámez, *El Victorial: Crónica de Don Pero Niño, conde de Buelna*, ed. Ramón Iglesia (Madrid: Espasa-Calpe, 1940), 101–3.

39. Carpenter, *Alfonso X and the Jews*, 34–35; *Siete Partidas*, 7.24.11, ed. Burns, 5:1436.

40. On Calahorra, see Fernando Bujanda, "Documentos para la historia de la Diócesis de Calahorra," *Berceo: Boletín del Instituto de Estudios Riojanos* 2 (1947): 116; see also Enrique Cantera Montenegro, "Los mudejares en el marco de la sociedad riojana bajomedieval," in *Actas del III Simposio Internacional de Mudejarismo* (Teruel: Centro de Estudios Mudéjares, 1986), 32; on Tarragona, see Josep María Pons Guri, "Constitucions conciliars Tarraconensis (1229 a 1330)," *Analecta Sacra Tarraconensia* 48 (1975): 357; on Valladolid, see Ladero Quesada, "Los mudéjares de Castilla en la baja edad media," 287; relevant passages from Valladolid 1322 are in Fernández y González, *Estado social y político de los mudejares de Castilla*, 377–79.

41. Vincent Ferrer, *Sermons*, ed. José Sanchis y Sivera (Barcelona: Barcino, 1932–84), 3:14 (sermon 56); Nirenberg, *Communities of Violence*, 169.

42. Fernández y González, *Estado social y político de los mudejares de Castilla*, 400–404; also Carrasco Manchado, *De la convivencia a la exclusión*, 179–84. Queen Catalina was clearly advised by Vincent Ferrer; see Justin K. Stearns, *Infectious Ideas: Contagion in Premodern Islamic and Christian Thought in the Western Mediterranean* (Baltimore: Johns Hopkins University Press, 2011), 55.

43. Ordinance from 1443; see Carrasco Manchado, *De la convivencia a la exclusión*, 189.

44. *Memorias de Don Enrique IV de Castilla* (Madrid: Fortanet, 1913), 435.

45. Echevarría, *Fortress of Faith*, 175.

46. Ladero Quesada, "Los mudéjares de Castilla en la baja edad media," 287. Torres Balbás, *Algunos aspectos del mudejarismo urbano medieval*, 30, notes that the 1484 legislation forbade Muslim and Jewish resale of foodstuffs due to claims that they were driving up prices.

47. *Relación de los hechos del muy magnífico e más virtuoso señor*, 95.

48. Harvey, *Muslims in Spain*, 95.

49. Translation taken from *The Qur'an: First American Version*, trans. T. B. Irving (Brattleboro, VT: Amana Books, 1985), 54.

50. *Llibre dels Fets*, 2:210 (chap. 244); *Book of Deeds*, 211.

51. See, for example, the documents from the thirteenth and fourteenth centuries collected by Febrer Romaguera in *Cartas pueblas de las morerías valencianas*. Muslim communities continued to enjoy similar privileges in the fifteenth century, as in Oriola in 1431, where the Muslim community was promised a qadi, who would follow *sunnah* and *sharī'ah* (*xuna e xara*); along with a mosque, oven, bath, and butcher shop (Febrer Romaguera, *Les aljames mudèjars valencianes*, 208–10, doc. 59).

52. As Robert Burns has pointed out, *carnicería* was a blanket term that "comprehended all phases of the meat industry from slaughtering, skinning, and dressing to retail sales" (*Medieval Colonialism*, 43).

53. "Suma de los principales mandamientos y devademientos de la ley y çunna," in *Tratados de legislacion musulman*, 251; Gerard Albert Wiegers, *Islamic Literature in Span-*

*ish and Aljamiado: Yça of Segovia (fl. 1450), His Antecendents and Successors* (Leiden: Brill, 1994), 78.

54. For the capitulations of Taberna, see Ladero Quesada, *Los mudéjares de Castilla en el tiempo de Isabel I*, 276; for Baza and Huéscar, see Gallego Burín and Gamir Sandoval, *Moriscos del Reino de Granada*, 66, 165, 168; for Vélez Rubio, see Grima Cervantes, *Almería y el Reino de Granada*, 222; Harvey, *Muslims in Spain*, 47.

55. Monroe, *Hispano-Arabic Poetry*, 378.

56. Longás Bartibás, *Vida religiosa de los moriscos*, 264–70.

57. Rosa María Blasco, "Una carnicería regentada por moriscos en el arrabal de San Juan, de Elche," *Sharq al-Andalus* 2 (1985): 75–79.

58. Brian Catlos, *The Victors and the Vanquished: Christians and Muslims of Catalonia and Aragon, 1050–1300* (Cambridge: Cambridge University Press, 2004), 194.

59. Joaquim Miret y Sans, *Les cases de Templers y Hospitalers en Catalunya* (Barcelona: Imprenta de la Casa Provincial de Caritat, 1910), 138. See also Mutgé Vives, *L'aljama sarraïna de Lleida a l'edat mitjana*, 10–11.

60. *Documentos de Jaime I de Aragón*, ed. Ambrosio Huici Miranda and María Desamparados Cabanes Pecourt (Valencia: Anubar, 1976–88), 2:319; Burns, *Medieval Colonialism*, 47.

61. Burns, *Medieval Colonialism*, 47.

62. Febrer Romaguera, *Cartas pueblas de las morerías valencianas*, 41.

63. González Arce, "Cuadernos de ordenanzas y otros documentos sevillanos," 125.

64. Burns, *Medieval Colonialism*, 45.

65. Rents collected by the bailiff of Valencia from the Muslim community of Alfafara in 1416 include rents from the *carnicería* (Fernández y González, *Estado social y político de los mudejares de Castilla*, 406, doc. 78).

66. In 1403, Martí I granted all revenues of the Muslim butchery in Játiva to the local *aljama* in return for an annual payment (Febrer Romaguera, *Les aljames mudèjars valencianes*, 111–14, doc. 19). In 1496, income from the Muslim butchery in Castelló de la Plana helped to buy lights and other supplies for the mosque (this is reminiscent of a *waqf* arrangement), but the town also collected fees; see Carmen Díaz de Rábago Hernández, "Alimentación y religión en una morería valenciana bajomedieval: Castelló de la Plana," *Millars: Espai i historia* 15 (1992): 107.

67. Seigneurial rights in fifteenth-century Valencia included butcher shops in Mudejar communities. These are mentioned in confirmations of seigneurial holdings and in grants of concessions leased to both Christian and Muslim tax farmers. See Febrer Romaguera, *Les aljames mudèjars valencianes*, 75–78, 122–26, 134–49, 156–61, 164–78, 205–7, 215–26, 271–80, 286–90, 317–33. Two leases of concessions including Mudejar butcher shops involved property belonging to Rodrigo Borja (the future pope Alexander VI), his mother, and nephew (250–53, 266–71).

68. Basáñez Villaluenga, *La aljama sarracena de Huesca*, 241–42.

69. "Concedimus vobis . . . liceat construere, facere et tenere infra limites morarie prefate, ubi magis elegeritis, carniceriam, et in ea scindere et vendere carnes quascumque et quibuscumque volueritis." The translation is from Burns, *Medieval Colonialism*, 48; Burns includes selections from the original Latin, but the charter is reproduced in full by Francisco Roca Traver, "Un siglo de vida mudéjar," 208; Hinojosa Montalvo, *Los mudéjares*, 2:296–97; Febrer Romaguera, *Les aljames mudèjars valencianes*, 47–48.

70. Febrer Romaguera, *Les aljames mudèjars valencianes*, 311–13. Apparently the butchers' guild in Valencia had earlier tried to limit and regulate which meats Mudejars could butcher and when.

71. Garrido Atienza, *Las capitulaciones para la entrega de Granada*, 287; García-Arenal, *Los moriscos*, 28.

72. Joaquín Aparici Martí, "Tolerar y convivir: Carnicerías musulmanas en tierras de Castello," in *VIII simposio internacional de mudejarismo: De mudéjares a moriscos: una conversión forzada; Teruel, 15–17 de septiembre 1999; Actas* (Teruel: Centro de Estudios Mudéjares, 2003), 1:321.

73. Basáñez Villaluenga, *La aljama sarracena de Huesca*, 53 and 136–37; Basáñez Villaluenga, *Las morerías aragonesas*, 438.

74. Aparici Martí, "Tolerar y convivir," 327.

75. Not far from Teruel, in Daroca, evidence from 1472 and 1498 indicates that Christians continued to buy meat from Muslim butchers in spite of economic sanctions; see Aparici Martí, "Tolerar y convivir," 328.

76. Fernández y González, *Estado social y político de los mudéjares de Castilla*, 407–12, docs. 80 and 81.

77. Francisco Macho y Ortega, *Condición social de los mudéjares aragoneses (siglo XV)* (Zaragoza: Tip. la Academia, 1923), 280–82, doc. 64.

78. Hinojosa Montalvo, *Los mudéjares*, 2:294–95, doc. 225; María Teresa Ferrer i Mallol, *Les aljames sarraïnes de la governació d'Oriola en el segle XIV* (Barcelona: Consell Superior d'Investigacions Científiques, 1988), 269–70, doc. 106.

79. Given the mess, smell, and noise created by these activities, it was common to locate butcher shops near the town walls, or just outside them, and if possible near a river. Butchers also needed space to pasture animals before slaughter, as evident in 1376 when Pere IV blocked Huesca's attempts to prevent Muslim butchers from holding animals in the same grazing areas as animals destined for Christian butchers (Basáñez Villaluenga, *La aljama sarracena de Huesca*, 56). In 1498–99, there were disputes in Segorbe as to whether Muslim butchers could pasture their animals in the same holding pens as Christian butchers (Aparici Martí, "Tolerar y convivir," 326–27).

80. There were debates about whether it was permissable for Muslims (and Christians) to buy meat from Jewish butchers. In 1295, a joint ordinance by both Muslim and Christian local authorities in Tarrazona prohibited such sales, but this was later annulled by the king (Nirenberg, *Communities of Violence*, 172, citing Lourie, "Anatomy of Ambivalence," 43 n. 138). In 1333–34, Muslims in Zaragoza complained to the king that some Muslims were buying from a Jewish butcher, while Christians complained that low prices

in Muslim meat stalls were attracting Christian buyers (Nirenberg, *Communities of Violence*, 172–73).

81. Rosa Mayordomo Font, "Notas históricas sobre la carnicería de la aljama sarracena de Tortosa (siglo XIV)," in *Homenatge a la memòria del Prof. Emilio Sáez: Aplex d'estudis del seus deixebles i col·laboradors* (Barcelona: Universitat de Barcelona, 1989), 226, 228–31; Nirenberg, *Communities of Violence*, 171–72; Nirenberg also discusses other examples of community competition over butchers in Tortosa and Zaragoza in the years 1328–34 (172–73).

82. *Documentos municipales de Huesca, 1100–1350*, ed. Carlos Laliena Corbera (Huesca: Ayuntamiento de Huesca, 1988), 111.

83. Basáñez Villaluenga, *La aljama sarracena de Huesca*, 56–58, 182–84, doc. 47.

84. Mayordomo Font, "Notas históricas sobre la carnicería de la aljama sarracena de Tortosa," 228.

85. Boswell, *The Royal Treasure*, 102.

86. María del Carmen Barceló Torres, "La morería de Valencia en el reinado de Juan II," *Saitabi* 30 (1980): 53.

87. Coleman, *Creating Christian Granada*, 69. These rulings from 1524 and 1525 are contemporary with Francisco Núñez Muley's 1523 petition to Carlos V regarding rules for New Christian butchers in Granada.

88. Hinojosa Montalvo, *Los mudéjares*, 1:169 (Murcia); Barceló Torres, "La morería de Valencia," 53 (Valencia).

89. Aparici Martí, "Tolerar y convivir," 328 (Daroca).

90. Aparici Martí, "Tolerar y convivir," 325.

91. Aparici Martí, "Tolerar y convivir," 322; Díaz de Rábago Hernández, "Alimentación y religión en una morería valenciana bajomedieval," 107.

92. Aparici Martí, "Tolerar y convivir," 323–25.

93. Miller, *Guardians of Islam*, 117; David M. Freidenreich, "The Food of the Damned," in *Between Heaven and Hell: Islam, Salvation, and the Fate of Others*, ed. Mohammad Hasan Khalil (Oxford: Oxford University Press, 2013), 253–72.

94. *Documentos de Jaime I de Aragón*, 2:319; Burns, *Medieval Colonialism*, 47.

95. Febrer Romaguera, *Cartas pueblas de las morerías valencianas*, 89.

96. Burns, *Medieval Colonialism*, 45.

97. Basáñez Villaluenga, *Las morerías aragonesas*, 123, 154, 418; Mayordomo Font, "Notas históricas sobre la carnicería de la aljama sarracena de Tortosa," 228. In Tortosa, this permission only extended for four years, starting in 1298.

98. Basáñez Villaluenga, *Las morerías aragonesas*, 37.

99. Fernández y González, *Estado social y político de los mudéjares de Castilla*, 384–85, doc. 69; Burns, *Medieval Colonialism*, 48–49. Among measures to rebuild and repopulate the *morería* of Oriola in 1376 was the establishment of a Muslim meat stall, under the supervision of the Christian butcher of the town. Income from this facility registered in 1377 and 1378 indicates that it was up and running; see Ferrer i Mallol, *Les aljames sarraïnes de la governació d'Oriola*, 157.

100. In 1485, an agreement between a Christian nobleman (*escudero*) and representatives of the local Muslim community in Calatayud arranged that the noble, Antón de Oblitos, would provide meat of certain types to the *carrnecería de los moros* on a regular schedule and at preestablished prices; see Hinojosa Montalvo, *Los mudéjares*, 2:300–301, doc. 230.

101. José Madurell Marimón, "La confradía de la Santa Trinidad de los conversos de Barcelona," *Sefarad* 18 (1958): 81; Mutgé Vives, "La aljama sarracena en la Lleida cristiana," 105. In the same year, and perhaps related to the queen's ruling, the city of Lérida decreed that Muslims in the city were not allowed to kill more animals than were needed by Muslim buyers (Mutgé Vives, *L'aljama sarraïna de Lleida a l'edat mitjana*, 11–12).

102. And ten years after that, there would be further disputes in Teruel about Christians buying meat in the *morería* (see note 74 above).

103. Aparici Martí, "Tolerar y convivir," 327.

104. Febrer Romaguera, *Les aljames mudèjars valencianes*, 308–9, doc. 94.

105. Aparici Martí, "Tolerar y convivir," 321–22; also Díaz de Rábago Hernández, "Alimentación y religión en una morería valenciana bajomedieval," 105–6; Fernández y González, *Estado social y político de los mudejares de Castilla*, 390–91, doc. 72; Macho y Ortega, *Condición social de los mudéjares aragoneses*, 280–82, doc. 64.

106. Gallego Burín and Gámir Sandoval, *Los moriscos del Reino de Granada*, 66 and 172–73.

107. Gallego Burín and Gámir Sandoval, *Los moriscos del Reino de Granada*, 180–82.

108. Gallego Burín and Gámir Sandoval, *Los moriscos del Reino de Granada*, 204.

109. Gallego Burín and Gámir Sandoval, *Los moriscos del Reino de Granada*, 204.

110. In December 1526, however, the archbishop of Granada did receive orders from the emperor to implement the ordinances regarding butcher shops (Gallego Burín and Gámir Sandoval, *Los moriscos del Reino de Granada*, 213).

111. Aparici Martí, "Tolerar y convivir," 325, 332.

112. Ehlers, *Between Christians and Moriscos*, 97; Raphaël Carrasco, *La monarchie catholique et les morisques (1520–1620)* (Montpellier: Université Paul-Valéry Montpellier III, 2005), 47.

113. Mármol Carvajal, *Historia del rebelión y castigo de los moriscos*, 4.30 (pig), 4.23 (boy).

114. David Nirenberg, *Anti-Judaism: The Western Tradition* (New York: W. W. Norton, 2013), 205–7; cf. Miri Rubin, *Gentile Tales: The Narrative Assault on Late Medieval Jews* (Philadelphia: University of Pennsylvania Press, 1999), esp. 8–28.

115. Dolors Bramon, "Del Principat estant: Dos miracles montserratins sobre el bandolerisme morisc valencià," in *L'expulsió dels moriscos: Conseqüències en el món islàmic i el món cristià; 380è Aniversari de l'Expulsió dels Moriscos, Congrés Internacional, Sant Carles de la Ràpita, 5–9 de desembre de 1990* (Barcelona: Generalitat de Catalunya, 1994), 253–58; Cristian Berco, "Revealing the Other: Moriscos, Crime, and Local Politics in Toledo's Hinterland in the Late Sixteenth Century," *Medieval Encounters* 8 (2002): 135–59.

116. Sugar was widely enjoyed in fifteenth-century Europe, and especially in Iberia. See Bruno Laurioux, "Modes culinaires et mutations du goût à la fin du Moyen-Âge," in *Artes mechanicae en Europe médiévale*, ed. Ria Jansen-Sieben (Brussels: Archives et bibliothèques de Belgique, 1989), 199–222; Adele Fábregas García, *Producción y comercio de azúcar en el mediterraneo medieval: El ejemplo del reino de Granada* (Granada: Universidad de Granada, 2000).

117. Translations included the *Liber de ferculis et condimentis*, translated in Venice ca. 1300 by Jambonino of Cremona, from the *Minhāj al-bayān* of Ibn Jazla (died 1100, in Baghdad), and the *Tacuinum sanitatis*, translated from the *Taqwim al-Sihha* of Ibn Butlan (eleventh century, Syria). On medieval Islamic cooking and cookbooks, see Maxime Rodinson, A. J. Arberry, and Charles Perry, eds., *Medieval Arab Cookery* (Totnes, Devon: Prospect Books, 2001); Lilia Zaouali, *Medieval Cuisine of the Islamic World* (Berkeley: University of California Press, 2007); Melitta Weiss Adamson, *Food in Medieval Times* (Westport, CT: Greenwood Press, 2004), 115–24; David Waines, "Luxury Foods in Medieval Islamic Societies," *World Archaeology* 34 (2003): 571–80.

118. Roberto de Nola, *Libre del coch: Tractat de cuina medieval*, ed. Veronika Leimgruber (Barcelona: Universitat de Barcelona, 1977), 56–58; Roberto de Nola, *Libro de guisados*, ed. Dionisio Pérez (Madrid: Compañía Ibero-Americana de Publicaciones, 1929), 77, 79. Almond milk was used in Arabic cookbooks, but it became especially popular in fourteenth-century works on food and health, such as the *Regimen sanitatis* of Arnau de Vilanova, physician to Jaume II. See Melitta Weiss-Amer, "The Role of Medieval Physicians in the Diffusion of Culinary Recipes and Cooking Practices," in *Du manuscrit à la table: Essais sur la cuisine au Moyen Âge et répertoire des manuscrits médiévaux contenant des recettes culinaires*, ed. Carole Lambert (Montreal: Les Presses de l'Université de Montréal, 1992), 69–80.

119. *Manual de mugeres en el qual se contienen muchas y diversas reçetas muy buenas*, ed. Alicia Martínez Crespo (Salamanca: Ediciones Universidad de Salamanca, 1995), 58.

120. *Libre de Sent Soví (Receptari de cuina)*, ed. Rudolf Grewe (Barcelona: Barcino, 1979), 188.

121. Terence Scully, ed., *The Neapolitan Recipe Collection: Cuoco Napoletano* (Ann Arbor: University of Michigan Press, 2000), 68, 194; Martino de Como, *The Art of Cooking: The First Modern Cookery Book*, ed. Luigi Ballerini (Berkeley: University of California Press, 2005), 134–35.

122. *Libre de Sent Soví*, 182–83; Johanna Maria van Winter, "Arab Influences on Medieval European Cuisine," in *Spices and Comfits: Collected Papers on Medieval Food* (Totnes, Devon: Prospect Books, 2007), 81–85; Melitta Weiss Adamson, ed., *Regional Cuisines of Medieval Europe: A Book of Essays* (New York: Routledge, 2002), 127; Bernard Rosenberger, "Les pâtes dans le monde musulman," *Médiévales* 8 (1989): 81–82.

123. *Libre de Sent Soví*, 205–7; Roberto de Nola, *Libro de guisados*, 122, 142; Zaouali, *Medieval Cuisine of the Islamic World*, 44–45; Adamson, *Regional Cuisines of Medieval Europe*, 132–33.

124. Maxime Rodinson, "Les influences de la civilisation musulmane sur la civilisation européenne médiévale dans les domains de la consommation et de la distraction: L'alimentation," in *Convegno internazionale Oriente e Occidente nel Medieoevo: Filosofia e scienze* (Rome: Accademia nazionale dei Lincei, 1971), 479–500; Maxime Rodinson, "Maʿmūiyya East and West," *Petits propos culinaires* 33 (1989): 15–25; Toby Peterson, "The Arab Influence on Western European Cooking," *Journal of Medieval History* 6 (1980): 317–40; Freedman, *Out of the East*, 26–27; Giovanni Rebora, "La cucina medievale italiana tra oriente ed occidente," in *Studi in onore di Luigi Bulferetti* (Genoa: Università di Genova, 1989–90), 3:1431–1578; C. B. Hieatt, "How Arabic Traditions Travelled to England," in *Food on the Move: Proceedings of the Oxford Symposium on Food and Cookery, 1996* (Totnes, Devon: Prospect Books, 1997), 120–26; C. Anne Wilson, "The Saracen Connection: Arab Cuisine and the Medieval West, Part I," *Petits propos culinaires* 7 (1981): 13–22.

125. A cookbook attributed to the first-century Roman epicure Marcus Gavius Apicius was considered an important exemplar of Roman cuisine by the later fifteenth century. The text was first printed in Milan in 1498, with two Venetian editions shortly thereafter in 1500 and 1503. See *Apicius: A Critical Edition with an Introduction and an English Translation of the Latin Recipe Text Apicius*, ed. Christopher Grocock and Sally Grainger (Totnes, Devon: Prospect Books, 2006).

126. To reduce the risk of fire, ovens were usually built away from other buildings. In Valencia City under Jaume I, one public oven was located near the beach and another was outside one of the city's gates (this latter in the same location as an earlier oven "from the time of the Saracens"). Burns, *Diplomatarium*, 4:342 and 356–57, docs. 1290 and 1306; also 2:191–93, doc. 228.

127. Burns, *Diplomatarium*, 2:80–81 and 163–64, docs. 92 and 194.

128. Febrer Romaguera, *Cartas pueblas de las morerías valencianas*, 54. References to ovens continue in the fourteenth and fifteenth centuries in both the Crown of Aragon and Castile. For the reign of Jaume II, see Basáñez Villaluenga, *Las morerías aragonesas*, 195, 210, 211, 247. In 1476, a privilege from Haro mentions "los hornos de los moros donde cocían ollas y cántaros y otras cosas de tierra" (Domingo Hergueta Martín, ed. *Noticias históricas de la muy noble y muy leal ciudad de Haro* [Haro, 1906; repr., Logroño: Diputación de Logroño, 1979], 254).

129. Macho y Ortega, *Condición social de los mudéjares aragoneses*, 259, doc. 47; likewise, an oven was granted to the Muslim *aljama* in Bureta in 1482 (p. 287, doc. 71).

130. Macho y Ortega, *Condición social de los mudéjares aragoneses*, 288–89, doc. 71.

131. My thanks to Karen Graubart for sharing this unpublished material, which will appear in her *Republics of Difference: Racial and Religious Self-Governance in the Iberian Atlantic 1400–1650* (Oxford: Oxford University Press, forthcoming).

132. Ruth Pike, *Aristocrats and Traders: Sevillian Society in the Sixteenth Century* (Ithaca, NY: Cornell University Press, 1972), 160–61; Debra Blumenthal, *Enemies and Familiars: Slavery and Mastery in Fifteenth-Century Valencia* (Ithaca, NY: Cornell University Press, 2009), 93–95, 108–11; Carrasco, *La monarchie catholique et les morisques*, 47; García Fuentes, *Inquisición en Granada*, 322.

133. Weiditz, *Authentic Everyday Dress of the Renaissance*, plate 91.

134. *Romancero general*, 220; Julio Caro Baroja, *Ciclos y temas de la historia de España: Los moriscos del Reino de Granada* (Madrid: ISTMO, 1976), 146.

135. *Castigos e documentos para bien vivir ordenados por el rey don Sancho IV*, 130, 132; Francesc Eiximenis, *Llibres, mestres i sermons*, ed. David Guixeras and Xavier Renedo (Barcelona: Barcino, 2008), 238; my thanks to Robert D. Hughes for his assistance with this reference to *bunyols*.

136. García-Arenal, *Inquisición y moriscos*, 72; Ehlers, *Between Christians and Moriscos*, 96; Juan Aranda Doncel, *Los moriscos en tierras de Córdoba* (Córdoba: Monte de piedad y caja de ahorros de Córdoba, 1984), 224–25. William Childers describes the case of an Old Christian who was suspected of being a Morisco on the basis of being from Granada, speaking Arabic, and working as a *buñolero* ("Disappearing Moriscos," in *Cross-Cultural History and the Domestication of Otherness*, ed. M. J. Rozbicki and G. O. Ndege [New York: Palgrave, 2012], 57).

137. Carrasco Manchado, *De la convivencia a la exclusión*, 344.

138. Ronald Surtz, "Crimes of the Tongue: The Inquisitorial Trials of Cristóbal Duarte Bellester," *Medieval Encounters* 12 (2006): 529; Deborah Root, "Speaking Christian: Orthodoxy and Difference in Sixteenth-Century Spain," *Representations* 23 (1988): 118–34.

139. María Luisa Ledesma, *Vidas mudéjares (aspectos sociales de una minoría religiosa en Aragón)* (Zaragoza: Mira Editores, 1994), 90–91.

140. Magín Arroyas Serrano and Vicent Gil Vicent, *Revuelta y represión en los moriscos castellonenses: El proceso inquisitorial de Pedro Aman, morisco vecino de Onda* (Onda: Ajuntement d'Onda, 1995), 76.

141. García Fuentes, *Inquisición en Granada*, 309–11.

142. García Fuentes, *Inquisición en Granada*, 351–52.

143. Charles Perry, "Couscous and Its Cousins," in *Medieval Arab Cookery*, ed. Maxime Rodinson, A. J. Arberry, and Charles Perry (Totnes, Devon: Prospect Books, 2001), 235–38; Zaouali, *Medieval Cuisine of the Islamic World*, 45–46; Lévi-Provençal, *Histoire de l'Espagne musulmane*, 3:421; Rachel Arié, *L'Espagne musulmane au temps des Nasrids* (Paris: É. de Boccard, 1990), 378; Teresa de Castro Martínez, *La alimentación en las crónicas castellanas bajomedievales* (Granada: Universidad de Granada, 1996), 240–41.

144. Expiración García Sánchez, "Ibn al-Azraq: *Urŷūza* sobre ciertas preferencias gastronómicas de los Granadinos," *Andalucía Islámica* 1 (1980): 155, 161.

145. *Cerámica granadina: Siglos XVI–XX* (Granada: Fundación Rodríguez-Acosta, 2001), 69, 85, 112; Juan Martínez Ruiz, *Inventarios de bienes moriscos del Reino de Granada (Siglo XVI)* (Madrid: Consejo Superior de Investigaciones Científicas, 1972), 46.

146. García Fuentes, *Inquisición en Granada*, 142–43, 166, 183–84, 223.

147. Henry Kamen, *Inquisition and Society in Spain in the Sixteenth and Seventeenth Centuries* (Bloomington: Indiana University Press, 1985), 107.

148. Díaz de Gámez, *El Victorial*, 101–3.

149. Martorell and Galba, *Tirant lo Blanc*, ed. Riquer, 445, 497; trans. Rosenthal, 230, 260 (chaps. 137 and 148). Although the Valencian authors placed their hero's travels

in the eastern Mediterranean world, in fact the menu for these feasts reflected Iberian tastes.

150. Francesc Eiximenis, *Com usar bé de beure e menjar: Normes morals contingudes en el "Terç de Crestià"* (Barcelona: Curial, 1983), 112. My thanks to Michael Ryan for his assistance with this passage.

151. The early fourteenth-century Castilian *Siete Partidas* instructs that one should eat neatly with one's fingers, not taking too much food at once, lest the eaters "show themselves to be gluttons, which is characteristic of beasts"; it went on to stress the importance of washing the hands both before and after eating (*Las Siete Partidas* 2.7.5; trans. Scott, ed. Burns, 2:303). Utilitarian fork usage is linked to the spread of slippery pasta dishes, with specific reference to the fourteenth-century court of Naples, in Giovanni Rebora and Albert Sonnenfeld, *Culture of the Fork: A Brief History of Everyday Food and Haute Cuisine in Europe* (New York: Columbia University Press, 2001), 14–18. However, forks did not come into common everyday use until the later eighteenth century.

152. Leo Africanus, or Yuhanna al-Asad (originally named Hasan al-Wazzan), had been born in Granada in about 1490, and his family emigrated to North Africa after the conquest of this city in 1492. Leo was then captured by pirates and brought to Rome in 1520, where he converted to Christianity and became a protégé of Pope Leo X.

153. "In comparatione de li signori de la Europa pare quella vita de Affrica cosa vile & misera non per la parvita de la Robba ma per lo desordine in li coustumi per che magnano in terra sopra certe tavole basse senza tovaglie & nisuno hanno sarvietta in mano & quando magnano el cuscusu o qualche vivanda lo magnano in siema in un Piatto & magnano con le mano senza cochiaro. . . . Ma li Doctori & li homini de qualita vivono piu politamente. Ma uno gentilhomo Italiano vive piu politamente che nisuno signore de Affrica." Hasan al-Wazzan (Leo Africanus), *Libro de la Cosmographia et Geographia de Affrica*, V.E. MS 953, Biblioteca Nazionale Centrale, Rome, fol. 165r–v. My thanks to Natalie Zemon Davis, who very kindly provided copies of the relevant pages from the 1526 manuscript.

154. Constable, "Food and Meaning," 222ff. Also, on shared habits of sitting on the floor, see Luis Ramón-Laca Menéndez de Luarca, "El hogar morisco," *Oppidum* 1 (2005): 128–39.

155. It went on to stress the importance of washing the hands both before and after eating (*Siete Partidas*, 2.7.5; trans. Scott, ed. Burns, 2:303).

156. See above, notes 7 and 8.

157. Pedro Mártir de Anglería, *Una embajada de los Reyes Católicos a Egipto*, ed. Luis García y García (Valladolid: Consejo Superior de Investigaciones Científicas, 1947), 99–100.

158. "Quando an de comer se assientan todos en el suelo, assi hombres como mugeres, y puesto en medio el librillo, cada uno mete la mano por su parte, y tienen por gran peccado comer con la mano yzquierda. . . . No les permite su ley que coman con cucharas, sino con la mano derecha. Y des que han comido se lamen los dedos y friegen

las manos una con otra y en los braços, y desta manera se limpian, porque no acostumbran manteles ni pañizuelos." Luis del Mármol Carvajal, *Descripcion general de Africa* (Granada: Casa de Rene Rabut, 1573–99, vol. 3, fol. 4v).

159. "Comen con la mano todo género de comidas, aunque tengan necessidad de cuchara, la mesa y los manteles es el suelo con una estera o cuero que llaman Taifor. Los pañuelos son las lenguas con que lamen las manos, que es la mas suzia cosa del mundo." Diego de Torres, *Relación del origen y suceso de los xarifes y del estado de los reinos de Marruecos, Fez, y Tarudante*, ed. Mercedes García-Arenal (Madrid: Siglo Veintiuno Editores, 1980), 207.

160. "El Rey en lugar de servilletas, se suele limpiar en las cabezas de dos Negrillos, diziendo: Que aquellas servilletas son mejores, porque valen mas, y no se rompen, que las que usan los Reyes Christianos." Francisco Jesús María de San Juan del Puerto, *Mission historial de Marruecos* (Seville: Francisco Garay, 1708), 51.

161. "Ordinariamente no se sentava en silla ni comía de mesa, por guarda y cerimonia de la dicha secta de Mahoma." Archivo Histórico Nacional, Inquisición, leg. 192, no. 22; Cardaillac, *Morisques et chrétiens*, 19.

162. García-Arenal, *Inquisición y moriscos*, 73.

163. Boronat y Barrachina, *Los moriscos españoles y su expulsión*, 635.

164. Aznar Cardona, *Expulsion iustificada de los moriscos*, fol. 33r–v; Bleda, *Coronica de los moros de España*, 1023; see also above, note 18.

165. Pedro Herrera Puga, *Sociedad y delincuencia en el siglo de oro. Aspectos de la vida sevillana en los siglos XVI y XVII* (Granada: Universidad de Granada, 1971), 449; Manuel Espadas Burgos, "Aspectos sociorreligiosos de la alimentación española," *Hispania: Revista Española de Historia* 131 (1975): 550.

166. Ehlers, *Between Christians and Moriscos*, 130. This view was not universal, and some argued that Moriscos were hardworking taxpayers who did not seek charity and "were modest in their dress and food" (ser templados en su vestir y comida); see García-Arenal, *Los moriscos*, 68.

## EDITOR'S AFTERWORD

1. On women's roles in crypto-Jewish communities and inquisitorial persecutions targeting religious practices associated with the traditionally "female" domestic sphere, see Renée Levine Melammed, *Heretics of Daughters of Israel? The Crypto-Jewish Women of Castile* (New York: Oxford University Press, 1999); a comparative stance is adopted in her "Judeo-Conversas and Moriscas in Sixteenth-Century Spain: A Study of Parallels," *Jewish History* 24 (2010): 155–68. Mary Elizabeth Perry's *The Handless Maiden: Moriscos and the Politics of Religion in Early Modern Spain* (Princeton, NJ: Princeton University Press, 2005) similarly examines the roles and treatment of Morisca women.

2. "Stephen Harper 'Playing a Very Divisive Game' with Niqabs, Tom Mulcair Says," CBC News, September 21, 2015, http://www.cbc.ca/news/politics/canada-election-2015 -niqab-bloc-1.3236837. Fears of an Islamic "fifth column" secretly lurking within a society,

while accurately describing early modern Spanish concerns, are clearly also a factor in contemporary European and North American politics.

3. "France's Le Pen: Ban Non-Pork Meals in Schools," *Telegraph*, April 5, 2014, http://www.telegraph.co.uk/news/worldnews/europe/france/10746273/Frances-Le-Pen -ban-non-pork-meals-in-schools.html; Adam Taylor, "Inside Britain's Big, Dumb Halal Meat Scandal," *Washington Post*, May 8, 2014, https://www.washingtonpost.com/news /worldviews/wp/2014/05/08/inside-britains-big-dumb-halal-pizza-scandal/.

# BIBLIOGRAPHY

## MANUSCRIPT SOURCES

Amiens, Bibliothèque d'Amiens Métropole, MS 108 (Pamplona Bible).

Berlin, Staatsbibliothek, Preussischer Kulturbesitz, Depot Breslau 2 (*Facta et Dicta Memorabilia*).

Boston, Harvard Art Museums/Arthur M. Sackler Museum, 2002.50.43 (*Khamsah*, separated folio).

Cambridge, St. Johns College, MS Browne 1434 (*Khamsah*).

Escorial, Biblioteca de El Escorial, MS H.l.15 (*Lapidario*).

Escorial, Biblioteca de El Escorial, Codex T.I.6 (*Libro de Ajedrez*).

Harburg, Castle Harburg Oettingen-Wallerstein Collection, MS 1, 2, Lat. 4°, 15 (Pamplona Bible).

London, British Library, Or. 6810 (*Khamsah*).

Madrid, Archivo Histórico Nacional, Inquisición, leg. 192, nos. 22–23.

Milan, Biblioteca Ambrosiana, MS J.6 inf., SP II bis (*De balneis Puteolanis*).

New York, Morgan Library, MS G. 74 (*De balneis Puteolanis*).

New York, Morgan Library, MS M. 12 (Book of Hours).

New York, Morgan Library, MS M. 52(Book of Hours).

New York, Morgan Library, MS M. 61 (Book of Hours).

New York, Morgan Library, MS M. 85 (Book of Hours).

New York, Morgan Library, MS M. 261 (Book of Hours).

Paris, Bibliothèque Nationale de France, MS Lat. 8161 (*De balneis Puteolanis*).

Paris, Bibliothèque Nationale de France, MS Lat. 10525 (St. Louis Psalter).

Rome, Biblioteca Nazionale Centrale, V.E. MS 953 (Hasan al-Wazzan/Leo Africanus, *Libro de la Cosmogrophia et Geographia de Affrica*).

Valencia, Biblioteca Universitaria de Valencia, MS 860 (*De balneis Puteolanis*).

Vatican, Biblioteca Apostolica Vaticana, Arabo MS 368 (*Ḥadīth Bayāḍ wa Riyāḍ*).

## PRINTED PRIMARY SOURCES AND DOCUMENTARY CATALOGS

Abū Dāʾūd Sulaymān ibn al-Ashʿath al Sijistānī. *Sunan Abu Dawud: The Third Correct Tradition of the Prophetic Sunna.* Trans. Muḥammad Mahdī Sharīf. 5 vols. Beirut: Dar al-Kotob al-Ilmiyah, 2008.

Alfonso X [El Sabio]. *Lapidario and Libro de las formas & ymagenes.* Ed. Roderic C. Diman and Lynn W. Winget. Madison, WI: Hispanic Seminary of Medieval Studies, 1980.

———. *Songs of Holy Mary of Alfonso X, the Wise: A Translation of the "Cantigas de Santa Maria."* Trans. Kathleen Kulp-Hill. Tempe: Arizona Center for Medieval and Renaissance Studies, 2000.

Al-Himyarī. *La péninsule ibérique au moyen-age d'après le Kitāb ar-rawd al-miʿtār.* Ed. and trans. Évariste Lévi-Provençal. Leiden: Brill, 1938.

Al-Idrīsī. *Description de l'Afrique et de l'Espagne par Edrîsî.* Ed. and trans. R. Dozy and M. J. de Goeje. Leiden: Brill, 1866.

Al-Maqqarī, Ahmad ibn Muhammad. *Analectes sur l'histoire et la littérature des arabes d'Espagne.* Ed. R. Dozy et al. 2 vols. Leiden: Brill, 1855–61.

Al-Saqaṭī. *Un manuel hispanique de hisba.* Ed. G. S. Colin and Évariste Lévi-Provençal. Paris: Ernest Leroux, 1931.

Al-Shaqundī. *Elogio del Islam español (Risāla fī faḍl al-Andalus).* Trans. Emilio García Gómez. Madrid: Estanislao Maestre, 1934.

Al-Wansharīsī. *Al-Miʿyar al-muʿrib wa al-jamiʿ al-mughrib.* Rabat: Wizarat al-Awqaf, 1981.

Anglería, Pedro Mártir de. *Una embajada de los Reyes Católicos a Egipto.* Ed. Luis García y García. Valladolid: Consejo Superior de Investigaciones Científicas, 1947.

*Apicius: A Critical Edition with an Introduction and an English Translation of the Latin Recipe Text Apicius.* Ed. Christopher Grocock and Sally Grainger. Totnes, Devon: Prospect Books, 2006.

Arnau de Vilanova. *Regimen sanitatis ad regem aragonum.* Ed. Luis García-Ballester and Michael R. McVaugh. Vol. 10.1 of *Arnaldi de Villanova Opera medica omnia.* Barcelona: Seminarium Historiae Scientiae Barchinone (C.S.I.C.), 1996.

Aznar Cardona, Pedro. *Expulsion iustificada de los moriscos.* Huesca: Pedro Cabarte, 1612.

Bermúdez de Pedraza, Francisco. *Historia eclesiástica de Granada.* Facsimile with preliminary study by Ignacio Henares Cuéllar. Granada: Editorial don Quijote, 1989.

Bernáldez, Andrés. *Memorias del reinado de los Reyes Católicos.* Ed. Manuel Gómez-Moreno and Juan de M. Carriazo. Madrid: Real Academia de la Historia, 1962.

Bleda, Jaime. *Coronica de los moros de España.* Valencia: En la Impresion de Felipe Mey, 1618.

Bukhārī. *Ṣaḥīḥ al-Bukhārī.* Trans. Muhammad Muhsin Khan. 9 vols. Riyadh: Darussalam, 1997.

*Cartulaire général de l'ordre des Hospitaliers de S. Jean de Jérusalem (1100–1310)*. Ed. Joseph Delaville Le Roulx. 4 vols. Paris: E. Leroux, 1894–1906.

*Castigos e documentos para bien vivir ordenados por el rey don Sancho IV*. Ed. Agapito Rey. Bloomington: Indiana University Press, 1952.

Castillejo, Cristóbal de. *Obras*. Ed. J. Domínguez Bordona. 4 vols. Madrid: Espasa-Calpe, 1957–60.

*Catálogo de la documentación relativa al antiguo reino de Valencia*. Ed. Jesús Ernesto Martínez Ferrando. 2 vols. Madrid: Cuerpo Facultativo de Archiveros, Bibliotecarios y Arqueólogos, 1934.

Cervantes Saavedra, Miguel de. *Don Quixote*. Trans. Charles Jarvis. Oxford: Oxford University Press, 1992.

*The Code of Cuenca: Municipal Law on the Twelfth-Century Castilian Frontier*. Trans. James F. Powers. Philadelphia: University of Pennsylvania Press, 2000.

*Código de las costumbres escritas de Tortosa a doble texto*. Ed. Ramon Foguet, José Foguet Marsal, Victor Covián, and Juan Permanyer. Tortosa: Impr. Querol, 1912.

*Colección de cánones y de todos los concilios de la iglesia española*. 7 vols. Ed. and trans. Juan Tejada y Ramiro. Madrid: Imprenta de J. M. Alonso, 1849–62.

*Colección diplomática de Alfonso I de Aragón y Pamplona, 1104–1134*. Ed. José Ángel Lema Pueyo. San Sebastián: Editorial Eusko Ikaskuntza, 1990.

Como, Martino de. *The Art of Cooking: The First Modern Cookery Book*. Ed. Luigi Ballerini. Berkeley: University of California Press, 2005.

*Correspondencia del Conde de Tendilla*. Ed. Emilio Meneses García. 2 vols. Madrid: Real Academia de la Historia, 1973–74.

*Cortes de los antiguos reinos de Aragon y de Valencia y Principado de Cataluña*. Madrid: Real Academia de la Historia, 1896.

*Cortes de los antiguos reinos de León y de Castilla*. 5 vols. Madrid: Real Academia de la Historia, 1861–1903.

*Costums de Tortosa*. Ed. Jesús Massip i Fonollosa. Barcelona: Fundació Noguera, 1996.

Covarrubias Orozco, Sebastián de. *Tesoro de la lengua castellana o española, según la impresión de 1611, con las adiciones de Benito Remigio Noydens publicadas en 1674*. Ed. Martín de Riquer. Barcelona: Horta, 1943.

*Crónicas de los reyes de Castilla desde Alfonso el Sabio, hasta los Católicos Don Fernando y Doña Isabel*. Ed. Cayetano Rosell. Biblioteca de autores españoles 68, vol. 2. Madrid: M. Rivadeneyra, 1877.

*Decrees of the Ecumenical Councils*. Ed. Norman Tanner. 2 vols. London: Sheed and Ward, 1990.

Delicado, Francisco. *Retrato de la Lozana Andaluza*. Ed. Jacques Joset and Folke Gernert. Barcelona: Círculo de Lectores, 2007.

Desclot, Bernat. *Crònica*. Ed. M. Coll i Alentorn. 5 vols. Barcelona: Barcino, 1949–51.

Díaz de Gámez, Gutierre. *El Victorial: Crónica de Don Pero Niño, conde de Buelna*. Ed. Ramón Iglesia. Madrid: Espasa-Calpe, 1940.

Díez Daza, Alonso. *Libro de los provechos y dannos que provienen con la sola bevida del agua*. Seville: Alonso de la Barrera, 1576.

*Diplomatarium of the Crusader Kingdom of Valencia*. Ed. Robert I. Burns. 4 vols. Princeton, NJ: Princeton University Press, 1985–2007.

*Documentos de Jaime I de Aragón*. Ed. Ambrosio Huici Miranda and María Desamparados Cabanes Pecourt. 5 vols. Valencia: Anubar, 1976–88.

*Documentos del Archivo general de la villa de Madrid*. Ed. Ángel Pérez Chozas, Agustín Millares Carlo, and Eulogio Varela Hervías. Madrid: Artes gráficas municipales, 1932.

*Documentos municipales de Huesca, 1100–1350*. Ed. Carlos Laliena Corbera. Huesca: Ayuntamiento de Huesca, 1988.

*Documents arabes inédits sur la vie sociale et économique en occident musulmane au moyen âge*. Ed. Évariste Lévi-Provençal. Cairo: Institut français d'archéologie orientale, 1955.

Eiximenis, Francesc. *Com usar bé de beure e menjar: Normes morals contingudes en el "Terç de Crestià."* Barcelona: Curial, 1983.

———. *Llibres, mestres i sermons*. Ed. David Guixeras and Xavier Renedo. Barcelona: Barcino, 2008.

*English Historical Documents*. Vol. 3, *1189–1327*. Ed. Harry Rothwell. London: Methuen, 1975.

Escobar, Luis de. *Las quatrocientas respuestas a otras tantas preguntas*. Valladolid: Por Francisco de Cordoua y a costa de Francisco de Alfaro, 1552.

*Escribir y gobernar: El último registro de correspondencia del Conde de Tendilla (1513–1515)*. Ed. María Amparo Moreno Trujillo, María José Osorio Pérez, and Juan María de la Obra Sierra. Granada: Universidad de Granada, 2007.

Eymeric, Nicholas. *Directorium inquisitorum*. Ed. Francisco Pegnae. Venice: Apud Marcum Antonium Zalterium, 1607.

*Fatāwā Ibn Rushd*. Ed. Al-Mukhtar ibn al-Tāhir al-Talīlī. 3 vols. Beirut: Dār al-Gharb al-Islāmī, 1987.

Fernández de Palencia, Alfonso. *Guerra de Granada*. Trans. D. A. Paz y Meliá. Facsimile. Granada: Universidad de Granada, 1998.

Ferrer, Vincent. *Sermons*. Ed. José Sanchis y Sivera. 2 vols. Barcelona: Barcino, 1932–84.

*Fori antiqui Valentiae*. Ed. Manuel Dualde Serrano. Madrid: Consejo Superior de Investigaciones Científicas, 1950–67.

*Forum Conche, Fuero of Cuenca: The Latin Text of the Municipal Charter and Laws of the City of Cuenca, Spain*. Ed. George H. Allen. Cincinnati: University Studies published by the University of Cincinnati, 1909–10.

*Fuero de Plasencia*. Ed. Jesús Majada Neila. Salamanca: Librería Cervantes, 1986.

*El Fuero de Teruel*. Ed. Max Gorosch. Stockholm: Almqvist & Wiksells Boktryckeri, 1950.

*Fuero de Usagre (siglo XIII) anotado con las variantes del de Cáceres*. Ed. Rafael de Ureña y Smenjaud and Adolfo Bonilla y San Martín. Madrid: Hijos de Reus, 1907.

*Fueros de Navarra*. Ed. José María Lacarra and Ángel J. Martín Duque. 2 vols. Pamplona: Institución Principe de Viana, 1975.

Guerra de Lorca, Pedro. *Catecheses mystagogicae pro advenis ex secta Mahometana.* Madrid: Apud Petrum Madrigal, 1586.

Hurtado de Mendoza, Diego. *Guerra de Granada hecho por el Rei de España don Philippe II nuestro señor contra los moriscos de aquel reino, sus rebeldes.* Lisbon: Giraldo de la Viña, 1627. Trans. Martin Shuttleworth as *The War in Granada* (London: Folio Society, 1982).

Ibn ʿIdhārī al-Marrākushī. *Kitāb al-bayān al-mughrib.* Ed. G. S. Colin and E. Lévi-Provençal. 2 vols. Leiden: Brill, 1951.

Ibn al-Khaṭīb. *Historia de los reyes de la Alhambra: El resplandor de la luna llena acerca de la dinastía nazarí (Al-Lamha al-badriyya fī l-dawlat al-nasriyya).* Trans. José María Casciaro Ramírez and Emilio Molina López. Granada: Universidad de Granada, 2010.

———. *Libro del cuidado de la salud durante las estaciones del año, o, "Libro de higiene."* Ed. and trans. María Concepción Vázquez de Benito. Salamanca: Universidad de Salamanca, 1984.

Ibn Khaldūn. *The Muqaddimah.* Trans. Franz Rosenthal. 3 vols. New York: Pantheon Books, 1958.

———. *Muqaddimat ibn Khaldūn: Prolégomènes d'ebn-Khaldoun.* Ed. M. Quatremère. 3 vols. Paris: Benjamin Duprat, 1858.

Jaume [James] I of Aragon. *The Book of Deeds of James I of Aragon: A Translation of the Medieval Catalan "Llibre dels Fets."* Trans. Damian J. Smith and Helena Buffery. Aldershot: Ashgate, 2003.

———. *Llibre dels fets del rei en Jaume.* Ed. Jordi Bruguera. 2 vols. Barcelona: Barcino, 1991.

Juan de Aviñón. *Sevillana medicina que trata el modo conservativo y curativo de los que habitan en la muy insigne ciudad de Sevilla.* Seville: Imprenta de Enrique Rasco, 1885.

Juan Manuel. *Obras completas.* Ed. José Manuel Blecua. 2 vols. Madrid: editorial Gredos, 1982–83.

Lalaing, Antoine de. "Relation du premier voyage de Philippe le Beau en Espagne en 1501." In *Collection des voyages des souverains des Pays-Bas,* ed. M. Gachard, 1:121–318. Brussels: F. Hayez, 1876.

Leo Africanus [Jean-Léon l'Africain]. *Description de l'Afrique.* Trans. A. Épaulard. 2 vols. Paris: Adrien-Maisonneuve, 1956.

León, Andrés de. *Practico de morbo gallico.* Valladolid: Luis Sanchez, 1605.

León Pinelo, Antonio de. "Velos antiguos y modernos en los rostros de las mujeres: Sus conveniencias y daños." Ed. Enrique Suárez Figaredo. *Lemir* 13 (2009): 235–388.

*Libre de Sent Soví (Receptari de cuina).* Ed. Rudolf Grewe. Barcelona: Barcino, 1979.

*El Libro de la Cadena del Concejo de Jaca.* Ed. Dámaso Sangorrín y Diest-Garcés. Zaragoza: Imprenta de F. Martínez, 1920.

Llull, Ramon. *Libre de Meravelles.* Ed. M. Salvador Galmés. 4 vols. Barcelona: Editorial Barcino, 1931–34.

Lobera de Ávila, Luis. *Vergel de Sanidad que por otro nombre se llamava Banquete de nobles cavalleros, y orden de bivir*. Alcalá de Henares: Joan de Brocar, 1542. Reprinted as *Banquete de nobles caballeros*. Madrid: Reimpresiones Bibliográficas, 1952.

López de Corella, Alonso. *Secretos de philosophia y astrologia y medicina y de las quatro mathematicas sciencias*. Zaragoza: En la casas de George Coci a costas de Pedro Bernuz, 1547.

López de Villalobos, Francisco. *The Medical Works of Francisco Lopez de Villalobos, the Celebrated Court Physician of Spain*. Trans. George Gaskoin. London: John Churchill and Sons, 1870.

———. *El sumario de la medicina*. Salamanca: Antonio de Barreda, 1498.

———. *El sumario de la medicina con un tratado de las pestiferas bubas*. Ed. María Teresa Herrera. Salamanca: Ediciones del Instituto de Historia de la Medicina Española, 1973.

Lucas of Tuy. *Lucae Tudensis Chronicon Mundi*. Ed. Emma Falque. Corpus Christianorum, Continuatio Mediaevalis, 74. Turnhout: Brepols, 2003.

*Manual de mugeres en el qual se contienen muchas y diversas reçetas muy buenas*. Ed. Alicia Martínez Crespo. Salamanca: Ediciones Universidad de Salamanca, 1995.

Mármol Carvajal, Luis del. *Descripcion general de Africa*. 3 vols. Granada: Casa de Rene Rabut, 1573–99.

———. *Historia del rebelión y castigo de los moriscos del reino de Granada*. Ed. Cayetano Rosell et al. In Biblioteca de autores españoles 21. Madrid: Ediciones Atlas, 1852. Reprinted with new pagination as *Rebelión y castigo de los moriscos*. Málaga: Editorial Arguval, 1991.

Martínez Montiño, Francisco. *Arte de cocina, pasteleria, vizcocheria, y conserveria*. Barcelona: En la imprenta de Maria Angela Martí, 1763.

Martínez de Toledo, Alfonso. *Archipreste de Talavera o Corbacho*. Ed. J. González Muela. Madrid: Clásicos Castalia, 1982.

———. *Little Sermons on Sin: The Archpriest of Talavera*. Trans. Lesley Byrd Simpson. Berkeley: University of California Press, 1959.

Martorell, Joanot, and Martí Joan de Galba. *Tirant lo Blanc*. Ed. Martí de Riquer. 2 vols. Barcelona: Editorial Seix Barral, 1970.

———. *Tirant lo Blanc*. Trans. David H. Rosenthal. New York: Schocken Books, 1983.

Massa, Nicolò. *Liber de morbo gallico*. Venice: In aedibus Francisci Bindoni, ac Maphei Pasini, 1507 [1527].

*Memorias de Don Enrique IV de Castilla*. Madrid: Fortanet, 1913.

Metge, Bernard. *The Dream of Bernat Metge*. Trans. Richard Vernier. Aldershot: Ashgate, 2002.

———. *Lo somni*. Ed. Lola Badia. Barcelona: Quaderns Crema, 1999.

Muntaner, Ramon. *Crònica*. Ed. Enric Bagué. 2 vols. Barcelona: Barcino, 1951.

Münzer, Jerónimo. *Viaje por España y Portugal (1494–1495)*. Madrid: Ediciones Polifemo, 1991.

Muslim. *Ṣaḥīḥ Muslim*. Trans. ʿAbdul Ḥamīd Ṣiddīqī. 4 vols. Lahore: Sh. Muhammad Ashraf, 1971–75.

Navagero, Andrea. *Opera omnia*. Venice: Typographia Remondiniana, 1754.

Nola, Roberto de. *Libre del coch: Tractat de cuina medieval*. Ed. Veronika Leimgruber. Barcelona: Universitat de Barcelona, 1977.

———. *Libro de guisados*. Ed. Dionisio Pérez. Madrid: Compañía Ibero-Americana de Publicaciones, 1929.

Núñez Muley, Francisco. *A Memorandum for the President of the Royal Audiencia and Chancery Court of the City and Kingdom of Granada*. Trans. Vincent Barletta. Chicago: University of Chicago Press, 2007.

*Ordenanças de Sevilla*. Seville: Juan Varela, 1527.

*Ordenanzas de la Real Audiencia y Chancillería de Granada*. Granada: Sebastian de Mena, 1601.

*Ordenanzas para el buen régimen y gobierno de . . . la ciudad de Toledo*. Toledo: Imprenta de José de Cea, 1858.

*Ordinaciones de la Casa Real de Aragón*. Zaragoza: Impr. y Lit. De M. Peiro, 1853.

*The Pamplona Bibles: A Facsimile Compiled from Two Picture Bibles with Martyrologies Commissioned by King Sancho el Fuerte of Navarra (1194–1234); Amiens Manuscript Latin 108 and Harburg MS. 1, 2, Lat. 4°, 15*. Ed. François Bucher. 2 vols. New Haven, CT: Yale University Press, 1971.

Pérez de Ayala, Martín. *Sínodo de la Diócesis de Guadix y de Baza*. Facsimile with preliminary study by Carlos Asenjo Sedano. Granada: University of Granada, 1994.

*Primera crónica general de España*. Ed. Ramón Menéndez Pidal. 2 vols. Madrid: Editorial Gredos, 1955.

*Regesta de letras pontificias del Archivo de la Corona de Aragón*. Ed. Francisco J. Miquel Rosell. Madrid: Cuerpo de Archiveros, Bibliotecarios, y Arqueólogos, 1948.

*El registro del Merino de Zaragoza el Caballero Don Gil Tarín, 1291–1312*. Zaragoza: Imprenta del Hospicio Provincial, 1889.

*Relación de los hechos del muy magnífico e más virtuoso señor, el señor don Miguel Lucas, muy digno condestable de Castilla*. Ed. Juan Cuevas Mata, Juan del Arco Moya, and José del Arco Moya. Jaén: Universidad de Jaén, 2001.

*Repartimiento de Sevilla*. Ed. Julio González. 2 vols. Madrid: Consejo Superior de Investigaciones Científicas, 1951.

*Los repartimientos de Vélez-Málaga: Primer repartimiento*. Ed. María Teresa Martín Palma. Granada: Editorial Universidad de Granada, 2005.

Roig, Jaume. *"The Mirror" of Jaume Roig: An Edition and an English Translation of MS. Vat. Lat. 4806*. Ed. and trans. María Celeste Delgado-Librero. Tempe: Arizona Center for Medieval and Renaissance Studies, 2010.

Rojas Villandrando, Augustín de. *El viaje entretenido de Agustín de Rojas*. Ed. Manuel Cañete. 2 vols. Madrid: Rodríguez Serra, 1901.

*Romancero general (1600, 1604, 1605)*. Ed. Ángel González Palencia. 2 vols. Madrid: Consejo Superior de Investigaciones Científicas, 1947.

Sánchez de Arévalo, Rodrigo. *Compendiosa historia hispánica*. Rome: Udalricus Gallus, 1470.

Sandoval, Prudencio de. *Primera parte de la vida y hechos del emperador Carlos Quinto.*
Valladolid: Sebastian de Cañas, 1604. Republished in *Historia de la vida y hechos del
emperador Carlos V,* ed. Carlos Seco Serrano, in Biblioteca de autores españoles 81.
Madrid: Ediciones Atlas, 1951.

San Juan del Puerto, Francisco Jesús María de. *Mission historial de Marruecos.* Seville:
Francisco Garay, 1708.

Santa Cruz, Alonso de. *Crónica de los reyes católicos.* Ed. Juan de Mata Carriazo. Seville:
Escuela de Estudios Hispano-Americanos de Sevilla, 1951.

Schellig, Conrad. *In pustulas malas morbum quem malum de Francia vulgus appellat consilium.* Facsimile ed., in Karl Sudhoff and Charles Singer, *The Earliest Printed Literature
on Syphilis: Being Ten Tractates from the Years 1495–1498.* Florence: R. Lier, 1925.

*Segunda parte de las leyes del Reyno* [*Nueva Recopilación de las leyes del Reyno*]. Alcalá de
Henares: Andrés de Angulo, 1567.

*Las Siete Partidas.* Trans. Samuel Parsons Scott, ed. Robert I. Burns. 5 vols. Philadelphia:
University of Pennsylvania Press, 2001.

*Sínodo de la Diócesis de Guadix y de Baza, edición facsímil.* Ed. Carlos Asenjo Sedano.
Granada: Universidad de Granada, 1994.

Talavera, Hernando de. *Breve e muy provechosa doctrina christiana.* Granada: Meinardus
Ungut and Johann Pegnitzer, 1496.

Torres, Diego de. *Relación del origen y suceso de los xarifes y del estado de los reinos de Marruecos, Fez, y Tarudante.* Ed. Mercedes García-Arenal. Madrid: Siglo Veintiuno
Editores, 1980.

Torres, Pedro de. *Libro que trata de la enfermedad de las bubas.* Madrid: Luis Sanchez,
1600.

*Tratados de legislación musulmana.* Ed. Pascual de Gayangos. Madrid: Real Academia de la
Historia, 1853.

*Un tratado catalán medieval de derecho islámico: El llibre de la çuna e xara dels moros.* Ed.
Carme Barceló Torres. Córdoba: Universidad de Córdoba, 1989.

Usama ibn Munqidh. *The Book of Contemplation: Islam and the Crusades.* Trans. Paul M.
Cobb. London: Penguin, 2008.

Valencia, Pedro de. *Tratado acerca de los moriscos de España: Manuscrito del siglo VII.* Ed.
Joaquín Gil Sanjuán. Málaga: Algazara, 1997.

Vega, Lope de. *Obras completas de Lope de Vega.* 15 vols. Madrid: Biblioteca Castro, 1993–
98.

## SECONDARY SOURCES

Adamson, Melitta Weiss. *Food in Medieval Times.* Westport, CT: Greenwood Press, 2004.

———, ed. *Regional Cuisines of Medieval Europe: A Book of Essays.* New York: Routledge,
2002.

Aguilar García, María Dolores. "Mezquitas y baños de Málaga musulmana." In *Simposio internacional sobre la ciudad islámica*, 389–400. Zaragoza: Institución Fernando el Católico, 1991.

Ahmed, Leila. *A Quiet Revolution: The Veil's Resurgence, from the Middle East to America.* New Haven, CT: Yale University Press, 2011.

———. *Women and Gender in Islam.* New Haven, CT: Yale University Press, 1992.

Akbari, Suzanne Conklin. *Idols in the East: European Representations of Islam and the Orient, 1100–1450.* Ithaca, NY: Cornell University Press, 2009.

Alegría Suescun, David. *Agua y ciudad: Aprovachamientos hidráulicos urbanos en Navarra (siglos XII–XIV).* Pamplona: Gobierno de Navarra, 2004.

———. "Baños urbanos del patrimonio real en Navarra (siglos XII–XIV)." In *Usos sociales del agua en las ciudades hispánicas a fines de la edad media*, ed. María Isabel del Val Valdivieso, 315–65. Valladolid: Universidad de Valladolid, 2002.

Alonso, Álvaro. "Un poema erótico de Cristóbal de Castillejo: 'Estando en los baños.'" In *Venus venerada: Tradiciones eróticas en la literatura española*, ed. José Ignacio Díez and Adrienne L. Martín, 39–56. Madrid: Editorial Complutense, 2006.

Amer, Sahar. "Muslim Women: Western Literature." In *Women and Gender in Medieval Europe: An Encyclopedia*, ed. Margaret Schaus, 593–95. New York: Routledge, 2006.

Anderson, Ruth M. *Hispanic Costume, 1480–1530.* New York: Hispanic Society of America, 1979.

Andrés, Alfonso. "Monasterio de San Juan de Burgos." *Boletín de la Real Academia de la Historia* 71 (1917): 117–36.

Aparici Martí, Joaquín. "Tolerar y convivir: Carnicerías musulmanas en tierras de Castello." In *VIII Simposio Internacional de Mudejarismo: De mudéjares a moriscos; Una conversión forzada; Teruel, 15–17 de septiembre de 1999; Actas*, 1:315–32. Teruel: Centro de Estudios Mudéjares, 2003.

Aranda Doncel, Juan. *Los moriscos en tierras de Córdoba.* Córdoba: Monte de piedad y caja de ahorros de Córdoba, 1984.

Arco, Ricardo del. "El monasterio de Santa Cristina de 'Summo Portu.'" *Linajes de Aragón* 5 (1914): 101–20.

Arié, Rachel. "Acerca del traje musulmán en España desde la caída de Granada hasta la expulsión de los moriscos." *Revista de Instituto Egipcio de Estudios Islámicos* 13 (1965–66): 103–17.

———. "Le costume des musulmans de Castille au XIII\ :sup:`e` siècle d'après les miniatures du *Libro de Ajedrez*." *Mélanges de la Casa de Velázquez* 2 (1966): 59–69.

———. *L'Espagne musulmane au temps des Nasrides.* Paris: É. de Boccard, 1990.

———. "Quelques remarques sur le costume des musulmans d'Espagne au temps des Naṣrides." *Arabica* 12 (1965): 244–61.

Arrizabalaga, Jon, John Henderson, and Roger French. *The Great Pox.* New Haven, CT: Yale University Press, 1997.

Arroyas Serrano, Magín, and Vicent Gil Vicent. *Revuelta y represión en los moriscos castellonenses: El proceso inquisitorial de Pedro Aman, morisco vecino de Onda.* Onda: Ajuntement d'Onda, 1995.

Asher, Catherine B. "The Public Baths of Medieval Spain: An Architectural Study." In *The Medieval Mediterranean: Cross-Cultural Contacts,* ed. Marilyn J. Chiat and Kathryn L. Reyerson, 25–34. St. Cloud, MN: North Star Press, 1988.

Asín Palacios, Miguel. "El original árabe de la novela aljamiada 'El baño de Zarieb.'" In *Homenaje ofrecido a Menéndez Pidal,* 1:377–88. Madrid: Librería y Casa Editorial Hernando, 1925.

Barceló Crespí, María, and Guillem Rosselló Bordoy. *La ciudad de Mallorca: La vida cotidiana en una ciudad mediterránea medieval.* Palma: Lleonard Muntaner, 2006.

Barceló Torres, María del Carmen. "La morería de Valencia en el reinado de Juan II." *Saitabi* 30 (1980): 49–71.

Barrios Aguilera, Manuel. *Granada morisca, la convivencia negada: Historia y textos.* Granada: Editorial Comares, 2002.

———. "Religiosidad y vida cotidiana de los moriscos." In *Historia del Reino de Granada,* ed. Manuel Barrios Aguilera, 2:357–437. Granada: Universidad de Granada, 2000.

Basáñez Villaluenga, María Blanca. *La aljama sarracena de Huesca en el siglo XIV.* Barcelona: Consejo Superior de Investigaciones Científicas, 1989.

———. *Las morerías aragonesas durante el reinado de Jaime II: Catálogo de la documentación de la Cancelleria Real.* Teruel: Centro de Estudios Mudéjares, 1999.

Bayona i Prats, Lluís. "La rehabilitació en els monuments: El cas dels Banys Àrabs." *Revista de Girona* 139 (1990): 181–85.

Bazzana, André. *Maisons d'al-Andalus: Habitat médiéval et structures du peuplement dans l'Espagne orientale.* Madrid: Casa de Velázquez, 1992.

BBC News. "The Islamic Veil Across Europe." September 22, 2011.

Beinart, Haim. *Records of the Trials of the Spanish Inquisition in Ciudad Real.* 4 vols. Jerusalem: Israel Academy of Sciences and Humanities, 1974–88.

Benkheïra, Mohammed Hocine. "Tabou du porc et identité en Islam." In *Histoire et identités alimentaires en Europe,* ed. Martin Bruegel and Bruno Laurioux, 37–51. Paris: Hachette littératures, 2002.

Berco, Cristian. "Revealing the Other: Moriscos, Crime, and Local Politics in Toledo's Hinterland in the Late Sixteenth Century." *Medieval Encounters* 8 (2002): 135–59.

Berend, Nora. "Medieval Patterns of Social Exclusion and Integration: The Regulation of Non-Christian Clothing in Thirteenth-Century Hungary." *Revue Mabillon,* n.s., 8 (1997): 155–76.

Bernis, Carmen. *Indumentaria medieval española.* Madrid: Consejo Superior de Investigaciones Científicas, 1956.

———. "Modas moriscas en la sociedad cristiana española del siglo XV y principios del XVI." *Boletín de la Real Academia de la Historia* 144 (1959): 199–236.

———. *Trajes y modas en la España de los Reyes Católicos.* 2 vols. Madrid: Consejo Superior de Investigaciones Científicas, 1978–79.

Blasco, Rosa María. "Una carnicería regentada por moriscos en el arrabal de San Juan, de Elche." *Sharq al-Andalus* 2 (1985): 75–79.

Blumenthal, Debra. *Enemies and Familiars. Slavery and Mastery in Fifteenth-Century Valencia.* Ithaca, NY: Cornell University Press, 2009.

Bofarull y Sans, Francisco de. "Documentos para escribir una monografía de la Villa de Montblanch, leidos en la Real Academia de Buenas Letras de Barcelona." *Memorias de la Real Academia de Buenas Letras de Barcelona* 6 (1898): 425–578.

———. "Jaime y los Judíos." In *Congrés d'historia de la corona d'Aragó dedicat al rey en Jaume I y a la seua época*, 819–943. Barcelona: Stampa d'en Francisco Altés, 1913.

Borg, Alexander. "The Language of Folk Medicine—a Philological Note on the Pathology of Syphilis and Leprosy in a Morisco Arabic MS." *Korot* 21 (2011–12): 293–313.

Boronat y Barrachina, Pascual. *Los moriscos españoles y su expulsión.* 2 vols. Valencia: Imprenta de Francisco Vives y Mora, 1901.

Boswell, John. *The Royal Treasure: Muslim Communities Under the Crown of Aragon in the Fourteenth Century.* New Haven, CT: Yale University Press, 1977.

Bramon, Dolors. "Del Principat estant: Dos miracles montserratins sobre el bandolerisme morisc valencià." In *L'expulsió dels moriscos: Conseqüències en el món islàmic i el món cristià; 380è Aniversari de l'Expulsió dels Moriscos, Congrés Internacional, Sant Carles de la Ràpita, 5–9 de desembre de 1990*, 253–58. Barcelona: Generalitat de Catalunya, 1994.

Braudel, Fernand. *The Mediterranean and the Mediterranean World in the Age of Philip II.* Trans. Siân Reynolds. 2 vols. Berkeley: University of California Press, 1995.

Brundage, James A. *Law, Sex, and Christian Society in Medieval Europe.* Chicago: University of Chicago Press, 1990.

Bujanda, Fernando. "Documentos para la historia de la Diócesis de Calahorra." *Berceo: Boletín del Instituto de Estudios Riojanos* 2 (1947): 111–46.

Burguete Ors, Laura, and Josemi Lorenzo Arribas. "Limpieza y contaminación en la villa de Madrid durante la edad media: Casas de baño y tenerías." In *Agua y sistemas hidráulicos en la edad media hispana*, ed. Cristina Segura, 87–110. Madrid: Asociación Cultural al-Mudayna, 2003.

Burns, Robert I. "Baths and Caravanserais in Crusader Valencia." *Speculum* 46, no. 3 (1971): 443–58.

———. *The Crusader Kingdom of Valencia: Reconstruction on a Thirteenth-Century Frontier.* 2 vols. Cambridge, MA: Harvard University Press, 1967.

———. *Medieval Colonialism: Postcrusade Exploitation of Islamic Valencia.* Princeton, NJ: Princeton University Press, 1975.

———. "Women in Crusader Valencia: A Five-Year Core Sample, 1265–1270." *Medieval Encounters* 12 (2006): 37–47.

Butzer, Karl W., Elizabeth K. Butzer, and Juan F. Mateu. "Medieval Muslim Communities of the Sierra de Espadán, Kingdom of Valencia." *Viator* 17 (1986): 339–413.

Calleja Maestre, José María. "La expulsión de los moriscos en las artes plásticas." Extracts from a conference of the Asociación Amigos del Legado Andalusí, ed. Guillermo

Muñoz Vera (2010). http://www.arauco.org/SAPEREAUDE/terraaustralisincognita/historiasdealandalus/laexpulsionenlapintura.html.

Cantera Montenegro, Enrique. "Los mudejares en el marco de la sociedad riojana bajomedieval." In *Actas del III Simposio Internacional de Mudejarismo*, 21–38. Teruel: Centro de Estudios Mudéjares, 1986.

Cardaillac, Louis. *Morisques et chrétiens: Un affrontement polémique (1492–1640)*. Paris: Klincksieck, 1977.

Caro Baroja, Julio. *Ciclos y temas de la historia de España: Los moriscos del Reino de Granada*. Madrid: ISTMO, 1976.

———. "Los moriscos aragoneses segun un autor de comienzos del siglo XVII." In *Razas, Pueblos, y Linajes*, 81–98. Madrid: Revista de Occidente, 1957.

———. *Los moriscos del Reino de Granada (ensayo de historia social)*. Madrid: Instituto de Estudios Políticos, 1957.

Carpenter, Dwayne E. *Alfonso X and the Jews: An Edition of and Commentary on "Siete Partidas" 7.24 "De los judíos."* Berkeley: University of California Press, 1986.

Carrasco, Raphaël. *La monarchie catholique et les morisques (1520–1620)*. Montpellier: Université Paul-Valéry Montpellier III, 2005.

Carrasco Manchado, Ana Isabel. *De la convivencia a la exclusión: Imágenes legislativas e mudéjares y moriscos, siglos XIII–XVII*. Madrid: Sílex, 2012.

Carré, Antònia, and Lluís Cifuentes. "Práctica social, saber médico y reflejo literario de la cultura del baño en el contexto catalan medieval." *Anuario de Estudios Medievales* 39 (2009): 203–22.

Castillo Fernández, Javier. "Nuevos datos en torno a la ubicación de la judería de Baza y de sus baños árabes." *Miscelánea de estudios árabes y hebraicos: Sección de hebreo* 47 (1998): 57–74.

Castro, Américo. "Sentido histórico-literario del jamón y del tocino." In *Cervantes y los casticismos españoles*, 25–32. Madrid: Alianza Editorial, 1974.

Castro, Teresa de. "L'émergence d'une identité alimentaire: Musulmans et chrétiens dans le royaume de Grenade." In *Histoire et identités alimentaires en Europe*, ed. Martin Bruegel and Bruno Laurioux, 199–215. Paris: Hachette littératures, 2002.

———. "El tratado sobre el vestir, calzar y comer del arzobispo Hernando de Talavera." *Espacio, Tiempo y Forma* 14 (2001): 11–92.

Castro Martínez, Teresa de. *La alimentación en las crónicas castellanas bajomedievales*. Granada: Universidad de Granada, 1996.

Catlos, Brian A. *Muslims of Medieval Latin Christendom, c. 1050–1614*. Cambridge: Cambridge University Press, 2014.

———. *The Victors and the Vanquished: Christians and Muslims of Catalonia and Aragon, 1050–1300*. Cambridge: Cambridge University Press, 2004.

CBC News. "Stephen Harper 'Playing a Very Divisive Game' with Niqabs, Tom Mulcair Says." September 21, 2015. http://www.cbc.ca/news/politics/canada-election-2015-niqab-bloc-1.3236837.

*Cerámica granadina: Siglos XVI–XX*. Granada: Fundación Rodríguez-Acosta, 2001.

Childers, William. "Disappearing Moriscos." In *Cross-Cultural History and the Domestication of Otherness*, ed. M. J. Rozbicki and G. O. Ndege, 51–64. New York: Palgrave, 2012.

Clark, Raymond J. "Peter of Eboli, 'De Balneis Puteolanis': Manuscripts from the Aragonese Scriptorium in Naples." *Traditio* 45 (1989–90): 380–89.

Cohen, Jeffrey J. *Medieval Identity Machines*. Minneapolis: University of Minnesota Press, 2003.

Cohen, Mark. "What Was the Pact of 'Umar? A Literary-Historical Study." *Jerusalem Studies in Arabic and Islam* 23 (1999): 100–57.

Coleman, David. *Creating Christian Granada: Society and Religious Culture in an Old-World Frontier City, 1492–1600*. Ithaca, NY: Cornell University Press, 2003.

Constable, Olivia Remie. "Chess and Courtly Culture in Medieval Castile: The *Libro de ajedrez* of Alfonso X, el Sabio." *Speculum* 82, no. 2 (April 2007): 301–47.

———. "Clothing, Iron, and Timber: The Growth of Christian Anxiety About Islam in the Long Twelfth Century." In *European Transformations: The Long Twelfth Century*, ed. Thomas F. X. Noble and John Van Engen, 279–313. Notre Dame, IN: University of Notre Dame Press, 2012.

———. "Food and Meaning: Christian Understandings of Muslim Food and Food Ways in Spain, 1250–1550." *Viator* 44 (2013): 199–235.

———. *Housing the Stranger in the Mediterranean World Lodging, Trade, and Travel in Late Antiquity and the Middle Ages*. Cambridge: Cambridge University Press, 2003.

———, ed. *Medieval Iberia: Readings from Christian, Muslim, and Jewish Sources*. Philadelphia: University of Pennsylvania Press, 1997; 2nd ed., with the assistance of Damian Zurro, 2012.

———. "Muslim Spain and Mediterranean Slavery: The Medieval Slave Trade as an Aspect of Muslim-Christian Relations." In *Christendom and Its Discontents: Exclusion, Persecution, and Rebellion, 1000–1500*, ed. Scott L. Waugh and Peter D. Diehl, 264–84. Cambridge: Cambridge University Press, 1996.

———. "Muslim Women in Christian Spain." In *Women and Gender in Medieval Europe: An Encyclopedia*, ed. Margaret Schaus, 595. New York: Routledge, 2006.

———. *Trade and Traders in Muslim Spain: The Commercial Realignment of the Iberian Peninsula, 900–1500*. Cambridge: Cambridge University Press, 1994.

Contreras, Rafael. *Estudio descriptivo de los monumentos árabes de Granada, Sevilla y Córdoba, ó sea, la Alhambra, el Alcázar y la Gran mezquita de occidente*. Madrid: Ricardo Fé, 1885.

Corral Lafuente, José Luis. "El proceso de represión contra los mudéjares aragoneses." *Aragón en la Edad Media* 14–15 (1999): 341–56.

Corriente Córdoba, Federico. *Relatos píos y profanos del manuscrito aljamiado de Urrea de Jalón*. Zaragoza: Institución Fernando el Católico, 1990.

Cressier, Patrice. "Prendre les eaux en al-Andalus: Pratique et fréquentation de la Hamma." *Médiévales* 43 (2002): 41–54.

Daniel, Norman. *Islam and the West: The Making of an Image*. Oxford: Oneworld, 1993.

Danvila y Collado, Manuel. *La expulsión de los moriscos españoles*. Madrid: Librería de Fernando Fé, 1889.

Dedieu, Jean-Pierre. "Morisques et vieux-chrétiens à Daimiel au XVIᵉ siècle." In *Actes du II Symposium International du C.I.E.M. sur Religion, Identité et Sources Documentaires sur les Morisques Andalous*, ed. Abdeljelil Temimi, 1:199–214. Tunis: Institut Supérieur de Documentation, 1984.

Díaz de Rábago Hernández, Carmen. "Alimentación y religión en una morería valenciana bajomedieval: Castelló de la Plana." *Millars: Espai i historia* 15 (1992): 100–109.

Díez Jorge, María Elena. "Purificación y placer: El agua y las mil y una noches en los Baños de Comares." *Cuadernos de la Alhambra* 40 (2004): 123–50.

Dillard, Heath. *Daughters of the Reconquest: Women in Castilian Town Society, 1100–1300*. Cambridge: Cambridge University Press, 1984.

Dozy, Reinhart. *Dictionnaire détaillé des noms des vêtements chez les Arabes*. Amsterdam: J. Muller, 1845.

Drayson, Elizabeth. *The King and the Whore: King Roderick and La Cava*. New York: Palgrave Macmillan, 2007.

Echaniz Quintana, Ana María, Pedro J. Lavado Paradinas, Encarnación Martínez Martínez, Isabel Sáenz García-Baquero, and Ángel Zas Barriga. "Aguas mudéjares: Aguas para la salud." In *Actas del XI Simposio Internacional de Mudejarismo, Teruel, 18–20 de septiembre de 2008*, 325–44. Teruel: Centro de Estudios Mudéjares, 2009.

Echevarría Arsuaga, Ana. *The Fortress of Faith: The Attitude Toward Muslims in Fifteenth Century Spain*. Brill: Leiden, 1999.

———. *Knights on the Frontier: The Moorish Guard of the Kings of Castile (1410–1467)*. Trans. Martin Beagles. Leiden: Brill, 2009.

———. "Política y religión frente al Islam: La evolución de la legislación real castellana sobre musulmanes en el siglo XV." *Qurtuba* 4 (1999): 45–72.

Ehlers, Benjamin. *Between Christians and Moriscos: Juan de Ribera and Religious Reform in Valencia, 1568–1614*. Baltimore: Johns Hopkins University Press, 2006.

Epalza, Mikel de. *Baños árabes en el pais Valenciano*. Valencia: Generalitat Valenciana, Conselleria de Cultura, Educació i Ciència, 1989.

Espadas Burgos, Manuel. "Aspectos sociorreligiosos de la alimentación española." *Hispania: Revista Española de Historia* 131 (1975): 537–66.

Espinar Moreno, Manuel. "Apuntes de arqueología y cultura material Granadina: El baño del Albaicín (siglos XIII–XVI)." *Cuadernos de arte de la Universidad de Granada* 21 (1990): 71–86.

———. "Rentas y tributos de los baños de las tierras de Guadix: El baño de La Peza (1494–1514)." In *Actas del VI coloquio internacional de historia medieval de Andalucía*, 177–87. Málaga: Universidad de Málaga, 1991.

Evans, Helen C., and Brandie Ratliff, eds. *Byzantium and Islam, Age of Transition, 7th–9th Century*. New York: Metropolitan Museum of Art, 2012.

Fábregas García, Adele. *Producción y comercio de azúcar en el mediterraneo medieval: El ejemplo del reino de Granada*. Granada: Universidad de Granada, 2000.

Febrer Romaguera, Manuel Vicente, ed. *Les aljames mudèjars valencianes en el segle XV.* Valencia: Universitat de València, 2006.

———, ed. *Cartas pueblas de las morerías valencianas y documentación complementaria.* Zaragoza: Anubar, 1991.

Feliciano, María Judith. "Muslim Shrouds for Christian Kings? A Reassessment of Andalusi Textiles in Thirteenth-Century Castilian Life and Ritual." In *Under the Influence: Questioning the Comparative in Medieval Castile,* ed. Cynthia Robinson and Leyla Rouhi, 101–31. Leiden: Brill, 2005.

Fernández y González, Francisco. *Estado social y político de los mudéjares de Castilla.* Madrid: Imprenta a cargo de Joaquin Muñoz, 1866.

Ferrer i Mallol, María Teresa. *Les aljames sarraïnes de la governació d'Oriola en el segle XIV.* Barcelona: Consell Superior d'Investigacions Científiques, 1988.

———. *Els sarraïns de la corona catalano-aragonesa en el segle XIV: Segregació i discriminació.* Barcelona: Consell Superior d'Investigacions Científiques, 1987.

Fournier, Caroline. "Bains publics et mosquées dans les villes d'al-Andalus." In *I Congreso internacional: Escenarios urbanos de al-Andalus y el Occidente musulmán; Vélez-Málaga, 16–18 de junio de 2010,* ed. Virgilio Martínez Enamorado, 337–54. Málaga: Iniciativa Urbana de "Toda la Villa," 2011.

———. "Les bains publics d'al-Andalus, espaces de 'convivialité'? (IXᵉ–XVᵉ siècles)." In *La convivencia en las ciudades medievales,* ed. Beatriz Arízaga Bolumburu and Jesús Ángel Solórzano Telechea, 321–31. Logroño: Instituto de Estudios Riojanos, 2008.

Freedman, Paul. *Out of the East: Spices and the Medieval Imagination.* New Haven, CT: Yale University Press, 2008.

French, Roger, and Jon Arrizabalaga. "Coping with the French Disease: University Practitioners' Strategies and Tactics in the Transition from the Fifteenth to the Sixteenth Century." In *Medicine from the Black Death to the French Disease,* ed. Roger French et al., 248–87. Aldershot: Ashgate, 1998.

Freidenreich, David M. "The Food of the Damned." In *Between Heaven and Hell: Islam, Salvation, and the Fate of Others,* ed. Mohammad Hasan Khalil, 253–72. Oxford: Oxford University Press, 2013.

———. *Foreigners and Their Food: Constructing Otherness in Jewish, Christian, and Islamic Law.* Berkeley: University of California Press, 2011.

Fuchs, Barbara. *Exotic Nation: Maurophilia and the Construction of Early Modern Spain.* Philadelphia: University of Pennsylvania Press, 2009.

Gallego Burín, Antonio, and Alfonso Gámir Sandoval. *Los moriscos del Reino de Granada según el sínodo de Guadix de 1554.* Facsimile. Granada: Universidad de Granada, 1996.

Gallego Morell, Antonio. "La corte de Carlos V en la Alhambra en 1526." In *Miscelánea de estudios dedicados al profesor Antonio Marín Ocete,* 1:267–94. Granada: Universidad de Granada, 1974.

Gambra, Andrés. *Alfonso VI: Cancillería, curia, e imperio.* León: Centro de Estudios e Investigación "San Isidro," 1997.

García-Arenal, Mercedes. *Inquisición y moriscos: Los procesos del Tribunal de Cuenca*. Madrid: Siglo Veintiuno, 1978.

———. *Los moriscos*. Granada: Universidad de Granada, 1996.

———. *Moriscos y cristianos: Un enfrentamiento polémico (1492–1640)*. Madrid: Fondo de cultura económica, 1979.

———. "Los moros en las Cantigas de Alfonso X el Sabio." *Al-Qantara* 6 (1985): 133–51.

García-Arenal, Mercedes, and Fernando Rodríguez Mediano. "Médico, traductor, inventor: Miguel de Luna, cristiano arábigo de Granada." *Chronica Nova* 32 (2006): 187–231.

———. *Un oriente español: Los moriscos y el Sacromonte en tiempos de Contrarreforma*. Madrid: Marcial Pons Historia, 2010.

———. *The Orient in Spain: Converted Muslims, the Forged Lead Books of Granada, and the Rise of Orientalism*. Ed. and trans. Consuelo López-Morillas. Leiden: Brill, 2013.

García Fuentes, José María, ed. *La Inquisición en Granada en el siglo XVI: Fuentes para su estudio*. Granada: Universidad de Granada, 1981.

García Gómez, Emilio. *Cinco poetas musulmanas: Biografías y estudios*. Madrid: Espasa-Calpe, 1959.

García Mercadal, J., ed. *Viajes de extranjeros por España y Portugal desde los tiempos mas remotos, hasta fines del siglo XVI*. Madrid: Aguilar, 1952.

García Pardo, Manuela. "Las moriscas granadinas: Notas para su estudio." In *Famille morisque: Femmes et enfants*, ed. Abdeljelil Temimi, 116–30. Zaghouan: Fondation Temimi pour la Recherche Scientifique et l'Information, 1997.

García Sánchez, Expiración. "Ibn al-Azraq: *Urŷūza* sobre ciertas preferencias gastronómicas de los Granadinos." *Andalucía Islámica* 1 (1980): 141–62.

García y García, Antonio. "Jews and Muslims in the Canon Law of the Iberian Peninsula in the Late Medieval and Early Modern Period." *Jewish History* 3 (1988): 41–50.

Garrido Atienza, Miguel. *Las capitulaciones para la entrega de Granada*. Facsimile. Granada: Universidad de Granada, 1992.

Gil Sanjuán, Joaquín. "La inquisición de Granada: Visita a Málaga y su comarca en 1568." *Baetica* 1 (1978): 313–36.

———. "El parecer de Galíndez de Carvajal sobre los moriscos andaluces (año 1526)." *Baetica* 11 (1988): 385–401.

Girbal, Enrique Claudio. *Estudio histórico-artístico de los llamados baños árabes de Gerona*. Girona: Paciano Torres, 1888.

Gómez González, Cecilio, and Carlos Vílchez Vílchez. "Baños árabes inéditos de la época almohade (siglos XII–XIII) de la judería de Granada." *Actas del I Congreso de arqueologia medieval española* 3 (1986): 545–67.

Gómez Moreno, Manuel. *El Panteón Real de Las Huelgas de Burgos*. Madrid: Consejo Superior de Investigaciones Científicas, 1946.

González, Julio. *Reinado y diplomas de Fernando III*. Córdoba: Publicaciones del Monte de Piedad y Caja de Ahorros de Córdoba, 1986.

———. *Repoblación de Castilla la Nueva*. 2 vols. Madrid: Universidad Complutense, 1975.

————. "Repoblación de la 'Extremadura' leonesa." *Hispania* 3, no. 11 (1943): 195–273.

González Arce, José Damián. *Apariencia y poder: La legislación suntuaria castellana en los siglos XIII y XV.* Jaén: Universidad de Jaén, 1998.

————. "Cuadernos de ordenanzas y otros documentos sevillanos del reinado de Alfonso X." *Historia, Instituciones, Documentos* 16 (1989): 103–32.

González Jiménez, Manuel, ed. *Diplomatario Andaluz de Alfonso X.* Seville: El Monte, Caja de Huelva y Sevilla, 1991.

————. "Los mudéjares andaluces (ss. XIII–XV)." In *Actas del V coloquio internacional de historia medieval de Andalucia: Andalucia entre Oriente y Occidente (1236–1492),* ed. Emilio Cabrera, 537–50. Córdoba: Excma. Diputación Provincial de Córdoba, 1988.

González Palencia, Ángel. *Los mozárabes de Toledo en los siglos XII y XIII.* 4 vols. Madrid: Instituto de Valencia de San Juan, 1926–30.

Graubart, Karen. *Republics of Difference: Racial and Religious Self-Governance in the Iberian Atlantic 1400–1650.* Oxford: Oxford University Press, forthcoming.

Grieve, Patricia. *The Eve of Spain: Myths of Origins in the History of Christian, Muslim, and Jewish Conflict.* Baltimore: Johns Hopkins University Press, 2009.

Grima Cervantes, Juan. *Almería y el Reino de Granada en los inicios de la modernidad (s. XV–XVI).* Almería: Arráez Editores, 1993.

Harvey, L. P. *Muslims in Spain, 1500–1614.* Chicago: University of Chicago Press, 2005.

Hasenclever, Adolf. "Die tagebuchartigen Aufzeichnungen des pfälzischen Hofarztes Dr. Johannes Lange über seine Reise nach Granada im Jahre 1526." *Archiv für Kulturgeschichte* 5 (1907): 395–439.

Heine, Peter. *Food Culture in the Near East, Middle East, and North Africa.* Westport, CT: Greenwood Press, 2004.

Hergueta Martín, Domingo, ed. *Noticias históricas de la muy noble y muy leal ciudad de Haro.* Haro, 1906. Reprint, Logroño: Diputación de Logroño, 1979.

Herrera Puga, Pedro. *Sociedad y delincuencia en el siglo de oro: Aspectos de la vida sevillana en los siglos XVI y XVII.* Granada: Universidad de Granada, 1971.

Herrero Carretero, Concha. *Museo de telas medievales: Monasterio de Santa María la Real de Huelgas.* Madrid: Patrimonio Nacional, 1988.

Hieatt, C. B. "How Arabic Traditions Travelled to England." In *Food on the Move: Proceedings of the Oxford Symposium on Food and Cookery, 1996,* 120–26. Totnes, Devon: Prospect Books, 1997.

Hillgarth, Jocelyn. *The Spanish Kingdoms, 1250–1516.* 2 vols. Oxford: Clarendon Press, 1976.

Hinojosa Montalvo, José. *Los mudéjares: La voz del Islam en la España cristiana.* 2 vols. Teruel: Centro de Estudios Mudéjares, 2002.

Iversen, Reem F. "El discurso de la higiene: Miguel de Luna y la medicina del siglo XVI." In *Morada de la palabra: Homenaje a Luce y Mercedes López-Baralt,* ed. William Mejías López, 1:892–910. San Juan: Universidad de Puerto Rico, 2002.

Jódar Mena, Manuel. "El gusto por lo morisco como símbolo de identidad del poder: El caso del Condestable Iranzo en el reino de Jaén." *Revista de Antropología Experimental* 12 (2012): 335–48.

Kamen, Henry. *Inquisition and Society in Spain in the Sixteenth and Seventeenth Centuries*. Bloomington: Indiana University Press, 1985.

Kauffmann, C. M. *The Baths of Pozzuoli*. Oxford: Bruno Cassirer, 1959.

Krivatsy, Peter. "Nicola Massa's *Liber de morbo gallico*—Dated 1507 but Printed in 1527." *Journal of the History of Medicine and Allied Sciences* 29, no. 2 (1974): 230–33.

Ladero Quesada, Miguel Ángel. *Los mudéjares de Castilla en el tiempo de Isabel I*. Valladolid: Instituto "Isabel la Católica" de Historia Eclesiástica, 1969.

———. "Los mudéjares de Castilla en la baja edad media." *Historia, Instituciones, Documentos* 5 (1978): 257–304.

Lagardère, Vincent. *Histoire et société en Occident musulman au Moyen Âge: Analyse du "Mi'yār" d'al-Wanšarīsī*. Madrid: Consejo Superior de Investigaciones Científicas, 1995.

Lasmarías Ponz, Israel. "Vestir al morisco, vestir a la morisca: El traje de los moriscos en Aragón en la edad moderna." In *Actas: X Simposio Internacional de Mudejarismo, Teruel 14–15–16 septiembre 2005*, 629–42. Teruel: Centro de Estudios Mudéjares, 2007.

Laurioux, Bruno. "Modes culinaires et mutations du goût à la fin du Moyen-Âge." In *Artes mechanicae en Europe médiévale*, ed. Ria Jansen-Sieben, 199–222. Brussels: Archives et bibliothèques de Belgique, 1989.

Lea, Henry Charles. *A History of the Inquisition of Spain*. 4 vols. New York: Macmillan, 1906–7.

———. *The Moriscos of Spain: Their Conversion and Expulsion*. New York and London, 1901. Reprint, New York: Haskell House, 1968.

Ledesma, María Luisa. *Vidas mudéjares (aspectos sociales de una minoría religiosa en Aragón)*. Zaragoza: Mira Editores, 1994.

Leduc, Louise. "L'appui à la charte est maintenant majoritaire." *La Presse*, March 3, 2014. http://www.lapresse.ca/actualites/dossiers/charte-de-la-laicite/201403/03/01 -4744020-lappui-a-la-charte-est-maintenant-majoritaire.php.

Lee, Christina H. *The Anxiety of Sameness in Early Modern Spain*. Manchester: Manchester University Press, 2015.

Levi Della Vida, Giorgio. "Il regno di Granata nel 1465–66 nei ricordi di un viaggiatore egiziano." *Al-Andalus* 1 (1933): 307–34.

Lévi-Provençal, Évariste. *Histoire de l'Espagne musulmane*. 3 vols. Paris: Maisonneuve, 1950–53.

Levy-Rubin, Milka. *Non-Muslims in the Early Islamic Empire: From Surrender to Coexistence*. Cambridge: Cambridge University Press, 2011.

Lewis, Bernard. *Islam from the Prophet Muhammed to the Fall of Constantinople*. 2 vols. New York: Oxford University Press, 1974.

Longás Bartibás, Pedro. *Vida religiosa de los moriscos*. Madrid: E. Maestre, 1915.

Lopes de Barros, Maria Filomena. "Body, Baths and Cloth: Muslim and Christian Perceptions in Medieval Portugal." *Portuguese Studies* 21 (2005): 1–12.

López de la Plaza, Gloria. "Las mujeres moriscas granadinas en el discurso político y religioso de la Castilla del siglo XVI (1492–1567)." *En la España Medieval* 16 (1993): 307–20.

Lourie, Elena. "Anatomy of Ambivalence: Muslims Under the Crown of Aragon in the Late Thirteenth Century." In *Crusade and Colonization: Muslims, Christians, and Jews in Medieval Aragon*, essay 7. Aldershot: Variorum, 1990.

Macho y Ortega, Francisco. *Condición social de los mudéjares aragoneses (siglo XV)*. Zaragoza: Tip. la Academia, 1923.

Madurell Marimón, José. "La confradía de la Santa Trinidad de los conversos de Barcelona." *Sefarad* 18 (1958): 60–82.

Mami, Ridha. "Algunos ritos de los mudejares del siglo XV: Bodas, divorcios y circuncisión." In *Famille morisque: Femmes et enfants*, ed. Abdeljelil Temimi, 218–23. Zaghouan: Fondation Temimi pour la Recherche Scientifique et l'Information, 1997.

Manzano Martos, Rafael. "El baño termal de Alhama de Granada." *Al-Andalus* 32 (1958): 408–17.

Marín, Manuela. *Mujeres en al-Andalus*. Madrid: Consejo Superior de Investigaciones Científicas, 2000.

Martinell, César. "Los baños medievales en el Levante español." *Cuadernos de arquitectura* 2 (1944): 4–19.

Martínez, H. Salvador. *La Convivencia en la España del siglo XIII: Perspectivas alfonsíes*. Madrid: Ediciones Polifemo, 2006.

Martínez Ferrando, Jesús Ernesto. *Jaime II de Aragón: Su vida familiar*. 2 vols. Barcelona: Consejo Superior de Investigaciones Científicas, 1948.

Martínez Meléndez, María del Carmen. *Los nombres de los tejidos en castellano medieval*. Granada: Universidad de Granada, 1989.

Martínez Ruiz, Juan. *Inventarios de bienes moriscos del Reino de Granada (Siglo XVI)*. Madrid: Consejo Superior de Investigaciones Científicas, 1972.

Martínez San Pedro, María Desamparados. "La práctica de la circuncisión, un 'pecado' morisco." In *VII Simposio Internacional de Mudejarismo, Teruel, 19–21 de septiembre de 1996*, 467–74. Teruel: Centro de Estudios Mudéjares, 1999.

Martín García, Mariano. "Baños árabes de la provincia de Granada: El Baño de la Zubia." *Andalucía Islámica* 4–5 (1986): 307–15.

Mayordomo Font, Rosa. "Notas históricas sobre la carnicería de la aljama sarracena de Tortosa (siglo XIV)." In *Homenatge a la memòria del Prof. Emilio Sáez: Aplex d'estudis del seus deixebles i col·laboradors*, 223–31. Barcelona: Universitat de Barcelona, 1989.

Melammed, Renée Levine. *Heretics of Daughters of Israel? The Crypto-Jewish Women of Castile*. New York: Oxford University Press, 1999.

———. "Judeo-Conversas and Moriscas in Sixteenth-Century Spain: A Study of Parallels." *Jewish History* 24 (2010): 155–68.

Menéndez de Luarca, Luis Ramón-Laca. "El hogar morisco." *Oppidum* 1 (2005): 128–39.

Menéndez Pidal, Gonzalo. *La España del siglo XIII leída en imágenes*. Madrid: Real Academia de la Historia, 1986.

Menéndez Pidal, Ramón. *Documentos lingüísticos de España*. Madrid: Consejo Superior de Investigaciones Científicas, 1919.

———. *Rodrigo, el ultimo godo.* 3 vols. Madrid: Espasa-Calpe, 1942–56.

Mernissi, Fatima. *The Veil and the Male Elite.* Trans. Mary Jo Lakeland. New York: Addison-Wesley, 1991.

Miller, Kathryn. *Guardians of Islam.* New York: Columbia University Press, 2008.

Miranda Díaz, Bartolomé, and Francisco de Córdoba Soriano. *Los moriscos de Magacela.* Magacela: Ayuntamiento de Magacela, 2010.

Miret y Sans, Joaquim. *Les cases de Templers y Hospitalers en Catalunya.* Barcelona: Imprenta de la Casa Provincial de Caritat, 1910.

Mirrer, Louis. *Women, Jews, and Muslims in the Texts of Reconquest Castile.* Ann Arbor: University of Michigan Press, 1996.

Monga, Luigi, ed. *Un mercante di Milano in Europa: Diario di viaggio del primo Cinquecento.* Milan: Jaca Book, 1985.

Monroe, James T. *Hispano-Arabic Poetry: A Student Anthology.* Berkeley: University of California Press, 1974.

Monter, William. *Frontiers of Heresy: The Spanish Inquisition from the Basque Lands to Sicily.* Cambridge: Cambridge University Press, 1990.

Muñoz Sanz, Agustín. *Los hospitales docentes de Guadalupe: La respuesta hospitalaria a la epidemia de bubas del Renacimiento (siglos XV y XVI).* Badajoz: Junta de Extremadura, 2008.

Mutgé Vives, Josefina [Josefa]. "La aljama sarracena en la Lleida cristiana: Noticias y conclusiones." In *VII Simposio Internacional de Mudejarismo, Teruel, 19–21 de septiembre de 1996,* 101–11. Teruel: Centro de Estudios Mudéjares, 1999.

———. *L'aljama sarraïna de Lleida a l'edat mitjana: Aproximació a la seva història.* Barcelona: Consell Superior d'Investigacions Científiques, 1992.

Nader, Helen. *The Mendoza Family in the Spanish Renaissance, 1350–1550.* New Brunswick, NJ: Rutgers University Press, 1979.

Nirenberg, David. *Anti-Judaism: The Western Tradition.* New York: W. W. Norton, 2013.

———. *Communities of Violence: Persecution of Minorities in the Middle Ages.* Princeton, NJ: Princeton University Press, 1996.

———. "Conversion, Sex, and Segregation: Jews and Christians in Medieval Spain." *American Historical Review* 107 (2002): 1065–93.

Ocasio, Rafael. "Ethnic Underclass Representation in the *Cantigas*: The Black Moro as a Hated Character." In *Estudios alfonsinos y otros escritos en homenaje a John Esten Keller y a Aníbal A. Biglieri,* ed. Nicolás Toscano Liria, 183–88. New York: National Endowment for the Humanities, 1991.

Pagani, Samuela. "Un paradiso in terra: Il *Ḥammām* e l'economia della salvezza." In *Hammam: Le terme nell'Islam; Convegno internazionale di studi, Santa Cesarea Terme, 15–16 maggio 2008,* ed. Rosita D'Amora and Samuela Pagani, 133–58. Florence: Leo S. Olschki, 2011.

Passini, Jean. "El baño de Bāb al-Mardūm (o de la Cruz): Localización e identificación." *Al-Qanṭara* 31 (2010): 211–23.

Passini, Jean, Juan Manuel Rojas Rodríguez-Malo, and J. Ramón Villa. "Los baños extramuros de San Sebastián." *Al-Qanṭara* 18 (1997): 187–219.

Patton, Pamela Anne. *Art of Estrangement: Redefining Jews in Reconquest Spain.* University Park: Pennsylvania State University Press, 2012.

Peinado Santaella, Rafael Gerardo. *"Como disfrutan los vencedores cuando se reparten el botín": El reino de Granada tras la conquista castellana (1483–1526).* Granada: Comares, 2011.

Pérès, Henri. *La poésie andalouse en arabe classique au XI siècle.* Paris: Adrien-Maisonneuve, 1953.

Pérez de Colosía Rodríguez, Isabel. "La religiosidad en los moriscos malagueños." In *Actes du II Symposium Internacional du C.I.E.M. sur Religion, Identité et Sources Documentaires sur les Morisques Andalous,* ed. Abdeljelil Temimi, 1:181–98. Tunis: Publications de l'Institut Supérieur de Documentation, 1984.

Pérez de Colosía Rodriguez, María Isabel, and Joaquín Gil Sanjuán. *Málaga y la Inquisición.* Málaga: Diputación Provincial de Málaga, 1982.

———. "Los moriscos del Algarbe malagueño: Orígenes y presión inquisitorial." *Jábega* 56 (1987): 13–28.

Pernoud, Régine, ed. *Les statuts municipaux de Marseille.* Paris: Librairie Auguste Picard, 1949.

Perry, Charles. "Couscous and Its Cousins." In *Medieval Arab Cookery,* ed. Maxime Rodinson, A. J. Arberry, and Charles Perry, 233–38. Totnes, Devon: Prospect Books, 2001.

Perry, Mary Elizabeth. *The Handless Maiden: Moriscos and the Politics of Religion in Early Modern Spain.* Princeton, NJ: Princeton University Press, 2005.

Peterson, Toby. "The Arab Influence on Western European Cooking." *Journal of Medieval History* 6 (1980): 317–40.

Pike, Ruth. *Aristocrats and Traders: Sevillian Society in the Sixteenth Century.* Ithaca, NY: Cornell University Press, 1972.

Poirier, Guy. "A Contagion at the Source of Discourse on Sexualities: Syphilis During the French Renaissance." In *Imagining Contagion in Early Modern Europe,* ed. Claire L. Carlin, 157–76. Basingstoke: Palgrave Macmillan, 2005.

Pons Guri, Josep María. "Constitucions conciliars Tarraconensis (1229 a 1330)." *Analecta Sacra Tarraconensia* 48 (1975): 241–363.

Powers, James F. "Baths." In *Medieval Iberia: An Encyclopedia,* ed. Michael Gerli, 152–53. New York: Routledge, 2003.

———. "Municipal Baths and Social Interaction in Thirteenth-Century Spain." *American Historical Review* 84 (1979): 649–67.

Prieto Bernabé, José Manuel. "Aproximación a las características antropológicas de la minoria morisca asentada en Pastrana en el último tercio del siglo XVI." *Wad-al-Hayara: Revista de estudios de Guadalajara* 14 (1987): 355–62.

Puig i Cadalfalch, Josep. *Les bains de Girone, guide descriptive.* Barcelona: Imprenta de la Casa de Caritat, 1936.

———. "Els banys de Girone i la influencia moresca a Catalunya." *Anuari* 5 (1913): 687–728.

*The Qur'an: First American Version.* Trans. T. B. Irving. Brattleboro, VT: Amana Books, 1985.

Rebora, Giovanni. "La cucina medievale italiana tra oriente ed occidente." In *Studi in onore di Luigi Bulferetti*, 3:1431–1578. Genoa: Università di Genova, 1989–90.

Rebora, Giovanni, and Albert Sonnenfeld. *Culture of the Fork: A Brief History of Everyday Food and Haute Cuisine in Europe.* New York: Columbia University Press, 2001.

Régné, Jean. *History of the Jews in Aragon: Regesta and Documents, 1213–1327.* Jerusalem: Magnes Press, 1978.

Reilly, Bernard F. *The Kingdom of León-Castilla Under King Alfonso VII, 1126–1157.* Philadelphia: University of Pennsylvania Press, 1998.

———. *The Medieval Spains.* Cambridge: Cambridge University Press, 1993.

Renaut, Luc. "Recherches sur le henné antique." *Journal of Near Eastern Studies* 68, no. 3 (2009): 193–212.

Ricard, Robert. "Espagnol et Portugais 'marlota': Recherches sur le vocabulaire du vêtement hispano-mauresque." *Bulletin Hispanique* 53 (1951): 131–56.

Robinson, Cynthia, ed. *Medieval Andalusian Courtly Culture in the Mediterranean.* New York: Routledge, 2007.

Roca Traver, Francisco A. "Un siglo de vida mudéjar en la Valencia medieval (1238–1338)." *Estudios de Edad Media de la Corona de Aragón* 5 (1952): 115–208.

Rodinson, Maxime. "Les influences de la civilisation musulmane sur la civilisation européenne médiévale dans les domains de la consommation et de la distraction: L'alimentation." In *Convegno internazionale Oriente e Occidente nel Medieoevo: Filosofia e scienze*, 479–500. Rome: Accademia nazionale dei Lincei, 1971.

———. "Ma'mūiyya East and West." *Petits propos culinaires* 33 (1989): 15–25.

Rodinson, Maxime, A. J. Arberry, and Charles Perry, eds. *Medieval Arab Cookery.* Totnes, Devon: Prospect Books, 2001.

Romano, David. "Los judíos en los baños de Tortosa (siglos XIII–XIV)." *Sefarad* 40 (1980): 57–64.

Root, Deborah. "Speaking Christian: Orthodoxy and Difference in Sixteenth-Century Spain." *Representations* 23 (1988): 118–34.

Rosenberger, Bernard. "Les pâtes dans le monde musulman." *Médiévales* 8 (1989): 77–98.

Rubiera, María Jesús. *La arquitectura en la literatura árabe.* Madrid: Hiperión, 1988.

Rubin, Miri. *Gentile Tales: The Narrative Assault on Late Medieval Jews.* Philadelphia: University of Pennsylvania Press, 1999.

Rubio, Pedro María. *Tratado completo de las fuentes minerales de España.* Madrid: D. R. R. de Rivera, 1853.

Rubio García, Luis. *La procesión de Corpus en el siglo XV en Murcia y religiosidad medieval.* Murcia: Academia Alfonso X el Sabio, 1983.

Ruiz Moreno, Aníbal. "Los baños públicos en los fueros municipales españoles." *Cuadernos de Historia de España* 3 (1945): 152–57.

Ruiz Somavilla, María José. "Los valores sociales, religiosos y morales en las respuestas higiénicas de los siglos XVI y XVII: El problema de los baños." *Dynamis: Acta Hispanica ad Medicinae Scientiarumque Historiam Illustrandum* 12 (1992): 155–87.

Salicrú i Lluch, Roser. "La diplomacia y las embajadas como expresión de los contactos interculturales entre cristianos y musulmanes en el Mediterráneo occidental durante la baja edad media." *Estudios de Historia de España* 9 (2007): 77–106.

Sánchez Granjel, Luis. "El tema de la sifilis en la literatura médica española del siglo XVII." In *Capitúlos de la medicina española*, 77–86. Salamanca: Instituto de Historia de la Medicina Española, 1971.

Santo Tomás Pérez, Magdalena. "El agua en la documentación eclesiástica." In *El agua en las ciudades castellanas durante la edad media*, ed. María Isabel del Val Valdivieso, 13–40. Valladolid: Universidad de Valladolid, 1998.

———. *Los baños públicos en Valladolid: Agua, higiene y salud en el Valladolid medieval.* Valladolid: Ayuntamiento de Valladolid, 2002.

Sanz Gándara, Cristina. "El arrendamiento de los baños de una villa bajomedieval en el sudeste peninsular: Elche." In *El món urbà a la Corona d'Aragó del 1137 als decrets de nova planta: XVII Congrés d'Història de la Corona d'Aragó*, 2:371–78. Barcelona: Universitat de Barcelona, 2003.

Savo, Anita. " 'Toledano, ajo, berenjena': The Eggplant in *Don Quixote*." *La Corónica* 43, no. 1 (2014): 231–52.

Scully, Terence, ed. *The Neapolitan Recipe Collection: Cuoco Napoletano.* Ann Arbor: University of Michigan Press, 2000.

Sempere y Guarinos, Juan. *Historia del luxo y de las leyes suntuarias de España.* 2 vols. Madrid: Imprenta Real, 1788.

Serrano, Luciano. *El obispado de Burgos y Castilla primitiva desde el siglo V al XIII.* Madrid: Instituto de Valencia de San Juan, 1936.

Smarr, Janet Levarie. "Non-Christian People and Spaces in the *Decameron*." In *Approaches to Teaching Boccaccio's "Decameron,"* ed. James H. McGregor, 31–38. New York: Modern Language Association of America, 2000.

Squatriti, Paolo. *Water and Society in Early Medieval Italy, AD 400–1000.* Cambridge: Cambridge University Press, 1998.

Stearns, Justin K. *Infectious Ideas: Contagion in Premodern Islamic and Christian Thought in the Western Mediterranean.* Baltimore: Johns Hopkins University Press, 2011.

Stefanizzi, Serena."Sulla trasmissione di testi arabi nel 'De Balneis' (1553)." In *Hammam: Le terme nell'Islam; Convegno internazionale di studi, Santa Cesarea Terme, 15–16 maggio 2008*, ed. Rosita D'Amora and Samuela Pagani, 223–36. Florence: Leo S. Olschki, 2011.

Surtz, Ronald. "Crimes of the Tongue: The Inquisitorial Trials of Cristóbal Duarte Ballester." *Medieval Encounters* 12 (2006): 519–32.

Taylor, Adam. "Inside Britain's Big, Dumb Halal Meat Scandal." *Washington Post*, May 8, 2014. https://www.washingtonpost.com/news/worldviews/wp/2014/05/08/inside-britains-big-dumb-halal-pizza-scandal/.

*Telegraph.* "France's Le Pen: Ban Non-Pork Meals in Schools." April 5, 2014. http://www.telegraph.co.uk/news/worldnews/europe/france/10746273/Frances-Le-Pen-ban-non-pork-meals-in-schools.html.

Temimi, Abdeljalil. "Attachement des morisques à leur religion et à leur identité à travers les hadiths dans deux manuscrits morisques." In *Actes du II Symposium Internacional du C.I.E.M. sur Religion, Identité et Sources Documentaires sur les Morisques Andalous*, ed. Abdeljelil Temimi, 2 :151–61. Tunis: Publications de l'Institut Supérieur de Documentation, 1984.

Toaff, Ariel. "The Jewish Badge in Italy During the 15th Century." In *Die Juden in ihrer Mittelalterlichen Umwelt*, ed. Alfred Ebenbauer and Klaus Zatloukal, 275–80. Vienna: Böhlau, 1991.

Tolan, John. *Saracens: Islam in the Medieval European Imagination.* New York: Columbia University Press, 2002.

———. *Sons of Ishmael: Muslims Through European Eyes in the Middle Ages.* Gainesville: University Press of Florida, 2008.

Torres Balbás, Leopoldo. *Algunos aspectos del mudejarismo urbano medieval.* Madrid: Imprenta y Editorial Maestre, 1954.

———. "El baño de doña Leonor de Guzmán en el palacio de Tordesillas." *Al-Andalus* 24 (1959): 409–25.

———. "El baño de Torres Torres y otros levantinos." *Al-Andalus* 17 (1952): 176–86.

———. "El baño musulmán de Murcia y su conservación." *Al-Andalus* 17 (1952): 433–38.

———. "Crónica Arqueológica de la España Musulmana: Los baños públicos en los fueros municipales españoles." *Al-Andalus* 11:2 (1946): 443–45.

———. "La judería de Zaragoza y su baño." *Al-Andalus* 21 (1956): 172–90.

Torres Fontes, Juan. "Los baños de la reina." *Murgetana* 40 (1975): 63–74. ·

Vakulenko, Anastasia. *Islamic Veiling in Legal Discourse.* New York: Routledge, 2012.

Vallecillo Ávila, Manuel. "Los judíos de Castilla en la alta edad media." *Cuadernos de historia de España* 14 (1950): 17–110.

van Winter, Johanna Maria. "Arab Influences on Medieval European Cuisine." In *Spices and Comfits: Collected Papers on Medieval Food*, 81–89. Totnes, Devon: Prospect Books, 2007.

Vázquez de Benito, María Concepción. "La materia médica de Ibn al-Jatīb." *Boletín de la Asociación Española de Orientalistas* 15 (1979): 139–50.

Velázquez de Echeverría, Juan. *Paseos por Granada y sus contornos.* Granada: N. Moreno, 1764.

Vílchez Vílchez, Carlos. *Baños árabes.* Granada: Disputación de Granada, 2001.

Villanueva, Jaime. *Viage literario a las iglesias de España.* 22 vols. Madrid: Real Academia de la Historia, 1803–52.

Vincent, Bernard. "The *Moriscos* and Circumcision." In *Culture and Control in Counter-Reformation Spain*, ed. Anne J. Cruz and Mary Elizabeth Perry, 78–92. Minneapolis: University of Minnesota Press, 1992.

———. "Morisques et mobilité: L'exemple de Pastrana." In *Exils, passages et transition: Chemins d'une recherche sur les marges; Hommage à Rose Duroux*, ed. Anne Dubet and Stéphanie Urdician, 17–24. Clermont-Ferrand: Presses Universitaires Blaise Pascal, 2008.

———. "¿Qué aspecto físico tenían los moriscos?" *Andalucía moderna: Actas II Coloquios Historia de Andalucía, Córdoba, noviembre 1980*, 2:335–40. Córdoba: Monte de Piedad y Caja de Ahorros de Córdoba, 1983.

Viñuales Ferreiro, Gonzalo. "Aproximación al estudio de la comunidad mudéjar de Guadalajara en la Edad Media." In *Actas: X Simposio Internacional de Mudejarismo, Teruel, 14–15–16 septiembre 2005*, 501–12. Teruel: Centro de Estudios Mudéjares, 2007.

Vose, Robin. *Dominicans, Muslims, and Jews in the Medieval Crown of Aragon*. Cambridge: Cambridge University Press, 2009.

Waines, David. "Luxury Foods in Medieval Islamic Societies." *World Archaeology* 34 (2003): 571–80.

Walker Vadillo, Mónica Ann. *Bathsheba in Late Medieval French Manuscript Illumination: Innocent Object of Desire or Agent of Sin?* Lewiston, NY: Edwin Mellen Press, 2008.

———. "Emotional Responses to David Watching Bathsheba Bathing in Late Medieval French Manuscript Illumination." *Annual of Medieval Studies at the Central European University* 13 (2007): 97–109.

Weiditz, Christoph. *Authentic Everyday Dress of the Renaissance: All 154 Plates from the "Trachtenbuch."* Ed. Theodor Hampe. New York: Dover, 1994.

Weiss-Amer, Melitta. "The Role of Medieval Physicians in the Diffusion of Culinary Recipes and Cooking Practices." In *Du manuscrit à la table: Essais sur la cuisine au Moyen Âge et répertoire des manuscrits médiévaux contenant des recettes culinaires*, ed. Carole Lambert, 69–80. Montreal: Les Presses de l'Université de Montréal, 1992.

Wensinck, A. J. "The Origin of the Muslim Laws of Ritual Purity." In *The Development of Islamic Ritual*, ed. Gerald Hawting, 75–93. Aldershot: Ashgate, 2006.

Wiegers, Gerard Albert. *Islamic Literature in Spanish and Aljamiado: Yça of Segovia (fl. 1450), His Antecendents and Successors*. Leiden: Brill, 1994.

Wilson, C. Anne. "The Saracen Connection: Arab Cuisine and the Medieval West, Part I." *Petits propos culinaires* 7 (1981): 13–22.

Zaouali, Lilia. *Medieval Cuisine of the Islamic World*. Berkeley: University of California Press, 2007.

Zuwiyya, Z. David. "Arab Culture and Morisco Heritage in an Aljamiado Legend: Alhadit del baño de Zaryeb." *Romance Quarterly* 48 (2001): 32–46.

# INDEX

Afonso V, king of Portugal, 41

Africanus, Leo (Hasan al-Wazzan), 135, 137, 159n130, 190n152

Alba, Pedro de, 59

alcohol, prohibition against, 11, 107, 133, 180n17

aldifara, 35

Alexander VI, pope, 5, 183n67

Alfonso, prince of Aragon, 132

Alfonso I, king of Aragon, 75

Alfonso II, king of Aragon, 77, 88, 116

Alfonso III, king of León, 88

Alfonso V, king of Aragon, 44, 77, 98, 124

Alfonso VI, king of León-Castile, 8, 26, 69, 70, 75, 76, 101, 164n33, 181n32

Alfonso VII, king of León-Castile, 85, 88, 89, 171n111

Alfonso VIII, king of Castile, 70, 88, 89

Alfonso X, king of Castile, 15, 26, 27, 30, 31, 79, 81, 82, 84, 89, 112, 117

Alfonso XI, king of Castile, 76

Alhambra, 15, 28, 71–73, 76, 92, 100

al-Himyarī, 72

al-Idrīsī, 72

aljamiado, 72, 81, 85, 91, 100, 113, 158n129, 167n61

aljuba, 35, 37–38, 41–42, 44

almalafa, 19, 21, 23, 25, 30, 47–55, 147n15, 147n19. See also veil

al-Maqqārī, 72

almejía, 35, 44

Alpujarras rebellion, 7–8, 25, 54–55, 62, 101, 128

al-Saqatī, 73, 75

al-Shaqundī, 72

Anglería, Pedro Mártir de, 137

Apicius, Marcus Gavius, 131

Arabic, use of, viii, xiii, 1, 5, 7–8, 10, 11, 31

armbands, 38–40

Audiencia of Granada, 7, 16, 22, 23, 59

Avicenna, 76, 131

Ávila, Synod of, 155n97

Aviñon, Juan de, 76

Ayala, Martín Pérez de, 22

Aznar Cardona, Pedro, 107–8, 139

badges (star-, circle-, or moon-shaped), 10, 27, 31, 39–40

bakers, 110, 132–33

Baño de Comares, 71, 92, 100

Baño de Zaryeb, 72, 81, 85, 91, 100, 167n61, 176n179

bathing: as cause of weakness, 69, 101–2; health benefits of, 68, 71, 73, 75–77, 101–3

bathing stones, 67, 75, 79

Bathsheba, 67, 77–79, 95, 98–100

Baza, Synod of, 59

beards, 15, 17, 30–31, 33–35, 40, 41, 58, 59

Bellvís family, 36–37

Bermúdez de Pedraza, Francisco, 2, 105, 147n15, 150n17, 151n37

Bibles, illuminated, 78–79

Bleda, Jaime, 108, 139, 180n18

braided hair, threats to shave, 54

bread, 218, 225, 228, 230, 269, 270, 273, 283

burnūs, 38, 41, 42, 44

butchering, 2, 8, 20, 66, 84–85, 90, 93, 104–6, 109–10, 114–29, 132–33

butter, 106, 108, 109, 112, 113, 133

Calatrava, Order of, 88
canon law, 111, 112, 170n94
Cantigas de Santa María, 31, 78, 81
Castillejo, Cristóbal de, 100
Catalina, queen of Castile (regent for Juan II), 40, 90, 113, 122
Cervantes, Miguel de, 181n24
Charles V (Carlos I), emperor and king of Spain, 5, 7, 16, 21–22, 51, 53, 62, 64, 100, 104, 127–28
children, 8, 10–11, 18, 22, 26, 48, 51, 53, 58–59, 64, 85, 128, 138
Cid, beard of, 35
circumcision, 10, 11, 17, 18, 83, 127, 162n3
Cisneros, Francisco Jiménez de, 5–7, 20
clenxia (haircut), 37
Constitutions of Catalonia, 38
conversion, vii–viii, 4–10, 12, 16, 20, 26, 43, 46, 49, 63–64, 93–94, 105, 108–11, 113, 115, 118, 121, 125, 126, 132
cookbooks, 109, 130–31
copete (haircut), 30, 34, 37
Corbacho, 58, 98
Cortes, 30, 35–36, 38, 41, 43, 133, 154n82, 155n96
cosmetics, 57–59, 75, 101
couscous, viii, 2, 11, 104, 107–9, 111–12, 129, 133–35, 137, 138, 141
Covarrubias Orozco, Sebastián de, 69
cowl (capuz), 40

Delicado, Francisco, 100
Desclot, Bernat, 112
Deza, Pedro de, 16
dogs, Muslims compared to, 106

eating: from common bowls, 106, 134–36; with fingers, 104, 106, 133–35, 138; seated at tables, viii, 105, 137; seated on floors, 11, 104–6, 111, 135–38
Eboli, Peter of, 77, 95, 97
eggplant, 2, 108, 130, 141, 180n18, 181n24
Eiximenis, Francesc, 133, 135
Enrique II, king of Castile, 38, 44, 90
Enrique III, king of Castile, 155n96
Enrique IV, king of Castile, 40, 44, 113

Escobar, Luis de, 69
Espina, Alfonso de, 113
expulsion, vii, ix, xiv, 2, 4, 6, 8, 46, 60–63, 107, 128
Eymeric, Nicholas, 162n3

fasting, 2, 10–11, 64, 106–8, 114–15, 133
Felipe II, king of Spain, 56, 109, 128, 129
Felipe III, king of Spain, 8, 60, 139
Fernando and Isabel, "los Reyes Católicos," vii, 1, 3, 5, 8, 19, 40–41, 43, 46–47, 49, 51, 70, 86, 92–93, 100, 105, 117, 126, 137, 150n17, 157n113
Fernando I, king of Aragon (Fernando de Antequera), 42
Fernando II, king of Aragon. See Fernando and Isabel, "los Reyes Católicos"
Fernando III, king of Castile, 8, 88, 92
Ferrer, Vincent, 113, 160n163
figs, 107–9, 133
forks, xv, 135
fritters, 106, 108, 129, 133
fruit, 107–10, 113, 129, 133–34
fueros, 28, 65, 75, 82–83, 85, 89
funerals, 64

Galen, 76, 131
garceta (haircut), 34–40, 45, 62
Giunti, Tommaso, 102
goat, 108, 112, 113, 125, 130, 180n18, 181n28
Granada, Synod of, 54
Guadix, Synod of, 2, 22, 54, 59, 64, 65, 105, 137, 162n5
Guerra de Lorca, Pedro, 101
Guevara, Antonio de, 54, 58

ḥadīth, 11, 34, 58
Ḥadīth Bayāḍ wa Riyāḍ, 28–29, 159n133
hair styles, 10, 12, 15–18, 27–28, 30–31, 34–41, 43–45, 47, 54
halal meats, 2, 8, 107–8, 114–16, 120, 123, 125, 129, 133, 142
Hārūn al-Rashīd, 166n54
hats, 10, 20, 27, 43, 52, 54, 57
head covering, 23–25, 29, 38, 41, 43, 50–52, 56, 60, 158n129, 159n133

henna, xv, 2, 11, 12, 21, 31–33, 47, 57–60, 75, 100
honey, 106–9, 112–13, 129, 133
Hospitallers, 89, 132, 173n141
hot springs, 68, 73, 76–77, 92–93, 100–102, 165n43
hunting, 105, 107, 127

Ibn ʿAbdūn, 29, 72, 73, 166n61
Ibn al-Azraq, 134
Ibn al-Ḥājj, 73
Ibn al-Khaṭīb, 42, 158n129, 168n73
Ibn Butlan, 187n117
Ibn ʿIdhārī, 72
Ibn Jazla, 187n117
Ibn Khaldūn, 42
Ibn Rushd, 29
Ibn Saʿīd, 42
Innocent III, pope, 18–19, 31, 43
Inquisition, 4, 7, 9–13, 21–22, 46–47, 49, 50, 57–59, 63, 94–95, 100, 104, 106–9, 111, 112, 115, 129, 133–34, 138, 141–42
inter-religious sharing of food, 110–14, 133–35
Isabel I, queen of Castile. See Fernando and Isabel, "los Reyes Católicos"
Isabella of Portugal, empress and queen of Spain (wife of Charles V), 22, 54
Islamic law, 2, 8–10, 13, 30, 41–42, 58, 71, 73, 106, 108, 114–15, 117, 124, 134, 180n17, 182n51
Islamophobia, modern, 11–12, 142

Jaume I, king of Aragon, 8, 26, 34, 85–87, 90, 92, 112, 114, 116–17, 123, 132, 188n126
Jaume II, king of Aragon, 35–36, 76, 89, 112, 119–21, 124
Jeanne II, queen of Navarre, 174n145
jewelry, 11, 15, 22, 147n15
Joan I, king of Aragon, 37–39
Joan II, king of Aragon, 91, 121
Juan II, king of Castile, 40, 58, 90, 113
Juana, queen of Castile (wife of Fernando III), 88
Juana I, queen of Castile, 21, 23, 51–52, 126–27

La Cava, legend of, 81, 98
Lalaing, Antoine de, 51
Lange, Johannes, 51, 54, 57, 100
Lapidario, 79
lard, 107, 131
Lateran IV, 10, 15, 18, 19, 26–28, 30, 35, 37, 39, 43
León, Andrés de, 103
León, Pedro de, 139
Lérida, Synod of, 82
Libre de Sent Soví, 131
Libro de Ajedrez, 31–33, 50
Llull, Ramon, 44
Lobera de Ávila, Luis, 102, 131
Lope de Vega, 108
López de Corella, Alonso, 69
López de Mendoza y Quiñones, Iñigo, 44, 49, 52–53, 55
López de Villalobos, Francisco, 102
Lucas de Iranzo, Miguel, 44, 113
Luna, María de, queen and regent of Aragon (wife of Martí I), 39
Luna, Miguel de, 69, 102–3
luxury textiles and clothing, 23, 30–31, 34, 38–41, 44

Manuel, Juan, 81
María, empress (wife of Maximilian II), 103
María de Molina, queen of Castile (wife of Sancho IV), 88
María of Castile, queen of Aragon (wife of Alfonso V), 124
marlotas, 21, 23, 25, 30, 43, 44, 47
Mármol Carvajal, Luis del, 2, 7, 25, 59, 128, 137
Martí I, king of Aragon, 37, 39, 117, 183n66
Martínez de Toledo, Alfonso, 58, 81, 98
Martorell, Joanot, 98
Massa, Nicolò, 101
maurophilia, 44
Maximus, Valerius, 77, 95
Mendoza, Diego Hurtado de, 25, 55, 101
Mestre, Vicent (painter), 60
Metge, Bernat, 176n178

milk, 106–9, 133
milk, almond, 130
millers, 132–33
Muntaner, Ramon, 112
Münzer, Hieronymus, 100

napkins, viii, 135, 137–38
Navagero, Andrea, 51, 57, 100
Niño, Pero, 112, 134
Nola, Roberto de, 130–31
nudity, 73–75, 78–82, 95–100
Núñez Muley, Francisco, viii–ix, xiii–xiv, 1–4, 6–7, 9, 11–14, 16, 23–25, 49, 55, 59–60, 65–69, 73, 93, 95, 100, 103–5, 108–9, 111, 127–28

olive oil, 70, 108, 113
Ottoman sultan, pleas for help from, 6, 50, 115, 162n181
Ovens, as sources of revenue, 70, 75, 84–87, 90–91, 93, 109–10, 116, 132
Ovid, 95

Pact of 'Umar, 18, 29, 42
Palencia, Alfonso de, 100
Pedro I, king of Castile, 37–38
Pedro I, king of Portugal, 38
Pere II, king of Aragon, 87
Pere III, king of Aragon, 86–88, 112
Pere IV, king of Aragon, 36–38, 76, 87, 117, 119, 121, 124, 181n28, 184n79
Pinelo, Antonio de León, 56–57
poetry, 71, 73, 98, 100, 134, 162n181
pork, 2, 11, 106–8, 112, 114–15, 117, 126, 128–31, 133, 141–42
prostitution, 43, 73, 82, 89, 94, 100

Qur'ān, 11, 58, 107, 114, 129, 161n178

raisins, 107–9, 133
Ramadan, 2, 8, 107, 133
Ramiro II, king of Aragon, 85
Ramon Berenguer IV of Barcelona, 87
rape, 73, 82, 176n179
repartimientos, 75, 85, 87, 92
Ribera, Juan de, 128, 139

rice, 108, 113, 135, 180n18
ritual murder allegations, 128–29
ritual washing, Islamic, 2, 11, 64, 66, 68, 71, 73, 91, 94–95
Roig, Jaume, 81, 98

sábanas, 23, 48, 49, 54
Sacromonte prophecies, 102
Sánchez, Nuño, 89, 112
Sánchez de Arévalo, Rodrigo, 69
Sancho IV, king of Castile, 88, 106
Sancho VII, king of Navarre, 78
Sancho Ramírez, king of Aragon, 70
Sandoval, Prudencio de, 21
Santa Cruz, Alonso de, 19
Santiago, Order of, 89
Schellig, Conrad, 101
sexual activity and bathing, 63–68, 73, 75, 77–78, 82, 95, 98–101
sexual mixing, 10, 18–19, 43
shawls (mantos), 20, 22, 23, 47, 49, 50–52, 57, 155n97
shoes, 3, 13, 15–16, 18, 20, 23–25, 30, 40, 47, 73, 95, 105
Siete Partidas, 27, 82, 113, 135, 190n151
skirts (sayas), 20–21, 23, 47, 49, 52, 60
spices, 106, 113, 129, 130
spoons, 135, 138
squash, 130
sugar, 129–30
syphilis, xv, 101–3

table manners, viii, 4, 12, 105–7, 135, 137–39
tailors, 21–23, 52
Talavera, Hernando de, vii–viii, 4, 16, 20, 49, 56, 64, 93, 105, 114, 137, 139
Tarragona, Council of, 30, 35, 113
Templars, 35
Tirant lo Blanc, 98, 135
toca, 23, 43–44, 158n129
Toledo, Franciso de, 58
Torres, Diego de, 138
Torres, Pedro de, 103
Tortosa, Costums of, 35, 38

Tortosa, Synod of, 121
treaties, x, 6, 19–20, 50, 92–93
tripe and organ meats, 108, 122
turban, 18, 31, 43, 60, 158n129
Tuy, Lucas of, 69

Urraca, queen of León-Castile, 88
Usama ibn Munqidh, 167n61

Valencia, Pedro de, 107
veil, xv, 3, 10–12, 15, 19, 21, 23, 25, 31, 38,
    47–60, 67, 142; bans on, 3, 10–12, 21,
    23, 50, 142; use by Christian women,
    3, 25, 53–57

veil, half-, 56–57
Vilanova, Arnau de, 76, 187n118

weddings, 10, 13, 24, 45, 54, 64, 71, 104, 111,
    133, 134
Weiditz, Christoph, 47, 51, 133
wine, 98, 107, 112–13

Yça Gidelli (Īsa ibn Jābir), 42, 115
Yūsuf I, Naṣrid sultan, 73

zambra (dance), 3, 4, 11, 13, 134
Zamora, Synod of, 154n82
zaragüelles, 47, 49

# EDITOR'S ACKNOWLEDGMENTS

It remains to thank some of those who helped in the process of bringing this book to publication. I know that Remie intended to acknowledge all those who helped her, with her usual generosity, but unfortunately I am incapable of reconstructing her list of contacts in full and I will not even attempt a simulacrum of such a personal gesture. I do know that her research particularly benefited from a Guggenheim Foundation fellowship in 2012 and from support provided by the University of Notre Dame. Working through her research files, it also soon became evident to me just how widely and carefully she consulted with respected colleagues around the world and how much she appreciated receiving feedback at the various conferences where she presented early versions of her ideas. If you were among those who had the opportunity to discuss this project with her, rest assured that your comments had an impact on its development.

I would also like to recognize those who have helped me most directly over the months it has taken to finally bring this cornucopia of scholarship to harvest. First and foremost I am grateful to Matthew Bell for his patience, hospitality, and assistance. The kind encouragement of Remie's family made editorial work more of a pleasure than a chore, and I am deeply honored to have enjoyed their trust. John Van Engen, David Nirenberg, and Jerome Singerman provided invaluable advice and feedback on the finished manuscript. Alexandra Bain, Karen Graubart, Samira Farhoud, Julia Schneider, Ryan Szpiech, and Belen Vicens assisted with translation questions and research advice, as did another very helpful anonymous reviewer. Margaret Cinninger provided technical support and a warm welcome whenever I returned to the Medieval Institute at Notre Dame. The Medieval Institute, along with its staff, provided a most congenial setting for key phases of the work. Belen Vicens, Sarah Davis-Secord, and Elizabeth Koza organized conference sessions in Remie's memory at Kalamazoo and the Medieval Academy, which provided rewarding opportunities to reflect on her scholarship from a number of angles.

Because it overlapped with some of my existing research commitments, the project also derived support from an Insight Grant from the Social Sciences and Humanities Research Council of Canada and from St. Thomas University. My own family, Kim Vose Jones, Ryley Jones, and Owen Vose, supported and nurtured me throughout with characteristic generosity and good humor. To all the above and the many more who have shared in both the grieving and editing processes, thank you.